The 100 Best
Small Art Towns
in America

Discover Creative Communities,
Fresh Air, and Affordable Living

Third Edition

John Villani

John Muir Publications
Santa Fe, New Mexico

John Muir Publications, P.O. Box 613, Santa Fe, New Mexico 87504

Printed in the United States of America
Third edition. First printing September 1998.

Library of Congress Cataloging-in-Publication Data

Villani, John
        The 100 best small art towns in America : discover creative communities, fresh air, and affordable living / John Villani. —3rd ed.
                p.   cm.
        Includes index.
        ISBN 1-56261-405-3
        1. Art patronage—United States. 2. Artist colonies—United States. 3. Cities and towns—Ratings—United States. 4. United States—Description and travel. 5. Quality of life—United States.
I. Title.
NX503.V55   1998
700'.973—dc21
                                                98-16900
                                                CIP

Editors: Peg Goldstein, Heidi Utz, Nancy Gillan
Production: Janine Lehmann
Design: Janine Lehmann
Cover art: Tony D'Agostino
Typesetting: Marcie Pottern
Map: Michael Bain
Printer: Publishers Press

Distributed to the book trade by
Publishers Group West
Berkeley, California

For Dreamgal

Contents

Introduction

Small art towns have come to epitomize rural cultural coolness because who wouldn't want to visit a lively, open-minded town. In this book you'll find communities across the United States and Canada that are attracting a new wave of cultural tourists, immigrant artists, culturally minded retirees, art gallery owners, musicians, mobile career professionals, theater directors, restaurateurs, arts festival promoters, and coffee bar entrepreneurs.

A small art town is the type of community people love visiting on a weekend getaway. They might stay at a gorgeous B&B, have dinner in a great (but undiscovered) restaurant, wander around art galleries, antique shops, and flea markets, or perhaps visit and an annual Art in the Park festival.

A small art town is the sort of place urbanites move to after selling their condo and finding a renovated farmhouse on five forested acres. On weekends these new residents enjoy art gallery openings and local musicians performing at cafés. On weeknights there are jazz concerts and dance programs at the local arts center, or maybe a Tennessee Williams play at the restored, art deco theater downtown.

A small art town is the sort of place where people can find a true sense of community. Families value small art towns because they place a high priority on neighborliness and security. Kids can walk home from school in safety, and the local cops know the name of nearly every teenager in town. Crime rates are reassuringly low, rendering "armed response" lawn signs pointless.

A small art town is a great place to buy high-quality art at affordable prices. In a small art town gallery, people don't have to contend with the absurdly comic snobbery of buzz-cut, bleached, pierced, and black-jacketed gallery owners hiding behind paper-thin shields of elitist affectation. While urban art galleries whine about depressed art markets, small art town galleries representing equally skilled (if not the very same) artists thrive, because owners realize that neither the artists nor their collectors are well-served by the tired facade of urban art chic.

For the purposes of this book's third edition, a small art town has a full-time population of 65,000 or fewer. (The book includes university towns like Lawrence, Iowa City, and Athens, Georgia, which have part-time student populations approaching 30,000). With fewer than 100 residents, Round Top is the tiniest of the small art towns. With this edition, I have labored to broaden the community profiles to include all aspects of the visual arts, performing arts, and music. Both mainstream and alternative arts venues are covered.

Moving to a small town is not a panacea. When I arrived in Santa Fe in the late 1980s, one of the first nuggets of local wisdom tossed my way was, "This town either embraces you or spits you out." It's unreasonable to place too many expecta-

The Best Small Art Towns

B.C.

Salt Spring Island

Bellingham

Nelson

Alta.

Sask.

Man.

Port Townsend

Sandpoint

Olympia

Wash.

Flathead Valley

Mont.

N.D.

Cannon Beach

Walla Walla

Moscow

Missoula

Helena

Enterprise
Joseph

Ore.

Bozeman

Livingston

S.D.

Sun Valley

Idaho

Jackson

Ashland

Arcata
Eureka

Wyo.

Nebr.

Fort Bragg
Mendocino

Nevada City

Grass Valley

Mill Valley

Nev.

Park City

Loveland

Santa Cruz

Utah

Vail
Aspen

Colo.

Salida

Lawrence

Carmel

Telluride

Kans.

Calif.

Creede
Durango

Ojai

Flagstaff
Sedona

Taos

Santa Fe

Magdalena

N.Mex.

Okla.

Ariz.

Ruidoso

Truth or
Consequences

Bisbee

Tex.

Alaska

Big Bend region

Fredericksburg
Kerrville

Round
Top

Hawaii

Rockport

Homer

The 100 Best
Small Art Towns
in America

Northport, Alabama

For the past decade, the small art town of Northport on Alabama's Black Warrior River has been one of the South's best-kept art secrets. Scenic, laid-back Northport, just a bridge removed from the University of Alabama in adjacent Tuscaloosa, is known for its low cost of living and for the outstanding Kentuck Art Center. But what put Northport on the small art town map was nothing less than an art world explosion. The Kentuck Festival of the Arts practically overnight attracted hordes of art dealers, collectors, and gallery owners from around the world. Today the festival draws packs of art hounds, who crawl the town seeking art known locally as visionary folk art and known elsewhere as "outsider," "naive," and "primitive."

Lifestyle

Besides hosting one of the continent's premier art festivals (which has enabled hundreds of Alabama artists to afford better homes and studio space), Northport has become a smart and forward-thinking place whose business community has weighed in solidly behind the booming cultural tourism economy. The Kentuck Center's success has spawned artsy downtown offshoots—including the eclectic Globe Cafe and Hummer's on Main—as well as other art galleries, antiques stores, and clothing shops. These days, Northport is one of the nation's up-and-coming small art centers—a place where you're likely to bump into visiting gallery owners lunching at the Globe with one of the area's rising art stars.

But Northport remains a place where the downtown five-and-dime and the old-timey hardware store are important centers of daily life. You can still find a home here for $65,000 or historic residences in the nearby university town of Tuscaloosa for about twice that.

Arts Scene

Folk art here takes three forms. First, there's visionary folk art produced by art-world stars and internationally collected artists who live in and around Northport. Second is western Alabama's traditional folk art—pottery, canes, rocking chairs, and brooms. Last is the contemporary fine art created by craftspeople who sell their work into galleries in Boston, Miami, Seattle, and Santa Fe but who choose to live and work in laid-back, supportive Northport.

A new wave of non-folk artists is also moving into town. These are visual artists as well as digital, computer-based artists who've recently graduated from University of Alabama's art department and don't want to move to New Orleans (and perhaps be mugged on their way home from work).

Any North American art town would give its eyeteeth to host the Kentuck Festival of the Arts, which last year attracted 25,000 people to drool, buy, and fight over the work of more than 300 exhibiting artists. This late-October arts madhouse attracts a shoulder-to-shoulder crowd of art dealers from the nation's top folk-art galleries—dealers who line up with gallery owners and collectors, elbowing each other at Kentuck Park's main gate before the festival's 9 a.m. Friday opening. The Kentuck Art Center is home to seven studio artists, a sales gallery, exhibition gallery, and small museum, as well as a combined while two popular music festivals, Verde Valley Music Festival and Jazz on the Rocks, take place in October and September respectively.

Actors Repertory Theater, a professional company performing at the 99-seat community room of the public library, stages four plays during its season and also brings comedy companies into Sedona for special appearances at Los Abrigados Resort. Sedona Arts Center has recently launched Theaterfest, its own professional company that uses the newly renovated Charles Raison Theater as its home. Southwest Theater is Sedona's summer company, staging three plays at the Tlaquepaque Arts and Crafts Village each season.

Art Talk

Barbara Antonsen, president and founder of the Sedona Arts Festival, says her event's focus is on the local community: "It's the largest event Sedona has, and as far as its impact on our youth I'd say it's also the most important event. All of our profits go right back into the community, primarily in the form of expenditures directly related to the arts education of our young people. The festival attracts around 5,000 people, which is more than half Sedona's popula-

tion. We draw all our entertainers from the Sedona area and have a children's area, as well as copresenting an exclusive juried show for about 15 artists who either live here or have some strong connecton to Sedona. And we have a national art show with 120 exhibitors, a very strong group of artists who come here to sell their work and also to meet the gallery owners from Sedona and Scottsdale who come here scouting for new talents."

Deni, a wood sculptor who relocated to Jerome four years ago, says her new hometown is tremendously supportive of the arts. "Jerome's the sort of place where artists meet each other over potluck suppers and where local artists volunteer to teach art classes in the school," she remarks. "I sell my work at the Jerome Artists Cooperative Gallery, which is a wonderful venue for this town's very eclectic forms of creative expression. The gallery has prospered from the very first week it opened and continues to do very well. Buyers come in here year-round from all parts of the country because Jerome is an historic place—a quiet and safe place where people can connect with true creativity that's not the result of artists working just to make sales to tourists."

Essentials

Population: 9,500
Art Events: Sedona Film Festival in March, Annual Pow Wow and Native American Arts Celebration and Sedona Hopi Show in May, Jazz on the Rocks in September, Verde Valley Music Festival, Sedona Arts Festival, Multi-Cultural Festival, and Jerome Homecoming in October
Art Spaces: Sedona Arts Center, Old Mingus Art Center, Jerome Artists Cooperative Gallery, Wolfwalker Gallery, The Jerome Gallery, Windrush Gallery, El Prado Galleries, Mountain Trails Gallery, Queen's Neighbor Gallery, Point of Sedona Gallery, Jordan Road Gallery, Esser Gallery, New West Galleries, Frog Pond Gallery,

Raku Gallery, Dirty Laundry Studio, De Wolf Fine Art, Gallery Margo, Kopavi, Sculptured Arts Gallery
Hangouts: The Muse Literary Cafe & Bookstore, Sedona Coffeehouse & Bakery, Oak Creek Brewing Company, Jimmy Jean Red Rock Coffee Beans
Bookstores: The Book Loft, The Muse Literary Cafe & Bookstore, Golden Word Book Centre, Storyteller Bookstore, The Worm Book & Music Store
Public Radio: KNAU FM 88.7
Chamber of Commerce: P.O. Box 478, Sedona, AZ 86339, (520) 204-1123

Eureka Springs, Arkansas

There just isn't any other small art town in the country like Eureka Springs in northwest Arkansas. Part of its charm lies in pure Arkansas hokiness: all-you-can-eat catfish joints, country music revues featuring schtickmeisters in overalls, fudge shops run by retirees, and a towering statue of JC on a Eureka Springs hillside. Another part of this community's appeal lies in its historic charm, with an entire downtown declared a National Historic District and a business district largely built on steep hillsides. Then there's a pastiche of New Age spiritualists (the town has several crystal shops), a large community of gays and lesbians (the town's Carnival parade is pure camp and wildness), and a sophisticated crop of new restaurants owned by chefs who made their reputations in swank metropolitan joints but then opted for life in the Ozarks. Finally, there are the artists, musicians, and art entrepreneurs in this kooky, delightful community of slightly less than 2,000 individualists, just an hour's drive from the college town of Fayetteville.

Lifestyle

Coffee bars, nightclubs, gallery walks, art classes, music festivals with national names in blues, rock, and folk, and a few dozen fine art galleries are just part of what makes Eureka Springs so extraordinary. It has been a spa town for more than a century, and you'll also find retreats specializing in aromatherapy, reflexology, and shiatsu.

Despite the town's popularity, northwest Arkansas is still a real estate bargain-hunter's dream. Newer homes inside the city limits average around $120,000. Historic mansions within walking distance of downtown run in the $150,000 range.

Arts Scene

Like many other towns with a cultural tourism economy, Eureka Springs quiets down during its three-month winter off-season. But once late March rolls around, its "Watch out, Baby," as the community cranks up its schedule of music festivals, art walks, free concerts in Basin Park, and a whirlwind of club bookings. National talent rotates in and out of town for gigs at venues like the Auditorium, Center Street South, and Basin Park Hotel.

Other than Eureka Theatre Company productions, the town doesn't offer much live theater—unless you count the Passion play, a religious piece performed in summer at a complex outside of town. Classical music is also lacking—though the new Eureka Springs Classical Music Festival has started bringing some national chamber music names to town for concerts at the Auditorium and Crescent Hotel.

But Eureka Springs is a live music and art gallery mecca, the sort of place where visual artists and musicians can build a solid base of income and use local success as a platform for opportunities elsewhere. A number of contemporary galleries have opened in recent years, and one of the best art spaces in town is the 51-member cooperative known as Professional Artists Alliance Gallery. The town has a monthly Gallery Walk, and an annual Studio Walk along White Street delivers hundreds of buyers directly into artists' work spaces.

The Fine Arts Festival in May is a month-long celebration of everything that's creatively funky about Eureka Springs. Events include poetry and art exhibits in local coffeehouses and cafés, special exhibits in galleries, performances and concerts in restaurants and clubs, and a series of parades that would make anyone familiar with P-Town's shenanigans feel right at home.

Art Talk

Nicole Post, gallery director of Gryphon's Roost, a contemporary art space, says the local tourism base is shifting. "We're seeing fewer busloads of older tourists and many more younger tourists coming into town for the galleries and nightclubs and health spas," says Post. "They're buying art while they're here, which is why new galleries selling good work are popping up all the time. Eureka Springs is a place where everyone fits in and peacefully coexists. The area has many many talented artists moving in from places like the West Coast and Southwest. They like living here and selling their work here, but keep their gallery ties in other places. The town needs to redirect its tourism promotion toward cultural tourists and realize that with a bit of help Eureka Springs can attract the same big-spending art buyers who also vacation in places like Santa Fe and Mendocino. "

Eleanor Lux, fiber artist and bead worker, says Eureka Spring's direction as an arts community is changing: "Some of the lower end gift shops are closing, and less people are coming here for things like the Passion play. Instead, what we're getting more of are visitors who come in from Texas, Oklahoma, and Arkansas to buy art. There's a new group of younger families with high incomes who are moving into town, and a new airport is opening in Rogers that should bring a boom in high-end residential home building and resort building. For artists, this has always been a place to sell a little bit of work, but with the new galleries opening up and with art sales growing, I think we're finally seeing Eureka Springs develop into a place where serious collectors come to buy art."

Essentials

Population: 1,950

Art Events: Fine Arts Festival and Blues Festival in May, Opera in the Ozarks in June and July, Southern Gospel Music Festival in August, Eureka Springs Jazz Festival and Ozark Folk Festival in September

Art Spaces: Mud Street Espresso, New Orleans Hotel Lobby Bar, Arkansas Craft Gallery, The Oasis, Zarks, Uptown Pottery, Cosmic Cup, Spring Wind Gallery, Mitchell's Folly, Rhinehart Gallery, 83 Spring Street, Bish Art Gallery, Maggie's, Basin Park Hotel, Quicksilver Gallery, Women's Work, Autumn Breeze, Cherokee Mountain Gallery, Crazy Bone Gallery, Wilson & Wilson Folk Art, Satori Arts, Chez Charles, Fairmont Gallery, Weaver Springs Gallery, Gryphon's Roost Gallery, Jim & Brent's Bistro, Cottage Inn, Morrison-Woodward Gallery, Center Street South

Hangouts: The Roxy, Center Street South, Basin Park Hotel, Cosmic Cup, Sparky's Roadhouse, Eureka Live, Inga's Vunderbar, Fat Tuesday's, Shaw's Tavern

Bookstores: Gazebo Bookstore

Public Radio: KUAF FM 91.3

Chamber of Commerce: P.O. Box 551, Eureka Springs, AR 72632, (501) 253-8737

Hot Springs, Arkansas

In some ways, Hot Springs still hews to the Arkansas school of tourism development. Long a stopping-off point on the region's family vacation map, Hot Springs offers up an alligator farm, aquarium, Passion play, and hillbilly musical extravaganza for visitors. There's even a wax museum whose two star attractions are life-size figures of Bill and Hillary Clinton . . . something everyone would shell out a few bucks to see.

But here in the hometown of President Clinton there's an arts revolution underfoot that even this one-time Hot Springs High School sax-playing senior class president couldn't have anticipated...an arts-based economic resurgence driven by the multi-tentacled and free-spending monster called cultural tourism. In less than a decade, this historic community of massive bathhouses and turn-of-the-century commercial buildings has developed into one of the nation's best places to find work by, of all things, contemporary Italian artists. But that's only the tip of the Hot Springs arts iceberg. Hots Springs has witnessed the fairly recent establishment of more than a dozen art galleries, a number of fine restaurants, and a new convention center also serving as a state-of-the-art performing arts center. In addition, local government and wealthy families have put their energy toward turning the massive and practically unused old Hot Springs High School into the William Jefferson Clinton Cultural Campus.

Lifestyle

Within a few years, when Hot Springs has its new convention center cranked up to full speed along with the Clinton Arts Center, life here is going to be as arts-focused as it is in communities such as Northampton, Eureka, and Charlottesville. As the community's South End arts district continues to sprout fine art galleries, sophisticated restaurants, home furnishings stores, and coffee bars, Hot Springs will ascend into position as the state's cultural center, siphoning off what's left of Little Rock's cultural tourism business.

Hot Springs remains an eminently affordable place to live. Retirees love the town for its safety, friendliness, and easy access to golf courses, trout streams, and lakes. Families tired of urban life have also helped turn Hot Springs into a fast-growing area, and homes in the $75,000 range aren't hard to find.

Downtown Hot Springs, where the South End arts district borders the town's lovely Bathhouse Row and its string of mammoth spa buildings, once symbolized this community as a healing center in a state of decline . . . a place where cathouses, juke joints, and bookie parlors thrived. After law officers broke up the decades-long party, downtown slid downhill, until a group of artists and art gallery owners, led by Carolyn Taylor, Benini, Malinda Herr-Chamblis, Linda Palmer, and Lorraine Benini, moved into town.

Today, a thriving gallery scene has turned around not only Hot Springs' economic fortunes but also its once-sagging real estate market. Several celebrations of the arts and a monthly art walk have, over the years, built a significant cultural tourism business here. Today the arts sectors, downtown business sectors, and tourism sectors are all united

Profile

the canvas, I've started combining the different elements of what I've learned through my career. I'm doing comfortable and happy paintings of women having tea, images that are easier to look at, warmer and friendlier. And I'm gaining a fair amount of control over my media, which has started me doing landscapes.

"Now that I'm in Hot Springs I live on the side of a mountain in a home surrounded by trees and just a half-block from a wonderful hiking trail. My world has taken on a sense of being surrounded by nature, and it's fun to have subject matter like mountains and swimming holes just a few minutes' walk from my front door.

Katchen first came to Hot Springs on an arts writers trip. At the time, she barely knew where Arkansas was, let alone Hot Springs. She recalls: "I came here and thought it was a very nice town, but what got me back was an art gallery owner who wanted me to do an exhibition later that same year. By the time I returned to Hot Springs, so many positive changes had taken place in the town that I was compelled to start looking at real estate during my last two days here. I came back a month later and bought a home, packed up my things in L.A., and haven't regretted it for a single minute. There are so many things about living in a stable and supportive community that I love. Here I can own my own home, have a wonderful garden, and spend time playing with my dog—and that's just for starters.

"Hot Springs is the most nurturing place I've ever lived. It's green and lush and has a gentle change of seasons. I look at the town as a small, cosmopolitan oasis. Europeans love living here because Hot Springs' spas remind them of the great spas of Europe, and artists who have reached a certain level of independence in their careers find this a fantastic place to continue their work. . . . Hot Springs is impressive in terms of the range of different expressions that are represented in the galleries. Everything from Mary Cassat to abstract expressionism has a home here, and as long as an artist is working at a certain level of quality they are going to find themselves represented by one of the fine galleries here."

Katchen has been pleasantly surprised by the sales she's made in Hot Springs: "When I first moved here I assumed that I'd be making my income from selling through galleries elsewhere, but my originals have had a great year at the gallery representing me. Lots of Hot Springs people buy art, and we seem to be getting a steady flow of people from Dallas, Memphis, St. Louis, and Shreveport coming through town to buy. The drawbacks to living here are few, but I'd say the lack of good places for shopping and the absence of a bagel shop are at the top of my list."

Nelson, British Columbia

British Columbia's Kootenay Country offers the same sort of spectacular natural beauty that's drawn artists to places like West Virginia, northeast Oregon, and southern New Mexico. Some people note the "solace of open spaces" in these refuges, while others consider them ideal locales for the creation of art, the raising of families, and the pursuit of a better life.

Ringed by the soaring peaks of the Selkirk Mountains and nestled against the west arm of Kootenay Lake, the small art town of Nelson, British Columbia, certainly offers its 9,500 residents plenty of opportunities to commune with nature. Affordable, safe, and exceedingly friendly, Nelson is the sort of place artists love to call home. This popularity is due in no small part to the town's amazing stock of Victorian residences and a functional downtown loaded with massive historic buildings just aching to be turned into studio/galleries, rehearsal spaces, and Web site–driven business offices.

For artists turned off by the urban crunch of Vancouver, Calgary, and Edmonton, Nelson is increasingly becoming the alternative of choice. It's already developed a supportive and slightly funky arts scene that's dominated more by artists than by commercial galleries.

Lifestyle

Like many other western boomtowns, Nelson was built because of the rich veins of precious metals buried underneath it. And like its brethren mining towns of Creede, Bisbee, Park City, and Telluride, Nelson managed to beat the odds and hang onto its architectural legacy. Unlike these towns, though, Nelson never caught on as a cool place for the urban winter (or sum-

mer) crowd, even though first-rate ski areas—legendary for their massive snowfalls—are practically at the town's doorstep.

You can still slide into an average Nelson home for $125,000 U.S., live next door to working artists, and have easy access to one of the continent's greatest natural treasure chests. But typical winters in Nelson are wickedly cold and extremely white. From November through March, many local artists choose Mexico.

Arts Scene

As Nelson's reputation continues to spread, it's not only artists who are finding the town attractive. Cultural tourists from places like Vancouver and Spokane make a point of coming here to experience the local arts community. If they arrive during summer, those tourists are in luck—because they'll drop into the middle of Nelson's Artwalk, a 100-day event that rotates local artwork in and out of nearly 20 businesses ranging from retail stores to medical offices to pubs and coffee bars. Artwalk is one of those events that combines local art-council support with the free spirit of artists themselves and arrives at a perfect middle ground. A lot of Nelson art finds its way into the hands of collectors during Artwalk's run, and that makes local artists happy. Artwalk is also a great deal for the businesses exhibiting works, with business owners pocketing a 35 percent cut on everything that's sold.

Nelson's arts businesspeople have also done a great job establishing galleries in this community's historic downtown, with eight venues presently exhibiting local and regional art. These galleries are joined by increasing numbers of alternative venues (many of them

Honey in the Rock, Marcel Marceau, and Alvin Ailey.

While the Van Duzer concentrates on national and international acts, Humboldt County's local performers use a variety of venues, such as the Ink People Center for the Arts, Humboldt Arts Council's Carnegie Building, Dancenter, Manila Community Center, and Mateel Community Center. Theater is presented year-round and ranges from the Dell 'Arte School of Physical Theatre in Blue Lake to the weeklong summer Shakespeare at Benbow season. Northcoast Repertory Theatre and Ferndale Repertory Theatre both present mainstream dramas, comedies, and musicals in their own playhouses—Northcoast's being a 135-seat facility in downtown Eureka and Ferndale's being a 267-seat theater in that community's spectacular Victorian downtown. World Premier Theatre's experimental local productions are held above downtown Eureka's Lost Coast Brewery, while Pacific Center Theatre has earned a reputation for staging no-holds-barred productions during its four-play season at the Manila Community Center.

Classical music is performed by the Eureka Symphony, which presents its season of three concert pairs at Christ Episcopal Church. The HSU music department's faculty, students, and visiting artist give concerts at Fulkerson Recital Hall. The art council holds its Sunday concert series of recitals, chamber music, and chorale music at the Carnegie Building.

Two nonprofit art centers serve Eureka: Ink People Center for the Arts and the Humboldt Arts Council's Carnegie Building. Ink People, which operates in unharmed sections of an earthquake-damaged school building, is a vibrant exhibition facility, an arts education center offering workshops in painting, weaving, printmaking, and photography, and a performance space for poetry readings, plays, and films. Ink People also helps administer programs such as the Redwood Coast Writers' Center, artist Duane Flatmo's mural painting

program with at-risk youth, the region's Hmong cultural preservation project, and the Persephone Healing Through Art Program. The Humboldt Arts Council's recent takeover of Eureka's 1904 Carnegie library building has finally provided the council with exhibition and performance space. A current renovation project will modernize these spaces and provide three art classrooms and a youth art gallery space. The council, recipient of a huge Lila Wallace grant, also administers projects such as ArtLine, which tours CenterArts performers through local schools. The region's other premier, nonprofit exhibition facilities are the College of the Redwoods Art Gallery and the Reese Bullen, Foyer, and Windows Cafe Galleries on the HSU campus.

Downtown Eureka's Old Town historic district has parts that are as pretty as Seattle's Pioneer Square. The district has attracted substantial investment through local government programs. Galleries have come and gone in this part of Eureka, though several have managed to survive Old Town's stretches of slow business.

One constant in both Eureka and Arcata is that businesses hang local works of art on their walls—the result of Ink People's Alternative Gallery Project, which has enlisted more than two dozen business participants. At least that many businesses work independently with local artists of their choosing to exhibit changing shows on their walls.

Some artists live along the edges of downtown, while others, such as Hobart Brown, prefer Ferndale or other outlying communities where the loudest sound is that of wind rustling through redwood trees. Throughout Humboldt County it seems as though art confronts you at nearly every turn. Galleries, community art centers, murals, artists studios—all clustered within the powerful embrace of ocean breezes and the mighty redwoods. If ever there were a more beautiful place to create art or live as an artist, I have yet to see it.

Art Talk

Roy Furshpan, director of CenterArts, say the key to his group's success has been local audience enthusiasm: "Over the years people here have developed a tremendous amount of trust in us for presenting quality, affordable performances, and I think our 50 percent increase in season subscriptions over the past few years is proof of that. Now, for the first time, we're experiencing sellouts of shows months before they take place, and that's causing us to take a serious look at either expanding the number of shows we present or thinking about expanding the size of our facility. This is a very open-minded community, one where audiences respect performers and encourage them to present their very best, which is why the artists themselves want to keep coming back here year after year. We try to do everything well, from our family shows to our avant-garde performances, and we make every possible effort to keep our ticket prices low enough so that nearly everyone can afford to come and participate. The support we receive from the university and from local business is very strong and allows us to present acts that normally don't have a chance to perform in rural communities. We're moving into year-round programming, and that is just one more indication of the commitment people from this community have toward the arts."

Bruce Braly, coowner of Humboldt's Finest, says there's a good reason why Eureka has turned into a strong arts community. "We have artists who arrived here in the sixties," he says, "people so good at what they do that their work can and does sell anywhere they want it to, and their groundbreaking efforts at selling their work locally paved the way for hundreds of artists who came later. This isn't much of a tourist market, though the cultural tourists who come into town tend to buy the most expensive works. We're isolated, and that makes the area a great place to work but also gives the art created here an honesty that's hard to find in more heavily visited places. The biggest collector base is made up of local people, and because they have been around this strong art for years they tend to be very discriminating in what they buy and demand good value for their purchases. There's a lot of local interest in art that's created for art's sake, and [it] doesn't have to be functional or decorative to find a buyer. I'm not so sure Eureka could handle having more galleries, because there is a limited amount of money spent on art by local people."

Janette Guyette, owner of the Madison Art Gallery inside the Cream City Mall, says her innovative approach to displaying art has brought unexpected results: "I was a paralegal for years, but now I own this antiques mall and art gallery, which allows me to display art in a roomlike setting. I represent around twenty local artists and find Humboldt County to be the sort of place where people will spend substantial amounts on art, provided they think it makes a strong creative statement. Having art displayed around antiques means that people will sometimes come in here looking for a chair, spot the chair they like, see a painting on the wall next to it, and walk out with both. It's great, I feel like I'm selling art right in my own home."

Hobart Brown, owner of the Hobart Gallery and founder of the Kinetic Sculpture Race, was interviewed on a cellular phone in a field outside Perth, Australia. He explains his project, which began in Humboldt County: "I've spent the past couple of years starting Kinetic Sculpture Races around the world, and I think the one we're staging here in Southwest Australia will be the biggest yet. People here, as in places like Poland and the U.S., are in love with the idea of creating these wonderful machines that are essentially the expression of man's sleeping genius. I like to say that when it comes to the Kinetic Sculpture Race, we're in the hero business, not the racing business. . . . Our race awards go to first place, last place, middle of the pack, and all sorts of other competitors, and we'll bring the top Australian finisher to Ferndale for the world championships, which take place in late May."

Essentials

Population: Eureka, 27,600; Arcata, 16,000
Art Events: Arts Alive openings on first Saturdays, Humboldt International Film Festival in April, Kinetic Sculpture Race and Bebop & Brew in May, Jazz on the Lake, Summer Art Festival, and Art & Wine in the Park in June, Mad River Festival in June and July, Reggae on the River in August, Maskibition, Junk Art Exhibition, Redwood Art Association Fall Exhibition, and Pastels on the Plaza in October
Art Spaces: Reese Bullen Gallery, College of the Redwoods Art Gallery, Ink People Center for the Arts, Carnegie building, Las Truchas Gallery, Hagopian Gallery, Ferndale Arts Cooperative, Madison Art Gallery, Mateel Arts Cooperative Gallery, Hobart Gallery, Arcata Storefront Gallery, Old Town Art Gallery, Foyer Gallery, Windows Cafe Gallery, Trinidad Art Gallery, Gallery Loft at Humboldt's Finest, Ambiance Gallery, 308 Showcase Gallery, Moonstrike Gallery

Hangouts: Lost Coast Brewery, Eel River Brewing Co., Six Rivers Brewing Co., Humboldt Brewery, Jambalaya, Sunnyside Pub, Club West, Eureka Inn
Bookstores: J. J. Perry's, Northtown Books, Eureka Bookstore, Fortuna Book Co., The Book Rack, Going Places, Booklegger's, Arcata Books, Blake's Books
Public Radio: KHSU FM 90.5
Chamber of Commerce: 2112 Broadway, Eureka, CA 95501, (707) 442-3738

Grass Valley and Nevada City, California

Known as northern California's Gold Country, the spectacular landscape surrounding Grass Valley and Nevada City has for decades served as a getaway for Bay Area urbanites. The area offers easy access to both the city and to Sierra Nevada ski areas, hiking trails, and trout streams. On weekends when Mother Nature cooperates, Nevada County is flooded with Bay Area and Sacramento day-trippers, who enjoy white-water rafting, cross-country skiing, mountain biking, and hiking along backcountry trails.

Nevada City, a gold mining town, was once one of the continent's wealthiest communities. To this day the deep mine shafts below Grass Valley yield enough gold to keep a sizable portion of the local population employed. While both communities have historic districts, smaller Nevada City has the higher concentration of intact Victoriana.

Lifestyle

The region was one of the first places to experience the "lone eagle" phenomenon—telecommuting professionals moving to the area and establishing home offices. In recent years, the area has also become a bedroom community for those who work in Sacramento and can tolerate the hour-long commute in each direction.

The region's real estate values have played a variety of tunes in recent years. But lately homes in Grass Valley have been holding fairly steady in the $175,000 range. In historic Nevada City prices tend toward the $190,000 level, though in both communities craftsman's specials are available for around 25 percent less.

Arts Scene

The visual arts market here is in a state of growth. While Nevada City and Grass Valley aren't yet the sort of places where artists can earn a majority of their income selling into the local market, the towns are on the cusp of developing a commercial gallery concentration that will make collectors' mouths water.

The Miners Foundry Cultural Center, a performance space used for local theater and music, has recently turned part of its lobby into a gallery in response to the demands of local artists. The North Columbia Schoolhouse, a venue 16 miles from Nevada City, has developed a strong reputation for the quality of its one-artist and group exhibitions. The area's premier visual arts exhibition venue is the Museum of Ancient and Modern Art, a facility in nearby Penn Valley exhibiting local and regional work, as well as offering art classes for kids.

There has been even stronger support for theater than for visual arts, with several drama companies active on the local scene. Some use the intimate, 99-seat Studio Theatre in downtown Grass Valley, while others stage performances at the 250-seat Nevada Theatre in Nevada City. The Nevada County Community Players present year-round family entertainment, while the similarly oriented Chris Harada Productions stages a few plays yearly and concentrates on art education in local schools. Foothill Theatre Company presents five yearly productions and some locally written work at the Nevada Theatre, as well as an outdoor Shakespeare festival in September at the Fred Forsman Amphitheatre. Community Asian by some dance and music presenters who occasionally rent out the facility—tops out at 109. During the summer months there are free concerts on Mill Valley's plaza.

One of the region's better nightclubs, Sweetwater, is located right in the center of Mill Valley. The club brings in much of the same musical talent that works its way through the Bay Area's competitive and professional music scene. Other Mill Valley nightclubs presenting live music are the 2AM Club and Panache. In nearby San Rafel, a 15-minute drive from here, clubs such as the Panama Hotel, Fourth Street Tavern, and Caffe Valeska also present live music.

Art Talk

Susan Cummins, gallery owner, says Mill Valley is home to serious art collectors. "My gallery has been in business for 13 years, representing a national group of contemporary artists to a collector base that's mostly in the southern Marin communities," she says. "This is a very culturally alive town, a place where well-traveled and successful people like to live and support a wide range of quality arts events. I'd rather have a gallery here than in San Francisco because in Mill Valley I can have a street-level space that's easy to find and that encourages people to walk in and look around."

Julia James, executive director of Artisans Gallery, says her art space serves a unique purpose in Marin County's arts scene: "Our focus is on the emerging artist, and over the years there have been many artists who have used Artisans Gallery as a springboard for getting commercial gallery representation in San Francisco and Carmel. We're really a part of the history of this area, and our shows, especially our invitational exhibitions, are always big successes. Keeping a retail space in Mill Valley open is a challenge because most of our sales are to local people and not to tourists. But we're creative and we work hard, and that's what makes the difference."

Essentials

Population: 14,000

Art Events: First Tuesday Art Walks, Mountain Play in May and June, Art Paint-Off in August, Mill Valley Arts Festival in September, Mill Valley Film Festival in October

Art Spaces: O'Hanlon Gallery, Artisans Gallery, Susan Cummins Gallery, At the Top, Robert Green Fine Arts, Sunnyside Cafe, Outdoor Art Club

Hangouts: The Coffee Roasterie, Peet's Coffee, Caffe Valeska, Depot Bookstore & Cafe

Bookstores: Depot Bookstore & Cafe, Book Passage, Borders

Public Radio: KQED FM 88.5

Chamber of Commerce: P.O. Box 5123, Mill Valley, CA 94941, (415) 388-9700

Ojai, California

Ojai was hip before the '50s beatnik heyday, New Age before the Beatles ever set foot in India, and artsy before potter Beatrice Wood was a flapper. To this day, Ojai remains a treasured retreat for film and music stars—people who need to be reasonably close to Hollywood yet want to spend as much time as possible away from the urban crunch and wrapped in the embrace of a laid-back community. Artists, spiritualists, retirees, and urbanites holed up in Ojai's many retreats have all staked their claim to this spectacular community near the 7,500-foot Pine Mountain, which is why the town has restricted its rate of growth and works overtime to preserve its historic charm.

Lifestyle

Ojai has so many centers for personal growth and reflection that other towns could consider using therapy as an economic development tool. The Ojai Institute, Ojai Foundation, Krotona Institute of Theosophy, Ojai Yoga Center, Ojai Valley Dharma Center, and World University of American are the better known centers, and there are at least a dozen others offering every kind of alternative medicinal practice known to man.

Does it work? Well, Ojai does have a very low crime rate. Its residents are certainly friendly enough . . . and it's a great place to buy art. And, surprise of surprises, the town even has affordable homes starting in the $150,000 range—though $225,000 will buy what's considered a more "average" place. Call it karma or whatever you wish, Ojai is exactly the sort of place artists want to call home.

Arts Scene

Ojai has a vibrant commercial gallery scene, with an emphasis on pottery and ceramics—a reflection of the stature and influence of artists such as Beatrice Wood and Otto Heino. Wood, until her death in 1998, exerted a powerful spiritual influence on the valley's artists, especially women artists.

Downtown Ojai's mission-style Arcade is a blocks-long series of archways framing the doorways to the town's best galleries. Several of these galleries have developed national reputations for exquisite fine crafts. In all, there are around two dozen commercial galleries in Ojai, as well as the Ojai Center for the Arts, which operates a nonprofit exhibition space focusing on local and regional work. Six miles away in the much larger community of Ventura are several contemporary galleries representing artists from Ojai and the surrounding region.

Ojai's performing arts scene is typical for a community of its size—but the quality is higher. The arts center's performance space serves as a venue for community theater productions by companies such as the Flying H Group, Theater 150, and Theatre4.comm. The First Baptist Church and Ojai Presbyterian Church are venues for classical and chorale concerts. The Ojai Music Festival, a series of classical concerts, takes place over several days in May at the Libbey Bowl. The Bowlful of Blues Festival uses the same stage for its October concert series.

Local Hero Books & Cafe is one of Ojai's most active live-music and poetry-reading venues. Nicholby's and a sushi bar named Go Fish also present evening music performances.

Art Talk

Teri Mettala, director of the Ojai Center for the Arts, says Ojai is finally living up to its arts reputation. "Up until a couple of years ago, people would visit Ojai and be disappointed that there weren't art galleries and places to go shopping," Mettala notes. "But for better or worse, our downtown is now filled with galleries and places that sell things to tourists, and I see this community becoming a gallery center like Carmel in a few years. The art center opened its doors in 1939 and continues to serve Ojai's literary, visual, theater, and music arts needs by providing a venue for classes, performances, and exhibitions. We are attracting a new generation of visual artists who enjoy living here, who make some of their sales locally, and who use Ojai as a base from which they work with galleries and art festivals throughout the state. And we're attracting a lot of film industry people as a place for their weekend homes."

Gail Childress, owner of G. Childress Gallery, says Ojai is finally capitalizing on its arts reputation: "For years people realized a lot of great artists lived in the area, but until we started the Ojai Studio Artists Tour 14 years ago, there really wasn't a way to connect with those artists because many of them had national and international arts careers but just lived here quietly. Now, we're getting more galleries and music festivals, which is great because the galleries can sell to the people who come to Ojai to stay at the spas. This is a surprisingly supportive community for the artists who live here, and what I see is a congenial group that's respectful of each other's work and helpful, sort of like an art family."

Essentials

Population: 8,150
Art Events: Ojai Music Festival in May, Summer Art Stroll in June, Ojai Studio Artists Tour and Bowlful of Blues in October
Art Spaces: The Pottery, Ojai Center for the Arts, Blue Moon Fine Art, Beatrice Wood Studio, HumanArts Gallery, Massarella Pottery & Gallery, Milagro's Nest Gallery, Ojai Frameworks Gallery, Primavera, Nancy Rupp Studio, Carter Studio Gallery, Carlton Gallery, Childress Gallery, Buenaventura Gallery, Nomad Gallery, Ojai Valley Gallery, Bagier Gallery, Upstairs Gallery, Casa de la Luna, Back Arbor Gallery, Gallery One One One, Sweet Art Gallery

Hangouts: Local Hero Books & Cafe, Cuyama Buckhorn, Java & Joe, Cafe Voltaire, Ojai Cafe Emporium, 66 California, Nicholby's, Go Fish, Shields Brewing Company
Bookstores: Bart's Books, Book Mall, Ventura Bookstore, Local Hero Books & Cafe, Krotona Quest Bookshop
Public Radio: KCRW FM 102.1, KFCA FM 88.7
Chamber of Commerce: P.O. Box 1134, Ojai, CA 93024, (805) 646-8126

Santa Cruz, California

California's original Surf City has all the right ingredients for great small art town: a fabulous oceanside climate, a major university (University of California-Santa Cruz), a two-hour drive to San Francisco's airport, a surfing museum, 29 miles of beaches, towering redwoods, and a couple dozen wineries. For decades, a stellar list of musicians, painters, actors, and writers have holed up in Santa Cruz's mountains and beachfronts, creating works that premier locally and then nationally. The downside for most artists is limited local sales opportunity, but most artists overcome that problem by using laid-back Santa Cruz as a launching pad for gallery representation in nearby San Francisco, Carmel, and Saratoga.

Lifestyle

Fishing is still part of the local economy, and one of the great aspects of life here is the fresh seafood served at local restaurants. Strolling the beaches at Santa Cruz, Aptos, and Capitola are favored pasttimes, as is hiking through redwood groves in the region's many state and local parks. The area is an agricultural paradise, with many flowers and exotic plants found in few other places. Artichokes and strawberries are important crops, and choppers regularly scour the mountainsides looking for marijuana plantations. With a little luck, it's possible to find a home in the $150,000 range here, but it's likely to have lingering signs of damage from 1989's massive earthquake.

Art Scene

While a few Santa Cruz galleries sell contemporary paintings and landscapes, fine crafts and jewelry are the biggest sellers here. Many area coffeehouses and restaurants serve as alternative venues for those artists who prefer to go it alone. The university has two venues: Smith Gallery for local and regional work and Senson Gallery for national shows. The Santa Cruz Art League's Main Gallery and Off-Site Gallery are among the more prominent venues exhibiting local work. The Art Museum of Santa Cruz organizes local, regional, and some national exhibitions at its Solari and Octagon Galleries, as well as youth and adult art classes. For many artists, the highlight of each year comes in October during the Open Studios Tour—three consecutive weekends in which potential buyers traipse through area studios.

Performing arts, especially theater, are huge in Santa Cruz. Shakespeare Santa Cruz is a seven-week outdoor Bard blowout held in the redwood-rimmed Sinsheimer-Stanley Festival Glen on the UCSC campus and at the college's Performing Arts Theater. Cabrillo Stage at Cabrillo College presents a strong season of mainstream theater. Soquel Creek Community Theatre, performing at the Capitola Theatre, does the same. Actor's Theatre, an innovative company focused on new, local, and expermental works, stages its season, as well as a New Plays Festival, at its 97-seat playhouse.

In nearby San Juan Bautista, the highly regarded El Teatro Campesino, a touring company, presents plays dealing with social, ethnic, and cultural issues. Bay Shore Lyric Opera presents its five-production season at the Capitola Theatre, while the Santa Cruz Symphony uses the Civic Auditorium for its eight-concert season.

The region's most prominent musical

Profile

toward something that's moving along smoothly," he explains. "I guess I'm like a cattle herder when it comes to the way I run my studio. . . . On any given day I want my attention to be able to turn toward whatever it is my mind wants to take on that day. And whatever I don't want to do stays shoved in a corner until I'm ready to deal with it.

"A sculptor can refine and refine any idea until the end of time. But one of the skills you've got to be able to pick up is knowing that point at which you can answer 'yes' to the question of whether you've honestly done everything you can to a piece, and whether that piece is ready for molding. One of the drawbacks to working in bronze is the fear that you'll send a piece out to the foundry that has some flaw in it. There's nothing so awful as running into a gallery and seeing something you've done that has a problem on it that needs to be fixed, but that's permanently there in bronze for everyone to see forever."

Kreutzer observes that artists must also be skilled businesspeople. He says, "It's tough being an artist and managing a busy studio. But in an operation like this where I've got collectors dropping by the studio, commissioned pieces I'm working on, and the regular pieces I do that are going out to a dozen galleries, there are always going to be interruptions—that's just the way it is. A lot of the success an artist achieves in a career depends on some very fine points that are discussed at the time a piece is sold, and it's necessary to have myself available to deal with questions coming in from my galleries when they're trying to close on the sale of a piece. It's the middle of the day, and it's a constant interruption, but it's just part of the profession."

And success doesn't come easy, as Kreutzer explains: "It takes about $180,000 in income each year in order to establish yourself in Loveland and get to the point where you've got a net annual income of $50,000. In other words, you've got to get out there and sell a lot of bronze if you want to be financially secure, and it helps to know how to write grant proposals for those 'percent for the arts' programs."

Finally, Kreutzer believes in Loveland and feels that this small art town has yet to see its best days as an arts center. "Loveland continues to be the sort of place artists want to move to, because we're continually building our reputation and profile as a sales and education center for the arts," he says. "We've got a slew of foundries and a great academy of the arts. . . . This is an easy place to work, a supportive place to work, and it's a whole lot cheaper living here than in Santa Fe."

Salida, Colorado

alida, a town whose traditional business district was nearly abandoned in a 1980s headlong rush toward fringe-area, strip-mall development, was smart enough not to rip apart the turn-of-the-century brick commercial buildings in its historic downtown. As a result, slowly and surely, this community is becoming a Rocky Mountain region small art town success story. The renaissance has also been fueled by Salida's booming outdoor-recreation economy—an entrepreneur-driven industry dedicated to environmental and historic preservation. There's still plenty of room for arts entrepreneurs here, where tourism dollars flow during summer's awesome weather and winter's rapidly developing ski season (Monarch Ski Area is a 30-minute drive away).

Lifestyle

Though Salida is hemmed in by more than a dozen "fourteeners" (Rocky Mountain peaks higher than 14,000 feet), the valley sheltering this small art town has a surprisingly temperate climate. There's winter snow aplenty, but nothing approaching the 5-foot blanket that usually covers places like Vail. Salida's banana-belt weather means local gardeners can take advantage of a longer-than-average growing season, while schoolkids don't have to depend on snowmobiles to get them to and from classes.

With the state's largest amount of downtown footage listed on the National Historic Register, Salida is loaded with quaint Victorian residences on tree-lined neighborhood streets . . . and some houses can still be snagged in the $85,000 range. Residences fronting the white-water kayaker's wet dream–paradise Arkansas River run about twice that, but there you can paddle back and forth to work (at least during part of the year). In recent years Salida has become a fave with Denver retirees seeking a taste of old Colorado yet wanting decent (two-hour) access to their Mile High Stadium season seats.

Arts Scene

Being an artist here means doing studio work part of the day, then heading out to white-water kayak, downhill ski, cross-country ski, or mountain bike the rest of the day. Salida's weather is spectacular and sunny, providing local landscape painters with inspiration galore in the form of unparalleled alpine vistas.

The community's visual arts galleries have started taking root. Because of winter's ever-improving flow of cultural tourists, most galleries now stay open in the coldest months, selling a respectable amount of art and cultivating the same buyers who attend popular events such as the Salida Art Walk in June or nearby Buena Vista's Art in the Park in July. Surprisingly, contemporary art in the form of painting, ceramics, sculpture, and high-end jewelry does well here, as do more traditional landscape and floral works. Nearly a dozen art galleries are surviving here, and several restaurants and a hip coffeehouse make a habit of hanging local art on their walls.

The community's nonprofit art space is the Steam Plant Cultural Arts Center, a spectacular structure built along the Arkansas River in 1887 to provide power to Salida's commercial district. The plant has been converted into not only a visual arts exhibition space but also a community theater and outdoor sculpture garden. The Steam Plant presents a summer series of music, theater, and storytelling and continues to raise funds to complete its structural renovation.

For several years Salida has presented a July and August classical music series, combining musicians from the Aspen Music Festival and the Alpine Orchestra to create the six-concert Salida-Aspen Concert Series. The High Country Fine Arts Association offers a musical production each summer at John Held Auditorium, along with a children's theater show. On weekends, local musicians and imported Colorado Springs and Denver bands perform at Victoria Tavern.

Art Talk

Geraldine Alexander, manager of cultureclash gallery, says Salida has developed a reputation for contemporary art: "We're a place that likes unusual things—I guess because we're in the gallery all day and have to live with the work ourselves, so why not just have work we can enjoy instead of just work we think is going to sell. There are a number of good contemporary artists living in Salida who used to not have a place to show and sell their work locally but who did well in other parts of the state. Once we began exhibiting their work in this gallery, the work sold—which was surprising to some people, but also rewarding in that it proved something the artists here felt all along was possible. We're still a seasonal art market, but in the past few years the galleries are coming to be seen as important members of the business community, and we're being given a seat at the table, so to speak."

According to Marcy, owner of Soho Gallery and the Art Studio, Salida's Colorado cultural tourists are its strongest art buyers. "I've been here 16 years, and it's only been recently that locals have started buying my work. Weekends bring in lots of people from Colorado Springs and Denver who want to buy a painting before they go home," Marcy says. "The galleries always have some turnover, but it seems as if the moment one closes there's another opening in its place. Our growth has been slow but steady, and the past two years have been much faster. We could use an arts festival in early fall, maybe an outdoor event in the park, but there would need to be a consensus among the gallery owners and artists to work together if something like that was going to be a success."

Essentials

Population: 5,200

Art Events: Salida Art Walk and FIBark in June, Art in the Park and Art of the Rockies Association Exhibition in July, Salida-Aspen Concert Series in July and August, Chaffee County Open Award Art Show in September

Art Spaces: Laughing Ladies Cafe, Soho, Old Courthouse Gallery, Willow Tree Gallery, Il Vicino, cultureclash, American Traditions, Tierra Madre, The Art Studio, Cornucopia Bakery, Clay Basket, The Other Art Studio, Thistle & Sage, Beacon Gallery, Trembling Aspen Gallery, The View Art & Music, Green Cat

Hangouts: Victoria Tavern, Laughing Ladies Cafe, Bongo Billy's, Crooked Hearts, Jackson Hotel, First Street Cafe, Gold Star BBQ & Beer Garden, Crossroads Cafe, Daylight Donuts

Bookstores: First Street Books, Adventure Media, All Booked Up, Creekside Books & Art

Public Radio: KRZA FM 88.7

Chamber of Commerce: 406 W. Hwy. 50, Salida, CO 81201, (719) 539-2068

Telluride, Colorado

Tirelessly promoting itself through what has to be the most comprehensive festival calendar of any small art town, Telluride has earned a reputation as a place where something fun is always going on—or just about to. A beautiful mining town turned one of North America's top ski resorts, Telluride is surrounded by sheer alpine peaks and characterized by a small downtown lined with Victorian homes and turn-of-the-century, two-story, brick commercial buildings. Its strong economy has spun off satellite communities such as Mountain Village, connected to Telluride by "the G," a free gondola that transports skiers during daylight hours and at night carries folks to and from restaurants, nightclubs, and workouts at The Peaks, a fitness spa located at 9,500 feet in the San Juan Mountains.

Lifestyle

Telluride is a fantastic place to live—if you can afford it. Condos here sell for $200,000; small homes on downtown's sunny side command $300,000 and up (about 10 percent less on the shady side). Telluride's saving grace for residents has been its deed-restricted housing developments that market affordable homes to locals earning at least 80 percent of their income in town. With most of the festival action happening between May and October, what Telluride doesn't get much of is a chance to quiet down (as Vail and Steamboat Springs do) after ski season ends. Parking is a nightmare, and Telluride's tow-truck drivers have gotten rich. . . as have its valet-parking pros.

Telluride is home to one of America's best small-town art centers, the Ah-Haa School for the Arts. This centrally located exhibition, lecture, and education facility, offers adult classes in everything from intaglio printmaking to poker strategy (an art form everyone can relate to!), as well as year-round youth art classes and local writers' meeting space.

Arts Scene

Best-known on the local arts scene are the "big three": Telluride Jazz Celebration, Telluride Film Festival, and Telluride Bluegrass Festival, each one hugely successful and drawing thousands of visitors. While most art towns would be happy to have any one of these high spots on their annual calendars, Telluride has gone even further, also developing a chamber music festival, theater festival, outdoor Shakespeare season, performing arts festival, and a dance festival built around a month-long Joffrey Ballet Company residency. The Telluride Society of Performing Arts is responsible for luring the Joffrey into town and for promoting Telluride as a mecca for dancers and ballet stars—which is why there are now more dance performances here than in any other small art town of comparable size.

During winter, when the festivals are planning their next year's programs, the small, beautiful, and historic Sheridan Opera House presents touring national theater, music, and dance. Telluride Repertory Theatre performs at the Fred Shellman Memorial Stage, while its six-play season runs throughout the calendar year.

There's great nightlife in Telluride, courtesy of such spots as Fly Me to the Moon Saloon, a presenter of touring national jazz, rock, touring bands gigging at Margaritaville, the Green Parrot, Hogs Breath Saloon, and Turtle Kraals and live jazz at the Pier House Wine Gallery, Coffee & Tea House, and Godfather's.

Art Talk

Joan McGillis, artistic director of the Key West Theatre Festival, says that the community views cultural tourist attractions as important to its economic health: "The Tourism Development Commission helps fund local theater because cultural tourism keeps people in town for longer stays. Our customers are tourists, but we also have a huge base of local support that largely comes from people who have moved here from cities and were used to attending theater in their former home towns. By presenting quality work—new work—at the festival, we've been able to present a schedule of seven productions and six play readings and have audiences turn out for what we're doing."

"People are surprised when they come into a space like this and see all original paintings, because the town's other galleries mix posters and prints in with their originals," says Wanda Sobran, former director of the Gallery on Greene. "That's frustrating to artists like Greg, my husband, who only does original work. We've brought a group of traditional and impressionist artists into this gallery, two of whom live in Key West and the others who have strong Florida connections. There's not a large group of tourist art collectors for this type of work who know about us yet, but more people are starting to find us."

Essentials

Population: 25,000
Art Events: Key West Crafts Show in January, Old Island Days Art Festival in February, Underwater Music Festival in July, Fantasy Fest and Key West Theatre Festival in October, Gay Arts Festival in December
Art Spaces: Barrington Gallery, Haitian Art Gallery, Caribbean Gallery, East Martello Museum, Gallery on Greene, Gingerbread Square Gallery, Guild Hall Gallery, Harrison Gallery, Island Arts Co-op, Joy Gallery, Kennedy Gallery, Key West Art Center, Lucky Street Gallery, Baron Folk Art, Woodenhead Gallery, Kudu Galley of Tribal Arts, Whitehead Street Pottery

Hangouts: Coffee & Tea House, Java Lounge, Kelly's Caribbean Bar & Grill, Key West Brewery, Sippin', Cafe Noir, Margaritaville, Turtle Kraals, Green Parrot
Bookstores: Blue Heron Books, Caroline Street Books, Key West Island Bookstore, Upstart Crow Books, Waldenbooks, Valladares & Son
Public Radio: WLRN FM 91.3
Chamber of Commerce: 402 Wall St., Key West, FL 33040, (305) 294-2587

New Smyrna Beach, Florida

White sand dunes, protected beaches that are part of a 57,000-acre national seashore, nesting loggerhead turtles, and affordable housing combine to make New Smyrna Beach a small art town with an extremely bright future. Located within easy driving distance of the art museums, performing arts centers, and professional theaters of Daytona Beach, New Smyrna Beach is a unique visual arts mecca—a place where international contemporary art blends seamlessly with a developing local arts scene of surprising integrity.

Cultural tourists are pleasantly surprised when they encounter New Smyrna Beach's arts scene at events such as the springtime Images Art Festival, an important showcase for emerging local talent. The Atlantic Center for the Arts, with its beautiful campus on Turnbull Bay, provides New Smyrna Beach with the sort of resource that Haystack Mountain School of Crafts provides for Deer Isle, Maine. The center was spearheaded by painter/sculptor Doris Leeper, who envisioned a refuge where midcareer artists could work closely alongside international masters.

Lifestyle

While residences with views of the Intracoastal Waterway run $150,000 and up, artists can still find comfortable digs a few blocks from the beach for about half that price. This is a quiet, safe community of bicycle paths, pristine public beaches, public golf courses, and friendly neighbors—a perfect antidote for artists and art lovers escaping the northern winter's chill. You can watch space-shuttle launches from local beaches or take the kids to Mickeyland in just over an hour. Summer weather is predictably brutal—a perfect time to visit all those relatives up north.

Arts Scene

New Smyrna Beach's oldest arts presence, the Artists' Workshop Gallery, is a vital force for its member artists, providing exhibition space and workshops. A new visual arts space, Arts on Douglas, represents the work of 55 Florida contemporary artists. The other big news on the community's arts scene is the completion of the Leeper Studio Complex on the ACA's 67-acre ecological preserve. The complex holds a theater, resource library, and four studio spaces.

One of America's art treasures, the ACA is noted for its Master Artists-in-Residence program, which brings in visual artists, composers, playwrights, photographers, choreographers, poets, and sculptors three at a time for three-week residencies. Midcareer artists apply for inexpensive ACA workshop residencies with the master artist of their choosing. Tonia León, Bernard Rands, Merce Cunningham, Faith Ringold, Alex Katz, Peter Matthiessen, and William Wegman are among the masters who have completed ACA residencies since its 1977 founding. When the master artist is a performer, ACA's amphitheater or the 150-seat Joan James Harris Theater hosts concerts, dance performances, and recitals. A new exchange program has brought artists here from Japan and has sent master artists and midcareer artists from ACA to Japan for residencies.

Harris House, a renovated Lutheran parish house in downtown New Smyrna Beach, serves as ACA's exhibition, education, and outreach center. The emphasis here is on local and regional art, with many of Florida's most prominent artists exhibiting as well as teaching classes for adults and children. Harris House is also used for poetry readings, art lectures, and community meetings.

Art Talk

According to Meghan Foley, manager of Arts on Douglas, the community's art reputation is becoming more diverse. "People in Florida know about the Atlantic Center, but they don't yet associate New Smyrna with being a place like Sarasota that has lots of galleries," Foley says. "But we feel committed to selling regional work as well as helping to develop the careers of the 55 Florida artists we represent. Our openings are huge events, with 250 people showing up each month for the shows—

and that's helped to raise local awareness of what we're doing and what the art is like. What we're waiting for is for cultural tourists to get off the beaten path and find us."

Lisa Sumner-Messersmith, manager of ACA's Harris House, says her organization's outreach programs serve a large segment of the community: "If you considered all of our art classes, exhibitions, lectures, weekend art programs, and outreach programs into local schools, it would be more than 10,000 residents served. The community has become a gathering point for artists wanting a better quality of life, not just artists from Florida but from across the country. The town's business community is acutely aware of how the arts draw people to New Smyrna Beach, and living here I get the feeling the community is improving all the time."

Essentials

Population: 20,000
Art Events: Images Art Festival and Jazz Festival in Riverside Park in spring, Loggerhead Turtle nesting season April to October, Florida International Festival every two years
Art Spaces: Harris House, Atlantic Center for the Arts, Arts on Douglas, Artists' Workshop, Anthony Bell Creations, Bruneau Art & Frame Gallery, Jonah's Cat Art Gallery, Southeast Museum of Photography, Museum of Arts & Sciences, African American & Caribbean American Museum of Art, Ormond Memorial Art Museum

Hangouts: Riverfront Brewing Company, Euro Cafe, Riverview Charlie's
Bookstores: Brown's Bookstore, Book Barn, Barnes & Noble, Books-a-Million, Mandala Books
Public Radio: WUCF FM 89.9
Chamber of Commerce: 115 Canal St., New Smyrna Beach, FL 32168, (904) 428-2449

Panama City and Seaside, Florida

Mother Nature has been extremely generous to this swath of white-sand beaches on the crystal-clear Gulf of Mexico, and except for an occasional hurricane there's little here to upset artists. Linked to the rest of the world by miles of wind-tossed palms, Panama City's 37,000 residents enjoy a first-rate arts scene that includes nonprofit and commercial galleries, theater, performing arts, and orchestral concerts. Home to an air force base, Panama City is a favorite of retired military personnel, and local housing costs are affordable.

Seaside, a planned "new urbanism" community 25 miles west of Panama City, has architectural and spiritual roots harkening back to turn-of-the-century America. It is much pricier than Panama City and tends to attract both retired and family-raising urban refugees. Though it has filled out with second homes and rental cottages, Seaside is an artists' community in its own right, with art galleries, music festivals, and an attractive and inspiring atmosphere for midcareer artists. Since Seaside opened in the mid-1980s, its galleries have flourished—and they're expected to continue doing so as this innovative community expands to its full planned size.

South Walton County's "Emerald Coast," which includes Panama City and Seaside, is home to nearly two dozen art galleries representing local and regional work. Making a living in Panama City as an artist means tapping into the Emerald Coast's gallery scene and selling like mad during such events as ArtsQuest and the Grayton Beach Arts Festival at Eden State Park.

Lifestyle

Surf's up—and while you're at it, grab a fishing pole. On the Florida Panhandle, laid-back Panama City may not be a year-round swimming hole like Key West, but its daytime winter temperatures in the 60s are perfect for everything from golf to setting up an easel at favored spots such as St. Joseph's Bay, St. Andrews Point, and nearby historic De Funiak Springs. A huge wintering Canadian population has a big impact on the local arts economy.

Average home costs in Panama City hover around $80,000, with "handyman's specials" available for considerably less and beachfront addresses starting around $125,000. Community schools have some art education, though Panama City is the sort of place where many parents favor private academies and after-school art programs.

Arts Scene

The gemstone of Panama City's performing arts scene is its art deco masterpiece, the Martin Theatre, a 450-seat, 1936 movie palace that was restored to its full WPA glory in 1990. Home to both a performing arts series and a resident professional theater ensemble, the Martin relies on popular music to bring audiences to its two-month performance series. The Martin Theatre Presents series includes a Floyd Cramer concert, a big-band show, and a 1950s retro act. The Martin Resident Ensemble's four-play season runs September through April. Besides its usual evening performances, the company presents each play as an educational experience for community schoolkids.

Panama City's community theater is the

Profile

lot of glass. Our philosophy is to keep our prices as low as possible as a way to encourage people to not only buy the glass we make but also to take it home and use it. If it's too expensive, people will feel intimidated when they use it to serve a salad, so we try to overcome that obstacle with low prices. We just try to keep the rent paid and our furnace going, and let things take care of themselves."

Jack and Mary began working together in college and moved to Garfield six years ago. "Our first studio was in LaGrande, Oregon, and we did a lot of wholesale to galleries," Mary says. "I think it was our fate to end up in Garfield, to try and sustain a glass business in a town of 500. From the very first day we opened we've been blessed with a huge amount of support. Our grand opening attracted 250 people, which hardly goes by unnoticed in a town this size. The television stations and newspapers in Spokane jumped all over it, and what this flow of visitors has done for Garfield's business community has been significant. The mayor owns the town's restaurant, and a lot of the people who come here to visit the studio end up stopping in there for a bite to eat. Believe me, the mayor thinks we're great."

"We work damn hard and we do okay," Jack Doebler adds. "Yeah, there is some luck involved in our success, but you've got to understand that Garfield is a community of hard-working people, and when they see that we too are hard-working individuals, they accord us some respect. We keep the studio quiet and efficient, not loud and confusing like most of the glass studios I've worked in, and that's what makes folks feel comfortable enough to keep coming back for visits.

"I worked two years in Seattle glass studios, and I found the whole scene there to be cliquey and repetitive. I mean, how many glass artists from San Diego to Vancouver are now working in some style that's directly derivative of Dale Chihuly's? We chose to do our own lives and our own art in a place that's spectacularly beautiful, safe, and quiet. Living in Garfield we have enough time to garden, take saunas, visit with friends, and play music," he says.

"Since we've moved into Garfield there's been a lot of interest from other people in opening up their own businesses in downtown and in restoring some of the old hotels and apartment buildings downtown. People are starting to take more of an interest in living here and making a living in a town like this, and that's got a lot of local folks talking very positively about the future."

Sandpoint, Idaho

Beautiful Sandpoint, a lakefront paradise in northern Idaho, is precisely the sort of environment sought by artists, retirees, lone-eagle professionals, and harassed urban families when they pack their bags and head out toward a better quality of life. Sandpoint's restaurants, coffee bars, movie houses, art galleries, and strong public schools are main attractions, as is the 90-minute drive to the airport in Spokane, Washington. Artists especially tend to fan out from Sandpoint to find solitude in smaller communities along the forested shoreline of crystalline Lake Pend Oreille—towns such as Hope, Clark Fork, and Bayview.

Lifestyle

Sandpoint is the type of place where newcomers buy log homes with huge stone fireplaces, then set out to equip their digs with Zapotec blankets, antler chandeliers, local art, and the mandatory Pathfinder parked in the driveway. The real estate market in Sandpoint is a fickle creature, and more than a few supposedly smart home builders have taken major beatings on log-palace "spec homes"—built in the hope that a witless Californian with a few million to burn will show up at an open house. Certainly there's been an escalation in home prices, but the rate of L.A. influx has slowed, and prices are now edging back to reality. Today, it's easy to find a family home in the $110,000 range.

Arts Scene

The past few years have brought a lot of changes to Sandpoint's performing and visual arts scenes. In fact, Sandpoint has become the inland Northwest's premier visual arts marketplace and has developed a concentration of galleries rivaling those in Sun Valley. That's the good news.

The good-and-bad news is that the Festival at Sandpoint has not worked as well as similar music festivals in Aspen, Jackson, and Hot Springs. Soaring deficits forced the festival's board of directors to adopt a popularity-or-perish strategy. They turned the once-classical festival into a three-week series of rock, world music, jazz, and kid's programs—with the Spokane Symphony's performances whacked back to one evening. That's left the Pend Oreille Art Council's eight-concert performance series—held September to April at the Panida Theatre, a 1927, 570-seat playhouse—as Sandpoint's sole connection to the world of contemporary opera, dance, and new music. But Sandpoint still has a higher-than-average enthusiasm for classical music, as evidenced by the large turnouts for the Edgewater's Concerts on the Lawn series in July.

With each passing summer, Sandpoint becomes more prominent on the Northwest cultural tourism map. This growth is the result of summer lakeside activity, winter ski action at Schweitzer Mountain Resort, and year-round activities at the galleries, Panida Theatre, and alternative venues. The galleries help keep tourists coming back, and alternatives to the galleries are springing up around town as well.

Art Talk

Diane Ragsdale, executive director of the Festival at Sandpoint, says the event's programs may be down, but overall attendance figures are up. "What we had to do was go back to our original mission of providing a festival for the people of Sandpoint, and that meant staging affordable programs that the community wanted," Ragsdale explains. "So we folded our music institute in favor of a conductor's seminar, trimmed back the number of orchestral performances to two, and found touring national acts that we could bring in here at reasonable prices. It's a refocusing on Sandpoint's needs, and since we don't have the resources or infrastructure to compete with festivals in metropolitan areas, we turned to doing what we can do best: be a great local festival. We're careful, we're trimmed back, and we're competing for ticket buyers in an area where the average income is not very high. As a result, we're once again an intimate festival that in the past year doubled its numbers of attendees."

Ceramics sculptor Leata Judd says the key to surviving as a visual artist in Sandpoint is to remain flexible. "You've got to have your work hit all the possible price levels and get your things into galleries in Spokane and Coeur d'Alene," Judd says. "I'm part of the Art Works, a 15-artist cooperative that has a gallery space in the Power House, which is a wonderful, sophisticated setting for art, but not the best place in town for foot traffic from tourists. We're considering moving somewhere closer to where the tourist action is, because from May to October there are a lot of sales taking place in the downtown galleries. Local people buy art in the off-season, but they rarely go above the $500 level. If you create expensive art, it usually waits for an out-of-town buyer."

Essentials

Population: 6,000

Art Events: Hearts for the Arts in February, Summer Sounds at Park Place from May to September, Art Walk at 17 venues from June to September, Concerts on the Lawn in July, Festival at Sandpoint in July and August, Sandpoint Arts & Crafts Fair in August

Art Venues: POAC Gallery, Northwest Artisans, Lyman Gallery, Janusz, Entree Gallery, Panhandle Art Glass, Eklektos Gallery, Hallan's Gallery, Selkirk Gallery, Haynes Studio/Gallery, Hen's Tooth Studio, Art Works, Shoot the Moon, Jean Mace Gallery, Art Works Co-op

Hangouts: Monarch Mountain Coffeehouse, Pend Oreille Brewing Co., 219 Club, Cafe Espress, Hydra, Power House Bar & Grill

Bookstores: Book Gallery, Books at Foster's Crossing, Bonner's Books, Vanderford's Books, Elfin Rhythm

Public Radio: KSPT FM 95.3, KPND FM 102.7

Chamber of Commerce: P.O. Box 928, Sandpoint, ID 83864, (208) 263-2161

Sun Valley, Idaho

The Pacific Northwest's priciest area is also a great small art town with a nice balance between the visual arts, theater, and music. Sun Valley is actually just a ski area—along with a small residential and commercial district at the base. A mile away is the town of Ketchum, which contains almost all the area's restaurants, galleries, bars, and shopping. Twelve miles down the Wood River Valley is the town of Hailey, another hotbed for galleries and retail shops.

Lifestyle

If you live in this part of Idaho, you've got access to some of the best that nature has to offer. Locals say that Sun Valley's snow and slopes are the continent's best—a point folks in Telluride, Taos, and Jackson find debatable. Actually, Sun Valley has developed into more of a year-round resort than many of its Rocky Mountain ski-town peers. And the rugged appeal of the area's spectacular landscape draws tourists as much as any summer music, opera, or arts festivals.

Success comes with a price, and here that translates into a valley-wide population and development explosion that has driven average home costs to the $263,000 level. The boom has raised the region's cost of living so much that farming towns 40 miles away are starting to feel the development heat.

Arts Scene

The valley's real estate boom has brought a new breed of gallery owners—many of whom have their roots in Seattle and Portland—selling art to second-home owners and cultural tourists. There are a half dozen commercial galleries in Hailey and more than a dozen in Ketchum, most of which deal in contemporary work at the higher price end. Some local artists have made a killing selling through the galleries, while others sell from studio/gallery setups and through alternative venues—including Iconoclast and Sun Valley Athletic Club—that rotate local shows monthly.

The area's most influential arts presence is the Sun Valley Center for the Arts and Humanities, which serves as an exhibition, art education, and occasional performance facility. The center also presents high-caliber music programs, such as a jazz series at River Run Lodge and the Chamber Artists Series—six concerts at a local church. Sun Valley Pro Musica presents its winter concerts at the Sun Valley Opera House, while the Sun Valley Summer Symphony's season of 12 free orchestral concerts and two chamber concerts takes place at Sun Valley Lodge. Jazz on the Green is a series of free summer concerts from June to August at Elkhorn Resort. Two other not-to-be-missed events are the Idaho Shakespeare Festival, which stages three September performances, and Saturday evening Ice Shows at Sun Valley Resort's outdoor skating rink.

Live theater has caught on in a big way in the valley. Laughing Stock presents musicals twice annually in the opera house, Sun Valley Repertory Company presents mainstream pieces at NexStage and Liberty Theatre, and Company of Fools stages plays in the art center's gallery space.

The valley's live music scene has been great ever since actor Bruce Willis bought The galleries in City Hall, the City Hall Annex, and College Square Mall.

Other visual arts offerings can be found at UNI, where the Kamerick Art Building gallery stages an ambitious exhibition program of both permanent holdings and touring national shows. The Museum of Art contains America's most extensive Haitian art collection, while its Grant Wood originals are among the nation's finest. Local artists exhibit their work in the Henry W. Myrtle Gallery, the Oster Regent lobby, the Storefront Gallery, Holland Galleries, and Cup of Joe.

Art Talk

Bruce Marquis, executive director of the Gallagher-Bluedorn Performing Arts Center, came to Cedar Falls after directing a similar complex in Lincoln, Nebraska. "I'm not known as the sort of person who plays it safe when it comes to programming," Marquis says. "Certainly, a center like the Gallagher-Bluedorn will have to respond to the needs of this community and the university, but it will also be a place that educates audiences about what's taking place in the performing arts world. We'll have a 1,600-seat main hall, a 300-seat recital hall, and a 125-seat organ gallery, among other educational facilities. I expect the center to be largely self-supporting after its initial few years, and I expect it to be nothing short of a major step forward for the arts in the Cedar Valley. Once we're open, people won't have to drive two hours to Iowa City for first-rate performing arts, I assure you."

Ann Hermann, owner of Cup of Joe, says Cedar Falls is loaded with visual art talent: "I never have to go outside of town to find good art for the exhibits we do. This is an anything-goes gallery setting in a surprisingly creative community, so what ends up on our walls is amazing. Our most popular exhibit is the 3-D Jesus show we do around the holiday season, but we also do some serious art. . . . The university has a great group of artists . . . and we've given a show to almost every art professor, as well as to students and the professional artists in Cedar Falls. It's not about sales . . . it's all about art."

Essentials

Population: 23,000

Art Events: Cinco de Mayo in May, Sturgis Falls Celebration in June, College Hill Arts Festival in July, Cedar Valley Arts & Crafts Show in September

Art Spaces: The Art Colony, Art & Frame on Main, Cup of Joe, Gallery One-Ten, Hearst Center for the Arts, Henry W. Myrtle Gallery, Holland Galleries, Main Gallery, Oster Regent Theatre, Storefront Gallery, UNI Gallery of Art, Waterloo Museum of Art

Hangouts: Brown Bottle, Nickers Grill, Olde Broom Factory, Steb's, Tally's Grand Cafe, Toad's Bar & Grill

Bookstores: B. Dalton, Bought Again Books, Hill Street News, University Book & Supply

Public Radio: KUNI FM 90.9

Chamber of Commerce: P.O. Box 367, Cedar Falls, IA 50613, (319) 266-3593

Iowa City, Iowa

Culture capitals exist in all sizes, but when it comes to the Midwest, few small art towns approach Iowa City. This is where small-town life meets big-city art standards . . . where 60,000 full-time residents smoothly integrate with 27,000 college students and cherry-pick from a harvest of major, minor, and experimental art events, exhibits, concerts, and festivals.

Said to be the nation's best-educated community, Iowa City is also a fun place to live, where life is affordable and the folks are friendly. There's nightlife, liberal politics, a strong local school system, mass transit, and a safe downtown perfect for artist studios. A half-day's drive gets you to Chicago, Memphis, and a half-dozen other urban areas. Expect to find lots of art galleries showing mostly local work—much of it created by University of Iowa grads who have decided that this is the perfect place to raise a family, advance a career, and build a future.

Lifestyle

As word of Iowa City's high quality of life spreads, so does its population rise. Outlying communities such as Coralville and, to a lesser extent, Downey are sprouting homes at a breakneck pace. What once was 25 miles of farmland between Iowa City and Cedar Rapids is filling in with malls and subdivisions—you'll even find rush-hour traffic along this stretch of I-380. Houses in Iowa City's older neighborhoods sell in the $120,000 range, while a subdivision home in Coralville averages about $5,000 more.

A recent trend has been a wave of retirees moving here from other parts of Iowa. These folks had one helluva great time here during their college years, and they now want to root for the Hawkeyes from season seats in Kinnick Stadium, take art classes at Arts Iowa City, catch one of Riverside Theatre's expertly staged plays, and soak in free summer jazz concerts at Pedestrian Plaza.

Arts Scene

Iowa City is not only an easy place for artists to live and work, it's also an arts-and-culture–lover's dream. Unlike nearby Cedar Rapids, which assembled its high-quality arts scene from local public and private dollars, Iowa City built and maintains the luxuries art lovers take for granted here with state funding.

On campus are numerous theaters and concert halls, most prominently the Iowa Center for the Arts, home to the 2,600-seat Hancher Auditorium, Clapp Auditorium, and the UI Museum of Art. Hancher presents a performing arts series loaded with classical music, world music, touring theater, and dance. It imports acts such as the Sydney Dance Company, Sweet Honey in the Rock, Kronos Quartet, and the Chieftans. The art museum covers all visual-art and fine-crafts bases, hanging historic and contemporary international work and celebrating important midwestern voices.

Classical music concerts are held in the senate chamber of the Old Capitol and at Harper Hall. Cedar Rapids Symphony stages its season at the Paramount Theatre. Families enjoy Iowa City Community Theatre's five-play season at the 4-H Fairgrounds, while a more issues-oriented approach guides Riverside

Theatre's September-to-June, six-play season. Performing in its 110-seat downtown playhouse, Riverside's professional resident company mixes new and classic material. On campus at the Thayer and Mabie Theaters, University Theaters presents its main-stage and gallery seasons of new works, locally produced plays, and commissioned pieces. No Shame Theatre, also on campus, uses Theatre B for its season of experimental works.

While the art museum is Iowa City's visual arts hub, the community also boasts numerous galleries and alternate exhibition venues. Even the Chamber of Commerce has a gallery. Arts Iowa City maintains a branch in Coralville, and during the warmer months hosts a Gallery Walk downtown. The region's cutting-edge contemporary space, CSPS in Cedar Rapids, hosts performances, concerts, and exhibits by local and national artists. The town's art-friendly library allows residents to borrow paintings and sculpture as they would check out a book.

Art Talk

"The level of sophistication and knowledge of the arts that exists in Iowa City is probably the best for any community this size anywhere in the country," says Mark Ginsberg, owner of M.C. Ginsberg, Inc. "The attitude here has allowed me to refine a national approach to collectors and develop two galleries representing national and international work. . . . People see us as a place that sells pieces normally associated with metropolitan area galleries. . . . I don't know why there aren't more galleries like this in Iowa, because the collectors certainly are here."

"Our audiences are part of an educated community, an older community, and an affluent community," says Ron Clark, artistic director and cofounder of Riverside Theatre. "We travel to New York, London, and elsewhere searching for the [innovative] material that will keep our audience coming back for more."

Essentials

Population: 60,000

Art Events: Arts RiverFest in April, UI Iowa Playwrights Festival in May, Iowa City ArtsFair in June, Iowa City Craft Show in September, Thieves Market and Iowa Independent Film & Video Festival in October

Art Spaces: Artifacts, Artists Concepts Gallery, Arts Iowa City, Arts Iowa City West, The Brewery, The Cottage, The Cottage West, Custom Surfaces Gallery, Drewlowe Gallery, First National Bank, Frame House Gallery, Gallery One, Gallery 202, Hancher Auditorium Gallery, Hudson River Frame Co., Iowa Artisans Gallery, Iowa City Chamber Gallery, Java House, Lorenz Boot Shop, M. C. Ginsberg, Summit Street Gallery, The Tobacco Bowl, Transitions Studio

Hangouts: The Brewery, Gabe's Oasis, Martini's, Mill Restaurant, The Que, The Sanctuary

Bookstores: The Bookery, Haunted Bookshop, Iowa Book & Supply, Murphy Brookfield Books, Northside Books, Prairie Lights Bookstore

Public Radio: WSUI AM 910

Chamber of Commerce: 325 E. Washington St. #100, Iowa City, IA 52244, (319) 337-9637

Lawrence, Kansas

Once a stop on the Underground Railroad, Lawrence has always been a bastion for free spirits—this college town was home to William S. Burroughs until his death in 1997. With 65,000 full-time residents and 25,000 University of Kansas students, Lawrence has the economic clout and infrastructure to support everything from a strong visual and performing arts scene to nightlife, brewpubs, body-piercing shops, natural food stores, Thai restaurants, used-record stores, and places selling hemp clothing. One of the nation's premier Native American colleges is also here, and you can even order a breakfast burrito in Lawrence without confusing the waitress. In recent years this art-conscious place has become a prime relocation spot for retirees and has also lured a new breed of entrepreneurs who have buffed up the tired side of downtown's Massachusetts Street and helped make Lawrence the Midwest's City of the Arts.

Lifestyle

Neighborhoods within walking distance of Lawrence's gleaming business district range from student ghettos to chic, upscale streets lined with elegantly restored Victorians. An average-size home costs $145,000 on the outskirts of town, but fixer-uppers near downtown can easily be found for half that.

For decades the community's old-money families have fought to keep downtown viable as Lawrence's shopping and socializing core, a battle that's paid off in the form of Massachusetts Street, one of the nation's best-preserved examples of pre-mall-crazy America. College students enjoy all the stores and music joints they need right downtown, and the rest of the community has everything it needs—from the outstanding Lawrence Arts Center to children's clothing stores, hardware stores, and bookshops. Meanwhile, the community's steady suburban expansion westward and an over-budget highway project have divided locals along pro- and antigrowth lines.

Arts Scene

Artists love to call Lawrence home—more for its great quality of life than for the strength of the local art market, which is developing slowly. The Lawrence Arts Center is central to the community's arts life—for the strong exhibitions at its Eastwood Gallery, the shows at its black-box performance space, an arts-based preschool, and year-round art classes for adults and kids.

Over 50 local artists sell their work through the Lawrence Art Guild's Riverfront Gallery, while many others opt to show work at alternative venues such as cafés and restaurants. Outside town are two bronze foundries, a studio glass gallery, and five commercial galleries showing fine crafts and contemporary prints, paintings, and sculpture. On campus, the Kansas Union Gallery and the Art & Design Gallery exhibit local and regional work, touring national and international shows appear at the Helen Foresman Spencer Museum of Art, and ethnographic exhibitions visit the Natural History Museum.

Ever since the Lied Center—a breathtaking, 2,020-seat performing arts center—opened its doors a few years ago, Lawrence has been saturated with the Lied's events. Nearly two for kids. Fredericks Auditorium holds Hanchey Gallery, with two exhibition spaces, and the Closet Gallery. The Hanchey hosts regional and touring national shows, and the Closet houses mostly faculty and student exhibitions. The best examples of Natchitoches's historic home furnishings style, crafted from locally grown cypress, are exhibited at Oliver's.

Art Talk

According to Fred Gianforte, painter and member of the Natchitoches Art Guild, the community is open-minded about art: "I'm a painter of nudes and floral landscapes, and even though my nudes don't appeal to everyone, the 10 percent or so of people who don't care for them always are respectful enough to make positive comments about my technique, along with their negative comments about my choice of subject matter. This is a community that encourages its residents to get involved in community life, which is why we're such an attractive place for young families looking to raise their kids in a low-crime setting. What could make Natchitoches an even better place for the arts would be to develop some sort of working artists' studio complex—a place that would help artists sell and attract more cultural tourists. And what we also need is a well-run private, commercial art gallery. We already get lots of buyers who come through town, and I'm amazed at the numbers of European tourists who visit here."

Jack Wann, artistic director of Northwestern Theatre, says his program is focused on teaching students survival skills they need for careers in theater. "I'm an equity actor, and so are several of the department's teachers," he says. "We know what it takes to find an agent, what it takes to succeed at an audition, and what's required of an actor in terms of mastering the skills of her or his craft. I like to say what we provide here is a combination of ammunition and art—when students graduate from this program they're ready for whatever the real world throws at them, and lots have gone on to work in New York or L.A. For people living here, a program like ours provides first-rate entertainment year-round. We've even started a summer season of two dinner-theater plays—musicals and comedies—like you'd see done in any other summer stock theater."

Essentials

Population: 17,000

Art Events: Jazz and Rhythm & Blues Festival in March, Melrose Plantation Arts & Crafts Festival in June, NSU Folklife Festival in July, Christmas Festival of Lights

Art Spaces: Hancher Gallery, Closet Gallery, Heritage Gallery, Martin's Roost, Louisiana Gallery, Cane River Crafts, Oliver's, The Landing, Papa's Bar & Grill, Cafe Isabella

Hangouts: Roque's Blues Hall, The Courtyard, Café Caffé, Papa's Bar & Grill

Bookstores: Book Merchant, Campus Corner

Public Radio: KLSA FM 90.7, KDAQ FM 89.9

Chamber of Commerce: P.O. Box 3, Natchitoches, LA 71458, (318) 352-6894

Belfast, Camden, and Rockport, Maine

Considered together, the art towns along the shores of Penobscot Bay in Maine's mid-coast region offer an incredible range of opportunities for cultural tourists, artists, and art-loving retirees. Add to these three towns Searsport to the north and Rockland to the south, and the regional arts scene will satisfy even the most avid arts hound.

This historic area is characterized by lighthouses, restored railway lines, sailing schooners, and hundreds of miles of pristine shoreline. Its abundant attractions include state parks galore, Camden's downhill ski area, u-pick raspberry and blueberry fields, community theaters and opera houses, an extremely healthy summer tourism season, and one of America's lowest crime rates. Artists come here to make a good living, enjoy a fine quality of life, and send their kids to progressive, results-oriented schools.

Lifestyle

As those elsewhere along Maine's coast, Penobscot Bay artists live and breathe for summer's lucrative tourism season. While this region has more year-round residents than strict summer havens such as Deer Isle, many artists still beat a hasty retreat southward after autumn's peak glory.

Take a drive down any country road for an impressive vista of gorgeous barns, waterfront views, moored lobster boats, and historic homesteads. Over the years, many of the area's historic structures have been restored. Homes in the $80,000 range are easy to find, with shorefront properties starting at around $105,000.

Arts Scene

Belfast, with its Institute for Advanced Thinking, Community Multi-Cultural Arts Project, Belfast Bay Brewing Company, and Belfast Arts Council, occupies the "progressive" high ground among the region's communities. Rockland serves as the area's well-financed link to the mainstream art world; its Farnsworth Art Museum contains substantial holdings of works by Andrew and Jamie Wyeth, Louise Nevelson, Marsden Hartley, Edward Hopper, and Maurice Prendergast. Rockland is also the site of the Olson House, the setting for Andrew Wyeth's famous painting *Christina's World.* The Farnsworth is currently constructing a Wyeth art center.

The region is loaded with art and fine crafts galleries, as well as artist-run studio galleries. Rockland also hosts Maine Coast Artists, which exhibits the work of established and emerging contemporary artists. The Rockport College MFA program offers some employment opportunities for artists, while the internationally respected Maine Photographic Workshop imports photojournalists and fine-art photographers into Rockport for its summer seminars.

On the music scene, Camden has begun booking jazz and classical concerts in its recently restored opera house. Rockport's opera house hosts the Bay Chamber Concerts, a year-round series of classical, jazz, and world music. Year-round productions in the Railroad Theater by the Belfast Maskers are enormously popular with local audiences, as are innovative performance and instructional programs presented year-round by the Belfast Dance Studio.

Art Talk

John Womer, president of Maine Coast Artists, notes, "We've just completed a top-to-bottom renovation of what had once been Rockport's firehouse and livery stables, so now we're able to offer year-round exhibition, education, and community programs in a three-story structure right downtown. The focus of our programs continues to be aimed toward the professional artist—emerging, mid-career, and late-career—but we're now making a major effort to work with local schools through a number of unusual programs aimed at the broader community. We see this as a way to maintain our commitment to Maine's contemporary arts community. The state has been an arts mecca for over a century, and what we do is exhibit the work of more than 400 artists, much of which is groundbreaking and not seen in commercial galleries. And, we extend ourselves toward emerging artists as well as late-career artists who are creating new work. Our juried crafts show and art exhibitions draw gallery owners from throughout the state and art buyers from across the nation, as well as a large number of European collectors, and we've successfully linked a number of our artists with commercial galleries."

Of Belfast, artist Harold Garde observes, "There is a supportive group of artists here that review other artists' work, and even though some galleries have closed, an even larger number have opened. Along the shore in Camden and Rockport there's been a huge impact from the expansion of Maine Coast Artists, and artists continue to move into the area—not only painters and sculptors but also musicians, photographers, and writers. So, we have older people who seek out the area's lifestyle and artists who are switching off the big-city fast track. Local living artists sell very well, and with more galleries opening up all the time, that situation continues to present lots of opportunities. There are even galleries opening up along the highways and doing well with serious work that's beyond sweet landscapes and seascapes."

Essentials

Population: Belfast, 6,300; Camden, 5,000; Rockport, 3,000

Arts Events: Bay Chamber Concerts in Rockport year-round, Belfast Arts in the Park and State of the Art exhibition at Maine Coast Artists in July, Rockland Artists Studio Tour in August, Rockport Folk Festival in September, Maine Coast Artists crafts show in October

Art Spaces: Artfellows, Bell the Cat, Institute of Advanced Thinking, and Spring Street Gallery in Belfast; Gleason Fine Art, Hector's Canine Gallery, and Old Post Office Gallery in Camden; Massachusetts House Gallery in Lincolnville; Between the Muse Gallery, Caldbeck Gallery, and Farnsworth Art Museum in Rockland; Maine Coast Artists in Rockport

Hangouts: Dos Amigos Cantina and Gilbert's Publick House in Camden; Blue Goose in Northport; Second Read Books & Coffee in Rockland

Bookstores: Canterbury Tales Books and Fertile Mind Bookshop in Belfast; Owl & Turtle Bookshop in Camden; Reading Corner and Second Read Books & Coffee in Rockland

Public Radio: WERU FM 89.9

Chamber of Commerce: Belfast Chamber of Commerce, P.O. Box 58, Belfast, ME 04915, (207) 338-5900; Camden and Rockport Chamber of Commerce: P.O. Box 919, Camden, ME 04843, (207) 236-4404

Deer Isle and Blue Hill, Maine

Down East Maine is home to one of the East Coast's premier art markets in the gallery-rich towns of Deer Isle (on Deer Island) and Blue Hill (on the mainland). Separated by 20 miles of spectacular seacoast along Penobscot Bay and Blue Hill Bay, these towns roar to life during the tourist-heavy warm months and hibernate (in other words, practically shut down) from mid-October to May.

Lobstering, hospitality, and cultural tourism are the region's economic mainstays. The seafood industry primarily employs long-time locals, while a large percentage of newcomers are involved in tourism and arts endeavors. Separated from Blue Hill and the mainland by a spectacular suspension bridge, Deer Island is an artist's inspirational haven. It is renowned for its isolation and its wealth of natural wonders—from lupines in spring to hours-long sunsets in summer to autumn's technicolor leaf season.

Lifestyle

Artists living in this region can have it both ways. They can sell or perform to a crush of moneyed tourists during the warmer months and use the dark frigid winter to create new works for the following summer season. Or they can just head south in winter for spiritual and creative renewal. While some year-rounder artists may look askance at their brethren who trade Maine's snows for Oaxaca's kaleidoscopic vibrancy or Florida's sun-soaked golf courses, the bottom line for artists here is to maximize their income while the cultural tourists are in town and to hold on tight until the tourism cycle revives itself in late spring.

Housing runs the gamut—from small, $100,000 homes in forested neighborhoods to seven-figure waterfront mansions occupied part-time by Boston lawyers and New York stockbrokers. But even for those without trust funds, it's still possible to live just a short walk from a rocky beach and to soak in a jaw-dropping sunset while paddling a kayak through pristine ocean waters.

Arts Scene

While numbers vary from year to year, Blue Hill supports around ten commercial galleries, while North Deer Isle and South Deer Isle (which together make up Deer Isle) support around 20 commercial galleries as well as the respected Haystack Mountain School of Crafts, which operates in summer. Many local artists were originally lured here by Haystack, either as students or as teachers, and decided to put down roots. The Haystack connection explains the high caliber of visual arts and fine crafts available in local galleries.

The region's most influential arts voices are WERU FM 89.9, a music-oriented public radio station broadcasting from nearby Ellsworth; the Maine Crafts Association, a statewide nonprofit artists organization and gallery headquartered in Deer Isle; and Egg Maine Music Magazine, a hip and inclusive quarterly. Speaking of music, local offerings include the top-notch Kneisel Hall Chamber Music Festival held on a bucolic 20-acre campus just five minutes from the center of Blue Hill, as well as a stellar schedule of bluegrass, folk, rock, reggae, and zydeco artists booked into Blue Hill's Left Bank Bakery and Cafe.

Every possible venue—from churches to coffee shops to high school auditoriums—is used for local performances. But the area really needs a first-rate, 400- to 700-seat performing arts center—the type of facility the "summer people" from Boston, New York, and elsewhere would be likely to support.

Art Talk

"One of Maine's assets is its number of artists and musicians, which from what I've heard is one of the highest per-capita ratios in the country," says Paul Woodfin, publisher of *Egg Maine Music Magazine.* "Winters here are long, and they give people lots of opportunity to get together and make music or create their own art. The artists and musicians we have are smart, hip, and important parts of their communities. Tourism produces a huge amount of income throughout the region, but because our population is small and tourism is seasonal, we're restricted as to what can happen year-round. Our music scene continues to grow, in part because the state backs art education projects, but for sure we could use a performing arts hall besides the Grand Theater in Ellsworth."

"Nancy and I retired here in 1989, after I taught art for 20 years at Deerfield Academy," say Dan Hodermarsky, a watercolorist living in Deer Isle. "This is a place where people can live the good life, where an artist can enjoy an extremely quiet winter and have a dramatically poetic environment to enjoy in the summer. I'm a watercolorist and paint everything from figurative pieces to landscapes and architectural paintings, and every so often the Turtle Gallery here gives me a show. Lots of my sales come through people visiting my studio, tourists who see my ad in the paper or hear about me. Like any artist, I'd like to sell more paintings, but for anyone who has self-confidence and lots of hustle, Deer Isle presents lots of opportunity. Some artists move away in winter, but I've found the people here to be so friendly that we prefer living here year-round."

Essentials

Population: Deer Isle, 2,800; Blue Hill, 2,600
Art Events: Antiques, Crafts and Collectibles Fair in July, Steel Band Street Dance and Seamark Artists' Studio Tour in August
Art Spaces: Liros Gallery, Peninsula Weavers, Deer Isle Artists Association, Blue Heron Gallery, Maine Crafts Association, Turtle Gallery, Green Head Forge, Dan Hodermarsky Studio, Mainstreet Studio Gallery, Leighton Gallery in Blue Hill

Hangouts: Left Bank Bakery & Cafe, Lily's Cafe & Catering
Bookstores: Blue Hill Books, Village Bookshop, Dockside Books & Gifts
Public Radio: WERU FM 89.9
Chamber of Commerce, P.O. Box 459, Stonington, ME 04681, (207) 348-6124

Portland, Maine

Arts in the seaport community of Portland, Maine's largest city with 64,000 residents, used to operate in the shadow of Boston's big money, big city arts scene. Today, with its resurgent economy and a downtown arts boom fueled by local political willpower and the talents of a new generation of artists, Portland stands tall as one of the nation's best small art towns. About the only thing Portland needs from Boston these days are cultural tourists. Every weekend, day-tripping urbanites swarm to Portland in search of great quality, affordable art, live music in Old Port, and performances by the Portland Symphony Orchestra (under the direction of maestro Toshiyuki Shimada).

Portland took the late '80s economic downturn squarely on its chin. A bustling real estate market, fueled by over-optimistic speculation, crashed and burned, dragging the city's job market (not to mention its civic pride) to all-time lows. About the same time, downtown's main drag, Congress Street, practically emptied out when a major department store and dozens of smaller businesses either high-tailed it out to the blacktop wonderland of suburban malls or folded up in the face of an influx of national retail chains.

Things began turning around in the early 1990s when the Maine College of Art (MCA) renovated what had been the state's largest department store into a five-story complex of classrooms, studios, exhibition spaces, and offices. The complex transformed Congress Street, providing a daily influx of more than 500 students, teachers, and staff. The expected boom in sandwich and cappuccino sales took place first, followed by a coordinated effort between the city and local arts organizations to use MCA's commitment as the starting point for a downtown arts corridor along Congress Street.

Today, Congress Street and its adjoining boulevards shine with new galleries, restaurants, coffee bars, boutiques, and other arts-related businesses. A forecast of continued decline has turned instead into an arts-based economic development success story.

Lifestyle

Including its outlying municipalities, the Portland metropolitan area has more than 200,000 residents. The state's best sandy beach, Old Orchard Beach, is just south of town, while two of New England's best ski areas, Sunday River and Sugarloaf USA, are around two hours north. Schools are strong, and while real estate values have escalated over the past couple of years, it's not hard to find a charming three-bedroom home with a yard and basement for less than $100,000.

Winters are at least five-month struggles against freezing temperatures and gloomy skies, with autumn arriving in mid-September and April sometimes disappointing gardeners anxious for the start of tomato growing season. "OK, it gets cold here in the winter, but somehow people just get used to it," says Deborah Krichels, executive director of the Portland Arts and Cultural Alliance, in a typically "Mainer" understatement. Just as gallery boppers in Seattle bundle up and waterproof themselves for that city's eminently successful First Thursday round of gallery openings, Portlanders make a point of thumbing their noses at some of the nation's most unforgiving winter weather. It's anything but unusual to spot groups of people walking around in 10-degree weather, chatting amiably, and acting as if they've got time to linger.

Recreational opportunities are many. The Sea Dogs, Portland's minor-league baseball team, is a farm club of the world champion Florida Marlins. The town is also home to a pro hockey team, a children's museum, and a children's theater company.

In its older quarters, Portland is very much a community of neighborhoods. You'll find microbrews on tap at small taverns and older cafés converted into culinary showcases by chefs from around the Northeast. As in other New England art towns, the culinary arts are flourishing in Portland. Never before has the community been blessed with such a wide range of ethnic eateries, as well as chic joints filled with local art and serving Maine's spectacular seafoods.

Arts Scene

Contemporary, traditional, and fine craft galleries, an art museum, professional theater, symphony, art school, studio spaces, nightclubs, recording studios, alternative art exhibition venues, summer music festivals— Portland has all the components of a great arts scene. Of course, there's no point in having an arts infrastructure in place if there aren't artists enough to fill the void. But one thing Portland is not lacking for is talent.

"The word's out about Portland being a happening place for the arts, a fun place to live, and somewhere where it's possible to start an arts career," says Mary Allen Lindemann, owner of Coffee by Design, a three-shop coffeehouse empire exhibiting and selling work by local artists alongside sacks of Guatemalan coffee beans. "You would be surprised at the resumes I get from young artists who are moving here from all over the country and need a day job to support the art they're creating at night. It may just be a word of mouth reputation, but Portland's got a good one."

On a national level, Portland's most prominent arts organization is the Portland Symphony Orchestra, which has been featured on NPR's *Performance Today.* The symphony's season runs from October into May and features a pops program and a chamber orchestra program, as well as Christmas and Fourth of July shows. Most performances are staged in the 1,909-seat Merrill Auditorium at City Hall, an impeccably restored 1912 concert hall that reopened in 1997 to national acclaim.

The Portland Concert Association stages its annual Great Performances series at the Merrill, with the likes of James Galway, Quartetto Gelato, and Opera Nazionale Italiana in a first-rate season from October to May. Merrill Auditorium also houses the Kotzschmar organ, a 6,613-pipe behemoth and one of the world's premier Austin organs. The Summer on the Kotzschmar concert series brings top organists from across the nation into Portland for performances costing only $5 a seat.

Portland Performing Arts, another organization that occasionally uses Merrill Auditorium but also employs venues such as the State Street Church and Portland High School, brings a wonderful selection of world, gospel, contemporary folk, and experimental modern music into Portland during its September through May season. The group also oversees the performance end of the House Island Project, a Lila Wallace Foundation effort aimed, among other things, at bringing ethnic performing arts companies to Portland. Puerto Rican drummers, Cambodian dancers, Québecois step dancers, and Greek folk musicians are but a few of the many artists featured.

Portland Stage Company, the state's largest professional theater organization, performs at the Portland Performing Arts Center off Congress Street. Some of Portland's other stage companies (Dark Water Theatre and

Once & Future Theatricals) use the 120-seat Oak Street Theatre or their own stages, as do Mad Horse Theatre Company and Portland Lyric Theatre. Says Mike Levine, producing director of Oak Street Theatre, "We don't do household name productions, but we've found a niche here with a supportive audience that turns out for newer American plays and strong dramas. We're in our fourth year and have a great audience with lots of younger people who buy tickets on the day of an event rather than for a season series."

In addition, three summer outdoor music festivals deliver lots of free entertainment to Portland residents: the Summer in the Parks series, the Congress Square series, and the Noontime Summer Performances series.

When it comes to visual arts, the Portland Museum of Art on Congress Square is universally regarded as the region's most influential organization. PMA's exhibitions run the gamut: international contemporary, European masterworks, Maine modernists, Andrew Wyeth, French Impressionism, and photography.

Running a close second to PMA is a gallery operated by the Institute of Contemporary Art at the Maine College of Art. ICA's offerings range from student and faculty exhibitions to international shows. The Maine Artists Space/Danforth Gallery is an artist-run organization presenting everything from contemporary drama to workshops, traveling exhibitions, electronic art, and member shows.

Galleries in Portland's downtown arts district tend to exhibit contemporary art, while galleries in the more heavily visited tourist magnet of Old Port tend toward traditional realism and crafts. June Fitzpatrick Gallery, Robert Clements Gallery, Danforth Gallery, Davidson & Daughters Gallery, and Pleasant Street Collective all show contemporary work. Spaces such as Exchange Street Gallery, Stein Contemporary Glass, Bayview Gallery, and Greenhut Gallery are in the Old Port district.

Alternative exhibition spaces, showing artists who for the most part haven't yet broken into the gallery system, are located all over the downtown arts district. Coffee by Design's two downtown locations are premier exhibition spaces, while businesses such as Stone Coast Brewing Company, Free Street Taverna, Portland Coffee Roasting Company, Perfetto's Restaurant, and Kutz Hair Salon all have rotating exhibitions of local work.

Art Talk

"For galleries, being on Congress Street brings more foot traffic, but I'm not sure if it brings more sales," says Rosemarie Frick, an independent curator. "Summer people and phone sales during the winter are what keep a contemporary gallery alive here. Artists move here for the quality of life and because they want to be part of a growing arts scene. Openings are well attended and happen on Thursday and Friday evenings."

Deborah Krichels, executive director of Portland Arts and Cultural Alliance, adds, "There's an amazing amount of support for the arts by our community's wealthier residents. Today it's the city itself that supports the arts, because the arts are seen as the key to downtown's revitalization. You can stroll from restaurants on Congress Street to the nightclubs in Old Port, and as more artsy businesses move onto Congress there's going to be even more pedestrian traffic downtown at night."

"Visitors from Boston day trip around here and buy art, but our base of local contemporary art collectors is small—and growing," says gallery owner June Fitzpatrick. "Older collectors are the most active, but I'm always willing to do layaways for younger collectors who can pay over time. We have so many artists here I wish I had a larger gallery, and from time to time I rent out alternative spaces to show especially worthy work. To find good artists all I have to do is open my door and they come in to see me—I don't have to leave town. My point of view is very optimistic about Portland's art scene. I've been open five years and I'm doing just fine."

Leo Pelletier is a gallery and frame shop owner. "I do a lot of art leasing around Portland to hospitals and offices," he says. "I find great new artists all the time and must have exhibited 200 of them in the past two years. ICA brought a new atmosphere to downtown, a good atmosphere that's helped the entire community."

Coffeeshop owner Mary Allen Lindemann notes, "Art is a large part of our mission, and we've broken through in the sense that our openings are well attended and written about in the newspapers. We've sold over 300 pieces of art through shows that rotate every six weeks and have matched lots of artists up with gallery owners from New York, San Francisco, and Boston—people who are on vacation who stop in here for coffee and immediately notice the work on our walls and want to meet the artists. We take a 20 percent commission and do mailings and press releases for our openings, as well as staff the openings and sell the work. I think that art becomes art for everyone when its shown in an atmosphere like this. Yes, it has built our position in the art community—but it's also allowed us to introduce art to people who never step foot in galleries or museums."

David Wells, gallery director, concludes, "Portland has a lot of creative energy and that's what's attracting artists to live here. There are a number of artists here who are working beyond traditional limits and who are expanding the limits of abstract art—they help give Portland's art scene a sense of excitement."

Essentials

Population: 64,000

Art Events: Noontime Summer Performance Series, Congress Square Series, Summer in the Parks performances, Annual Public Art Exhibition July through October, Sidewalk Art Festival in August, One World Portland in September, New Year's Portland in December

Art Spaces: Frost Gully Gallery, June Fitzpatrick Gallery, Greenhut Galleries, Jameson Gallery, Danforth Gallery, Robert Clements Gallery, Davidson & Daughters Gallery, ICA Gallery, Pleasant Street Collective, Portland Museum of Art

Hangouts: Coffee by Design, Stone Coast Brewing Co., Mesa Verde, Gritty McDuff's, Zoots, Asylum, Portland Coffee Roasting Company

Bookstores: Harding's Book Shop, Cunningham Books, Bookland, Books, Etc.

Public Radio: WMEA FM 90.1

Chamber of Commerce: 305 Commercial St., Portland, ME 04101, (207) 772-4994

Easton, Maryland

An edge city of Washington, D.C., and the cultural center of Maryland's Eastern Shore, Easton has always offered an outstanding quality of life. But recently, upscale cultural tourists and weekending urban professionals have discovered Eastern Shore art and housing. Thus, the Easton area can now support vibrant arts scenes, and resident artists can derive much of their annual income from regional sales, performances, and concerts.

Lifestyle

From Easton, a 90-minute drive will take you to the front door of a Georgetown (D.C.) jazz club. An even shorter drive will transport you to an Orioles game at Camden Yards. In Easton or one of the Eastern Shore's other safe and friendly communities, you'll also have the treasure of Chesapeake Bay at your fingertips. Easton's wildlife artists and decoy carvers (some of the nation's very best) enjoy year-round birding as well as a duck-hunting season of legendary bounty. For those who enjoy the water, it's possible to sail, fish, and go oystering in all but the coldest winter months.

The Eastern Shore's real estate market continues to boom, a mixed blessing for artists. In Easton, a home for $140,000 is considered a steal, while in tonier Chestertown, the going rates are even higher.

Arts Scene

Easton's arts scene is founded on four gems: the Historic Avalon Theatre, the Academy of the Arts, the Eastern Shore Chamber Music Festival, and the Waterfowl Festival. Nearby communities such as Oxford and Tilghman

Island offer a few galleries and art festivals, while St. Michael's contains the historic Chesapeake Bay Maritime Museum, complete with art festivals, rotating maritime art shows, and free summer concerts. In addition to the Chester River Craft & Art School, Chestertown sustains both a fine crafts gallery and a contemporary art gallery.

Despite its small population, Easton is diverse enough to support a metaphysical bookstore, a free summer music festival in Muskrat Park, the 400-acre Pickering Creek Environmental Center, and the November Waterfowl Festival, offering a multifaceted art show plus technical workshops in sculpture, painting, and decoy carving.

While the historic Tidewater Inn serves as an important exhibition space for regional artists, Easton's finest galleries are found within the Academy of the Arts, an enormously popular art education, exhibition, and studio complex. Housed in a converted schoolhouse, the academy's 24,000 square feet receive year-round use. Offerings include traveling shows from such places as the Baltimore Museum of Art, kids summer theater camps, a noontime classical concert series, local invitational art exhibits, and instruction ranging from dance to figurative painting to raku to kids printmaking workshops. One of the nation's most effective and impressive small-town art centers—serving more than 50,000 participants each year—the academy and its 250-plus annual programs are exceptional in their breadth of focus and community-wide impact.

For a dozen years the Eastern Shore Chamber Music Festival has gathered many of the nation's top soloists and chamber ensembles for two weeks of June concerts at the Historic Avalon Theatre. Once a twenties vaudeville house, this 400-seat jewel has now become much more than just the Eastern Shore's largest performing arts venue. It's the type of diverse facility every community lusts after—the sort of place that swings from classic movies to live radio shows to gospel concerts to contemporary American folk musicians to children's theater all year long.

Art Talk

"This is the sort of region where people driving through on weekends can suddenly decide to spend $8,000 on a sculpture or $4,000 on a painting," notes Chestertown gallery owner Carla Massoni. "Artists love living here, and there are 12 million people living within a 90-minute drive. We keep established name artists and lots of young artists in the gallery because collectors are always looking for something new. Towns in this area are linking their economic development to the arts—and it's working."

Performing arts presenter and Historic Avalon Theatre owner Ellen General works to keep the theater available to the entire community: "We just put in a public access television studio, and we've started presenting summer concerts in Idlewild Park, just to improve upon the cooperation that other arts organizations in the region are already demonstrating. Rehearsals, lectures, and public issues forums are all part of what we must do to have a truly multipurpose facility in this small community. We're hardly ever dark."

Essentials

Population: 11,000
Art Events: Mid-Atlantic Maritime Arts Festival and Oxford Fine Arts Fair in May, Chestertown Art in the Park in September, Waterfowl Festival in November, First Night in December
Art Spaces: Academy of the Arts, Carla Massoni Gallery, Chesapeake Bay Maritime Museum, Cultural Arts Gallery, Kerns Collection of Contemporary Crafts, Oxford Art Works, St. Michael's Cultural Center, Tidewater Inn, Troika Gallery

Hangouts: Decoy Lounge, Le Zinc, Time Out Tap & Grill
Bookstores: Compleat Bookseller, News Center, Rowens Bookstore
Public Radio: WSCL FM 89.5
Chamber of Commerce: P.O. Box 1366, Easton, MD 21601, (410) 822-4606

Martha's Vineyard, Massachusetts

Beaches, lighthouses, sunsets, and Mad Martha's ice cream parlors are what make this 100-square-mile island off the Massachusetts coast so popular with its 14,000 full-time residents. But the summer boom that surges the island's head count past the 100,000 mark, and a recent onslaught of million-dollar-plus trophy homes, are constant worries to artists and gallery owners concerned about their revered quality of life. Still, Martha's Vineyard remains a fantastic place for artists wanting to work in a relatively unspoiled setting just a 45-minute ferry ride from the mainland.

Lifestyle

The island's residents are clustered around the towns of Oak Bluffs, Vineyard Haven, and Edgartown—collectively known as Down Island. The towns of Gay Head, Chilmark, and West Tisbury on the island's west end are called Up Island.

Local taxes are highest Down Island, but wherever you set foot on Martha's Vineyard, the real estate market operates at sky-high levels. It's not unusual to meet artists who bought modest homes back in the 1970s and early '80s and now find themselves living in homes valued in the $500,000 range (and are working like mad to pay their property taxes!). Still, a small, three-bedroom house away from the waterfront and needing some work can sometimes be found for $150,000.

Island schools are quite good, and this being a heavily touristed area, there are fabulous restaurants on practically every street corner, as well as respectable year-round nightlife. It seems as if the island has at least one of everything: the brewpub is City Ale & Oyster House, the rib joint is Smoke 'n' Bones, the natural foods store is 24 Carrots, and the Mexican place is Zapotec Cafe. Regrettably, there appears to have been a population explosion in fudge shops and T-shirt vendors. Nonetheless, the island remains a great place for bike riding, sailing, fishing, and birding.

Arts Scene

Up Island, Down Island—it makes no difference where you are because art galleries are everywhere. Martha's Vineyard has one of the nation's healthiest visual arts marketplaces, and exhibition spaces here are loaded with work by local, regional, and national artists. Contemporary work and fine crafts both sell remarkably well, though both take a back seat to scenes of kite-flying kids on beaches, happy families on the seashore, lighthouses at sunset, and other traditional seascapes. There are dozens of galleries on the island as well as dozens of antiques stores. Martha's Vineyard Center for the Visual Arts in Oak Bluffs operates the Firehouse Gallery and offers year-round art classes in its converted firehouse.

Vineyard Playhouse flips back from a summer Equity company to a community theater company in winter. The playhouse presents an intriguing main-stage season at its 120-seat Vineyard Haven playhouse and July and August outdoor Shakespeare productions at 150-seat Tisbury Amphitheater. Kids enjoy a summer arts camp and year-round children's theater performances.

The Yard, a summer residency program, stages plays and dance performances at its Chilmark Theater, and the island's newest theater group, Island Actors Company, performs at Featherstone Meetinghouse for the Arts (also home to a full range of visual arts and fine crafts workshops and exhibits). Other companies are Island Theatre Workshop, Theatre Arts Productions, and Word Magic Ensemble.

The island's community orchestra, the Vineyard Sinfonietta, performs four yearly concerts as well as free Sunday afternoon rehearsals in summer. The Chamber Music Society presents year-round concerts, a ten-concert summer series, and music education programs in local schools.

Wintertide Coffeehouse, nonprofit and alcohol-free, is the island's funky, homegrown music center with folk, blues, jazz, and world music performances year-round. The Hot Tin Roof nightclub presents big-name national and regional rock, blues, and folk acts, while Atlantic Connection mixes live dance bands with DJ nights. The Ritz Cafe and the Lampost also offer live music. The island's bona fide jazz scene uses a variety of venues—Wintertide Coffeehouse (for Sunday jazz brunch), Lola's Southern Seafood, City Ale & Oyster, Aquinnah Restaurant, Farm Neck Cafe, Louis' Tisbury Cafe, and the Ritz Cafe.

Art Talk

"Things have gotten easier for artists since our tourism season expanded to run from late April into October," says Chris Dreyer, arts administrator, "but the high cost of living on the island compels most artists to hold down another job. There are lots of shared housing situations and few affordable places to live. Some newer galleries are doing well with expensive art that's not typical island landscapes, and the craft galleries seem to do very well. Our Firehouse Gallery has exhibitions that change weekly in July and August, and we do member shows and invitationals from May through September. The island is loaded with talented people, but they have to be talented in many ways just to survive."

According to gallery owner Holly Alaimo, "The island's new home owners have bought lots of local art for their homes and made it possible for galleries selling work other than island scenes to survive. Abstract, nonrepresentational art is still a more difficult sell, but many gallery owners feel a sense of commitment to the work and artists, so they keep it on their walls. In the heavily touristed areas, rents are too high to allow for much experimentation at the galleries, so there are new home-based exhibition spaces opening up and galleries going into areas where in the past you wouldn't expect to find them. The key to surviving here is to own your gallery space."

Essentials

Population: 14,000

Art Events: Vineyard Haven Art Walks monthly, Oak Bluffs Harbor Festival in June, All-Island Art Show and Jazzfest in August, Vineyard Artisans Festival on Labor Day and Thanksgiving weekends, Vineyard Craftsmen Annual Art & Craft Fair in October, First Night Celebration in December

Art Spaces: Firehouse Gallery, Featherstone Meetinghouse, Shaw Cramer Gallery, Gardner-Colby Gallery, Old Sculpin Gallery, Craven & Sanford Gallery, Etherington Fine Art (North Tisbury and Vineyard Haven), The Field Gallery, Dragonfly Gallery, Craftworks, Chilmark Pottery, The Christina Gallery, Kennedy Studios Gallery

Hangouts: Lola's Southern Seafoods, Jack's Pub, Wintertide Coffeehouse, Hot Tin Roof, The Ritz Cafe, Season's Pub

Bookstores: Bickerton & Ripley, Bunch of Grapes Bookstore

Public Radio: WGBH FM 89.7

Chamber of Commerce: P.O. Box 1698, Martha's Vineyard, MA 02568, (508) 693-0085

Nantucket, Massachusetts

E ver since turn-of-the-century summer stock actors boarded Nantucket's ferry seeking two months of relief from stifling July and August weather in Boston and New York City, this island off Cape Cod has been rightfully known as an artists' haven. Today, with milder-than-average winters and continuing growth of cultural tourism, Nantucket is also among New England's strongest art markets. This 3.5-by-14.5-mile hump of land in the Atlantic is a place of legendary pristine beaches, wandering bike trails that double as roads, and nearly a thousand historic homes ranging from colonial mansions to gray-shingled cottages built by long-dead whalers. The island, town, and county all share the name Nantucket.

Lifestyle

Growth is this town's fighting word. Out-of-control residential development—in the form of trophy homes built by weekenders from New York, Boston, and Hartford—sprawls across the island, creating a community of "have-a-lots" and "have-what-I-needs." Even ordinary real estate here is costly because owners can use it as lucrative summer rental property. Cottages in the $150,000 range are considered bargains, and an average-size home is more likely to cost $300,000.

From summer's start to its end, Nantucket is crowded and busy. Reservations are mandatory for everything from ferry travel to lunch breaks. Parking is horrendous—despite the island government's plea for visitors to leave their four-wheel-drives on the mainland and instead use one of the island's many taxicabs or rent a bicycle. Off-season begins at the close of Labor Day weekend and brings months of quiet, solace, and available parking spaces.

Arts Scene

Summer's cultural tourism wave supports more than 40 art galleries and provides gallery owners and artists with enough income to make it through the very slow (but steadily improving) off-season. Artists who paint seascapes, cottages, and lighthouses have traditionally been the best sellers in local galleries, but that's changing as a new breed of artists and art entrepreneurs enters Nantucket's visual arts market and pursues a decidedly contemporary pathway. The surprising success of spaces such as The (X) Gallery, Art Cabinet, Main Street Gallery, South Wharf Gallery, and Sailor's Valentine Gallery (for both visual arts and fine crafts) in exhibiting contemporary work has broadened Nantucket's somewhat introspective visual arts offerings and has encouraged more artists to move here and try their luck in this lucrative market.

This art town's most prominent art group is the Artists' Association of Nantucket, an organization that operates one of the island's best galleries (at 19 Washington Street), exhibiting contemporary work as well as works from its permanent 700-plus-piece collection. Year-round, the association sponsors art classes for children and adults—both beginners and experienced artists.

The year-round Theater Workshop of Nantucket performs at Bennett Hall. In summer its Star Series combines locally produced plays (including guest performances) with a festival of modern dance. Two other groups, Actors

Theatre of Nantucket and Island Stage, present summer stock plays. In the Performance Center, a converted Methodist church, Actors Theatre offers children's theater as well as adult material by the likes of A. R. Gurney.

Two classical music groups, the Nantucket Chamber Music Center and the Musical Arts Society, use the Unitarian Universalist Church for their concerts, while the First Congregational Church holds concerts drawing larger-than-average audiences. Nantucket High School's Walker Auditorium hosts touring recording artists such as James Taylor and Arlo Guthrie. During summer, Nantucket has a respectable nightlife scene, with bands appearing at such spots as The Muse, Rose & Crown, The Box, Harbor House, Cross Rip Coffeehouse, and the Tap Room.

Nantucket Island School of Design & the Arts offers a popular storytelling and summer Cultural Arts Lecture Series. The Nantucket Atheneum, the town's public library, also hosts a summer lecture series and exhibits local art in its gallery space. Historical lectures are held at the Egan Institute of Maritime Studies (at the Coffin School) and at the Whaling Museum.

Art Talk

Dörte Neudert, owner of Art Cabinet Nantucket, remarks: "I exhibit five contemporary European artists and have found a niche here selling contemporary work. I can walk to my gallery from my home in 10 minutes, expect to see my collectors when they're here on vacation, and meet new clients who have a developed taste in the arts. Artists here need to be daring and let collectors see their true signatures if they're going to be successes. If you offer this market quality, you'll do very well."

According to painter Joan Albaugh, "There are affluent, art-wise people from all across the country swarming over the island during the summer and lots of down time to paint during winter. Most artists exhibit at a gallery and also sell out of their studios during those three busy months. Nantucket has lots of restaurants and things to do in the off-season, but it's becoming overbuilt."

Essentials

Population: 7,000
Art Events: Harborfest in June, Folk Art & Crafts Show in July, Nantucket Arts Festival and Sandcastle & Sculpture Day in August
Art Spaces: East End Gallery, Artists Association of Nantucket Gallery, Atheneum Gallery, Nantucket Glass Works, Off Centre Cafe, The (X) Gallery, Arsenault Gallery, Hostetler Gallery, Sailors Valentine Gallery, Bill Rowe Gallery, Nantucket Gallery, Art Cabinet Nantucket

Hangouts: The Muse, Cross Rip Coffeehouse
Bookstores: The Hub, Mitchell's Book Corner, Nantucket Bookworks
Public Radio: WGBH FM 89.7
Chamber of Commerce: 48 Main St., Nantucket, MA 02554, (508) 228-1700

Northampton, Massachusetts

Though its population is barely 30,000, when it comes to the arts, the western Massachusetts town of Northampton has nearly everything a major metropolis would envy. For artists, art collectors, arts lovers, and cultural tourists, this truly is Paradise City. Set amid a cluster of college towns in the Connecticut River's Pioneer Valley, Northampton benefits enormously from local arts entrepreneurship and the arts-related infrastructure of colleges in nearby Amherst and South Hadley. Together, Northampton and the communities within a 15-mile radius offer a diverse restaurant, nightclub, and visual arts scene, including numerous art museums, performing arts centers, and alternative art spaces.

Fortunately for Northampton, the region's commercial and corporate center is in nearby Springfield, home to the Basketball Hall of Fame as well as highly regarded fine arts, science, and history museums. Springfield's status as a commercial hub helps ensure that historic Northampton won't be pressured by big city–style development.

Lifestyle

With Boston just a 90-minute drive east and the Hartford airport only 30 minutes south, Northampton allows easy access to the entire range of arts that the Northeast has to offer. Need to drop off a few paintings at your Soho Gallery? That's an easy day trip. Want to catch the Matisse show at Boston's Fine Arts Museum? You can leave home at 8 a.m. and still return in time for a late lunch at the Del Raye Bar & Grill, Northampton's head-turning new hot spot on Bridge Street.

Living here means choosing neighborhood life in the valley towns of Northampton and Amherst or opting for a more rural, laid-back existence in surrounding hill towns such as Chesterfield, Cummington, and Huntington. Your valley neighbors could be a university professor and her stay-at-home artist husband or a lesbian couple who own a downtown Northampton gallery and are raising an adopted son. Either way, you'll pay $150,000 for an average-size valley home or a similar price for a hill-town residence with wooded acres and stunning views. One unintended result of Northampton's reasonable housing costs and high arts accessibility is a quiet influx of summer snowbirds, retirees who spend six months skimming the warm-weather cream from the valley's arts scene, then head south for six months of Gulf Coast beach decadence.

Ski areas are within easy reach of Northampton, while more challenging slopes are a two-hour drive north. In summer dozens of lakes and ponds become swimming holes, the Connecticut River draws canoers and kayakers, and sun-worshipers drive two hours to Hampton Beach on New Hampshire's coast. Arcadia Nature Center, south of Northampton, is a 700-acre Audubon preserve, and adjacent Mount Tom Reservation offers cross-country ski trails through thousands of acres of forest.

Arts Scene

Northampton constantly improves its arts scene, either through art center, museum, and gallery expansion projects or through art festivals that feed locals' voracious art appetites. The Massachusetts International Festival of the in a league of its own. The club scene here would put most metropolitan areas to shame. Jazz, rock, disco, dance bands, and folk music are found at nightspots too numerous to list.

Art Talk

According to Elisabeth Richter, a photographer and acting gallery director, "It's sales versus aesthetics in most of the town's galleries, but at galleries like DNA you see work that's contemporary, cutting-edge, and controversial. Most openings are on Fridays, and on Saturdays there will be moderated public discussions about the art because the people who come to Provincetown specifically for the art tend to seek interaction and dialogue with the artists. Some gallery years are up, some are down, but artists continue moving here because it's such a beautiful and supportive place. Usually, an artist will sign up for a program at the Cape Cod School of Art or the Fine Arts Work Center and just decide to live here after their class is completed—though housing costs

have started limiting the range of artists who can actually afford to do that. Our gay community is permanent and visible, with a lot of economic and business clout."

William Evaul is a wood-block print artist and B&B owner. "I sell directly through my B&B, which works well as a place to introduce people to my art," he says. "In the past I've run the museum and the art association and would advise anyone coming here to first develop the heart for what they think they want to do. Artists continue to move here at all costs, and we have some turnover in the galleries because the owners aren't always ready to do the hard work it takes to be a success. This is still a great place to live for its national seashore, its beach forests, its ponds, its nice people, and its supportive community of artists. What we still need is committed art dealers who are effective communicators of the value of the art being created here—art dealers who have as much passion for their work as the artists have."

Essentials

Population: 3,700
Art Events: Portuguese Festival in June, Carnavale and Food & Wine Festival in August, Provincetown Fall Arts Festival in September, Halloween in October
Art Spaces: Berta Walker Gallery, Walker's Wonders, Julie Heller Gallery, Kir Priore Gallery, Eva de Nagy Gallery, Rice/Polak Gallery, DNA Gallery, Passions Gallery, Peter Coes Studio, Long Point Gallery, Rising Tide Gallery, Kennedy Studios, Cherrystone Gallery, Blue Heron Gallery, Wohlfarth Gallery, Addison Holmes Gallery

Hangouts: Lorraine's, Bubala's by the Bay, Iguana Grill, Club Euro
Bookstores: Bookworm, Provincetown Bookshop
Public Radio: WGBH FM 89.7
Chamber of Commerce: P.O. Box 1017, Provincetown, MA 02657, (508) 487-3424

Saugatuck and Douglas, Michigan

The largest concentration of art galleries anywhere in the upper Midwest is in the small art town of Saugatuck and the neighboring community of Douglas, nestled into the spectacular sand dunes along Lake Michigan. Certainly, cities such as Chicago, Minneapolis, and Detroit have their own arts districts loaded with Euro-cafés and trendy art galleries. But with more than two dozen galleries crammed into a few square blocks of each community's downtown, Saugatuck and Douglas have more in common with places like Carmel and Provincetown than most midwesterners realize. It's weekending cultural tourists and second-home owners from Chicago who have made all this possible in what was once a quiet summer retreat for Art Institute of Chicago faculty.

Lifestyle

Make no mistake, Saugatuck and Douglas are decidedly "summer towns" whose art gallery owners, innkeepers, and marina owners make the majority of their income from Memorial Day to Labor Day. Although in years past these towns have more or less shut down for winter, a concerted effort by innkeepers and gallery owners has started to generate a little more shoulder-season business and a gangbusters Christmas week.

Home prices have fluctuated in recent years but the overall trend has been upward, and today an average-size Saugatuck residence runs in the $150,000 range. Prices are somewhat lower in Douglas and a whole lot cheaper in nearby places such as the vineyard community of Fennville or the larger community of Holland, less than a half-hour's drive north.

Arts Scene

There's a five-play summer stock season at the Red Barn Playhouse (plays your granny would love) and the two-month Saugatuck Chamber Music Festival at All Saints Episcopal Church in July and August. All Saints also hosts an exceedingly popular Christmas performance by the Chicago Brass, as well as a Friday Summer Concerts Series featuring free chamber music at noon in summer.

Hope College, in nearby Holland, offers both a main-stage Summer Repertory Theatre season at DeWitt Center and an experimental theater season in the Studio Theatre. The Holland Area Arts Council coordinates a summer arts camp as well as year-round exhibitions at the DePree Art Center on the Hope College campus.

Though the Saugatuck/Douglas Art Club stages its share of events—such as its juried art show each July—the biggest player in the local arts scene is the Ox-Bow summer arts program. Ox-Bow's bucolic, 110-acre campus across the Kalamazoo River from downtown Saugatuck contains studios, classrooms, an exhibition gallery, lecture hall, and accommodations for student artists who complete residencies in painting, ceramics, glass, sculpture, printmaking, fine crafts, and performance art. Ox-Bow was the area's first arts presence, and there's a sense of pride among local artists and art business owners about parlaying the institution's all-too-brief annual presence into a thriving year-round arts industry.

Art Talk

Bob Neumann, owner of Global Bar & Grill, is a photographer who exhibits local artwork on the walls of his business. "Julie Line, my partner, is also a photographer, and when we first opened the Global we exhibited our own work on the walls, not so much as a way of selling it, but because we needed the spaces filled," Neumann notes. "Now, though, we have regular exhibitions with Friday evening openings about every month for local artists. Things really pick up around here in the summer when Ox-Bow is in session—there are artists everywhere you look. We also feature local music—jazz, blues, and acoustic—on weekends, and that helps bring in a strong crowd of our target audience, ages 25 to 50. Within a 100-mile radius of Saugatuck are all the artists and musicians we could ever want."

According to gallery owner Joyce Petter, Saugatuck could use more art galleries. "To me, this town has a little over a dozen real galleries, and if twenty more opened up that would just make things better for all of us," she says. "Winter business is absolutely getting better, because we've developed a number of very fine B&Bs and restaurants that attract visitors year-round. My gallery is 12,500 square feet and represents 52 local artists as well as national artists in visual arts, fine crafts, and sculpture. Saugatuck has a large and wealthy gay population who are part of the business community. People from Chicago, Detroit, Indianapolis, and St. Louis come here during July and August looking for art to buy and finding what they need right here. Our days of being an affordable little place on Lake Michigan are over, and lakefront property these days runs anywhere from $2,000 to $4,000 a foot, if you can believe it!"

Essentials

Population: Saugatuck, 1,000; Douglas, 1,100
Art Events: Fat Tuesday Parade in February, Red Barn Season June through August, Chamber Music Festival in July and August, Jazz Celebration in September, Art Stroll in October, Chicago Brass in December, U-pick season at Krupka's Blueberry Plantation
Art Spaces: ThirdStone Galleries, Good Goods Gallery, Vesuvius Gallery, Water Street Gallery, Australian Galleries, Bentley's Fine Art, DeGraff Fine Art, Animalia, Edward Scott Gallery, Ark Gallery, James Brandess Gallery, Highbanks Gallery, Button Gallery, Joyce Petter Gallery, Cain Gallery, Polka Gallery, Out of Hand Gallery, Delta Gallery, Karen Kendall Gallery, Karen Spoerl Sculpture

Hangouts: Billie's Boat House, Global Bar & Grill, Black River Bistro & Brewery, Coral Gables, Uncommon Grounds
Bookstores: Open Door, Village News, Reader's World
Public Radio: WBLU FM 88.9
Chamber of Commerce: P.O. Box 28, Saugatuck, MI 49453, (616) 857-1701

Grand Marais, Minnesota

The Grand Marais Art Colony and a spectacular stretch of Lake Superior shoreline have attracted artists, writers, and actors from Minneapolis and Duluth for more than 50 years. Not only has Grand Marais, a gateway to the Boundary Waters Canoe Area, recently drawn a new breed of art entrepreneurs, artists, musicians, and coffee-bar owners but it has also become the cultural tourism hub of Minnesota's fastest growing county.

The region's brief encounter with summer brings plenty of free-spenders into town, some of whom have bought large lakefront properties and erected a mixed bag of trophy homes. Local artists have prospered from the building boom, and today Grand Marais boasts a number of accomplished woodworkers, painters, sculptors, ceramacists, furniture-makers, and jewelers.

Lifestyle

This being Minnesota, Grand Marais is the sort of place where winners of fish-cake contests receive write-ups in the local newspaper. The town offers a safe, affordable, and friendly life, surrounded by the natural attributes of Lake Superior's North Shore. Snowmobile trails crisscross the winter landscape. A fine ski area at nearby Lutsen Mountain becomes a bike park in summer, and the spectacular Sawtooth Mountains sit to the west. The town is loaded with backcountry outfitters specializing in everything from birding excursions to king salmon fishing. These days, $400,000 lakeshore mansions are not uncommon, but year-rounders can easily find a cozy $70,000 place within walking distance of town.

Arts Scene

Founded by Birney Quick, an artist and instructor at the Minneapolis College of Art & Design, the Grand Marais Art Colony grew to be a favored summer getaway for art instructors from the University of Minnesota and other midwestern schools. Today the colony offers a summer workshop for mid-career artists, a weekend children's arts program, and year-round performances and instruction for aspiring artists. Nonprofit visual arts galleries are found at the colony and at Johnson Heritage Post, a gorgeous waterfront log structure. Both hang monthly exhibits by local and regional artists.

While Grand Marais boasts the highest commercial gallery concentration on the North Shore, galleries also prosper in nearby Lutsen, home to the Kah Nee Tah Gallery, and Tofte, home to the Coho Cafe's monthly shows and crowded openings. Native American artists exhibit at the Lodge, a casino resort at Grand Portage Reservation, while Grand Marais' eclectic traditional craftspeople and contemporary artists show and sell at Creative Nature, Silvertson Gallery, Eight Broadway, and he Artists' Point annual arts festival. North House Folk School is the region's center for traditional North Shore crafts.

Two outstanding organizations address the performing arts needs of this town of just 1,170. Grand Marais Playhouse, prosperous for nearly three decades, presents its June-to-October season of well-chosen drama and contemporary folk music at a converted church theater. The North Shore Music Association rolls out a 13-concert season of jazz, world ber Chorale, an a cappella choir whose shows at the Washington County Historical Courthouse are always sold-out affairs.

Stillwater is also well known as a center for specialized book publishers, with organizations such as Kisselburg Military Books, St. Croix Antiquarian Bookseller, and Loome Theological Bookseller headquartered here. Three commercial booksellers—Stillwater Book Center, Midtown Books, and Brick Alley Books—are located downtown among a dozen or so antiques shops.

Art Talk

Carole Trevis, glass artist and owner of Carved Elegance gallery, moved to Stillwater from the small art town of Santa Cruz. "I have lots of family here and developed an allergic reaction to earthquakes, so I came back to live in a place where the ground didn't move," Trevis explains. "I carry national fine crafts artists, some painters, and one potter, with some artists from here and some from the West Coast. Stillwa-ter's a good art market in the summer, but you really can't expect people to stroll along the streets of a Minnesota town in the middle of winter. Stillwater's popularity in the early and mid-1990s boosted rents on the south side of town to the point where there's a lot of turnover from year to year. . . . Things will rebound, but it will take a few years."

According to Cynthia Schreiner, co-owner with Bick Smith of the Grand Theatre, surviving in Stillwater is a matter of identifying your audience: "We get lots of business from people celebrating anniversaries and birthdays, and we do performances for groups in addition to our normal Friday-through-Sunday shows. We specialize in romantic comedies and small musicals, and by specializing we're able to present a quality theater experience that's lots of fun. Our atmosphere is intimate; we serve coffee and desserts to our audiences, and this works in Stillwater because we're a town with a unique character—and the only show in town."

Essentials

Population: 14,000
Art Events: Rivertown Art Festival and Afton Spring Art Fair in May, Stillwater Art Crawl in June, St. Croix Music & Arts Festival in July, Marine Art Fair in September, Fall Colors Fine Art & Jazz Festival and Visions of the Valley in October
Art Spaces: Washington County Historical Courthouse, Kelley Galleries, Dorothy Berge Gallery, Lakeview Hospital Art Gallery, Daily Grind, Phipps Center for the Arts, Carved Elegance, J. P. Laskin Co., Tamarack House Gallery, Railroad Art by Scotty

Hangouts: Tasteful Thymes Co., Daily Grind, Savories Cafe, Dock Cafe, Eno's, Esteban's Cafe, Cat Ballou's Saloon, Trump's Deluxe Bar & Grill, Supreme Bean, Harvest Inn, Meg's
Bookstores: Stillwater Book Center, Midtown Books, Brick Alley Books, Loome Theological Bookseller, Kisselburg Military Books, St. Croix Antiquarian Booksellers
Public Radio: KNOW FM 91.1
Chamber of Commerce: 423 S. Main St., Stillwater, MN 55082, (612) 439-7700

Ocean Springs, Mississippi

Mississippi's Gulf Coast has always attracted its share of eccentrics, including artists, actors, and writers seeking alternatives to city living. Ocean Springs, the home of painter Walter Inglis Anderson, sits across the bay from Biloxi, home of ceramacist George E. Ohr—both of whom were known in their day as crackpots. Today, these same artists are celebrated as geniuses who pushed the boundaries of art.

Live theater and several art galleries round out Ocean Springs' arts scene, while just a bridge away in Biloxi there's more live theater, a performing arts center, a community arts center, and several casinos hosting Vegas-style revues, rock acts, and jazz jams. A bit further west is historic Bay St. Louis, home to another half-dozen or so commercial galleries.

Lifestyle

Ocean Springs is a relaxed place to live, with average homes in the $85,000 range. What that buys is easy access to a historic, relatively unspoiled community that's also home to Davis Bayou of the Gulf Islands National Seashore. Happenings in big, bad Biloxi are just a short drive away, including the city's wild Mardi Gras Festival (second only to the Big Easy's) and concerts at casinos and the Mississippi Coast Coliseum. Those seeking more variety take their act an hour's drive west to New Orleans. The casinos that moved into this region in the early 1990s brought about a vastly improved employment and entertainment picture, providing the Gulf Coast with an unprecedented economic boost and raising everything from property values to art festival sales.

Arts Scene

The Walter Anderson Museum of Art continues to expand the reputation of Anderson—known primarily for his watercolor nature paintings, line drawings, and murals—who died in 1965. The museum owns much of his work and continues to acquire pieces. In recent years it has expanded its program of regional and national exhibitions, including the juried, biennial Cross-Currents show of national contemporary art. The museum also offers a summer art camp for kids. A measure of how highly Anderson is regarded in Ocean Springs is evident in the town's galleries, several of which specialize in his prints and mixed-media reproductions.

Though the George E. Ohr Arts & Cultural Center seems stuck on promoting itself as home to the legacy of "Biloxi's Mad Potter," the facility operates as a first-rate community arts center through its rotating Jambalaya Gallery exhibits, art lectures, black-tie Mad Potter's Ball in fall, and Fall Festival of the Arts. Finally, Ocean Springs has more than enough galleries to pull off a strong Art Walk each August.

Saenger Theatre for the Performing Arts is home to the Gulf Coast Opera Theatre and the Gulf Coast Symphony, while Gulfport Little Theatre offers both a main-stage season and the MusicMakers children's music theater program. Biloxi has two fine community theaters: Center Stage, with a September-to-May, five-play season, and Biloxi Little Theatre, which uses its own playhouse for a five-play season.

While some people cast casinos in a strictly negative light, they do give musicians and dancers a place to earn a paycheck. And events like the monthly jazz jams at Treasure

Bay in Biloxi give local musicians a chance to gig. Now if only someone would figure out a way to bring the Hard Rock Hotel into town ...that would ice the cake.

Art Talk

Joey Rice, curator at Walter Anderson Museum of Art, says her institution's programs are changing: "Our original mission was specific to Anderson's work, but since we've had a new director our shows have ranged farther afield into contemporary glass, wood sculpture, African American art, sculpture, and contemporary painting. There are people who visit here from as far away as Europe, specifically to see Anderson's work, and our broader exhibition programs haven't pleased everyone. So we've dedicated a new exhibition area to rotating displays of the more than 500 Anderson pieces in our collection, and we're bringing in these new shows as a way to promote Anderson's work to a new audience—to pull him out of that southern artist niche he's been in and present him as a nationally important artist whose work holds its own against anything out there."

According to Sharon McQuilken, owner of Art Who?/Who's Inn?, Ocean Springs's art scene is growing along with its population. "There's a huge amount of development taking place here now, and people moving into the area and into their $300,000 homes are looking for local art to put on their walls," she says. "We represent primarily southern contemporary artists working in all media, and buyers come in from New Orleans, New York, L.A., Memphis, and Atlanta. Our niche is that we don't exclusively sell art that relates to local scenes, and over the years we've been able to build a national collector base by being different—but it's still a bread-and-butter situation when it comes to the bottom line."

Essentials

Population: 17,500
Art Events: Art Fair for the Handicapped and ArtWave in June, Mississippi Gulf Coast Blues Festival in September, Collage Arts Celebration, Toast to the Coast Art Show, and Great Oaks Storytelling in October, Peter Anderson Arts Festival in November
Art Spaces: Walter Anderson Museum of Art, George E. Ohr Arts & Cultural Center, Studio of Joe Moran, Zervan Gallery, Local Color Gallery, Local Color Too Gallery, Whistle Stop Framing Gallery, Realizations, Gayle Clark Gallery, Art Who?/Who's Inn?, Shearwater Pottery, Gillespie Art Gallery, Wilson Community Center

Hangouts: Bayview Gourmet, Salvetti's Trattoria
Bookstores: Favorites Books, Spanish Trail Books
Public Radio: WMAH FM 90.3
Chamber of Commerce: P.O. Box 187, Ocean Springs, MS 39566, (601) 875-4424

Oxford, Mississippi

Oxford, an hour's drive from Memphis, has always attracted its share of creative professionals, cultural tourists, and free thinkers—and it has developed a diverse local arts scene in its own quietly hip way. To some artists, Oxford's best years were the late 1980s and early '90s, before the community popped up on travel writers' radar screens. But like many small art towns on the rise, Oxford remains an attractive place for relocating artists, culture-savvy retirees, self-employed lone eagles, and entrepreneurs bringing more restaurants, cafés, and galleries into town.

Home to the University of Mississippi, Oxford has achieved a smooth balance between the cultural needs of its 10,000 full-time residents and the entertainment needs of 10,000 students. If Ole Miss ever builds its performing arts center, and if Oxford ever builds its community arts center, this place could easily become a broad-based success story like Charlottesville.

Lifestyle

So far, Oxford's growth has been slow enough not to change this historic community's lovely character, yet steady enough to bring a measure of prosperity. Property values have been climbing, and today an average-size home in an outlying neighborhood runs around $90,000. Historic residences within walking distance of the William Faulkner statue (by sculptor William Beckwith) on Courthouse Square regularly command twice that.

Like most college towns, Oxford has a respectable nightlife, a situation that's greatly improved since the opening of Blind Jim's, a blues joint showcasing Mississippi's delta and country blues artists. One of the nation's most innovative bookstores, Square Books, thrives on Courthouse Square, with its brick main shop selling titles by hometown heroes such as Faulkner and John Grisham, its Coffee Bistro presenting folk musicians, and its Off Square Books selling remainders. There's a strong commitment to the arts in Oxford's public schools, and the university offers art classes to the community.

Arts Scene

Fine dining, respect for literary talent, great bars, a thriving local theater scene, and the university's museums, performing arts series, and sports—combine to make Oxford irresistible to artists. In recent years a number of national-caliber chefs have chosen to set up restaurants in Oxford, and though the town still abounds with catfish joints, these days nobody blinks when polenta replaces hush puppies as a side dish.

Southside Gallery, next door to Square Books, is nothing less than one of the South's premier contemporary art spaces. Its exhibitions cover everything from local to international art, giving Oxford's many established artists a sophisticated venue for strutting their latest stuff. Ten miles away in Taylor is another strong contemporary gallery, Taylor Arts, exhibiting everything from fine crafts to two- and three-dimensional works by local talent. Restaurants and coffee bars such as City Grocery, Bottletree Bakery, Downtown Grill, and Smitty's Cafe exhibit local art, and the Art on Display program also places rotating shows in restaurants and businesses.

On campus, the Marie Buie Museum exhibits traveling shows, while Bryant Hall Gallery center presenting local and regional exhibitions, art classes, and art lectures year-round. There are summer classical concerts at Bigfork's Sliter Park, while places such as Hale's Lake House, Sabo's, and Marina Cay Resort all present a variety of rock, blues, and jazz acts in summer.

Kalispell has developed a strong reputation in western realist art circles for the quality of bronze casting at its two foundries, Kalispell Art Casting and Arrowhead Bronze Foundry. The foundries have in turn drawn a number of professional sculptors to the area. Western realism remains the most prominent genre exhibited here, though in recent years a number of galleries have made a go of exhibiting contemporary art—a trend that will likely continue as more cultural tourists find their way here each summer.

Art Talk

Joe Abbrescia, artist and gallery owner, moved to Kalispell for its natural beauty. "I came here because this place is the epitome of Rocky Mountain paradise, and you can't beat it for a landscape painter," he says. "My wife Sue and I lived in Chicago but find Montana to be a very supportive place for the arts and for artists. Summers are prime time here, and Glacier National Park draws over a million people into the area, lots of whom want to take home some artistic statement about this place when they leave."

Mike Jenson, artist, gallery owner, and Whitefish mayor, says the local art market is seasonal and strong: "Skiers seem to want to get in here, ski, and leave. But summer tourists have time to buy art. There are a number of artists moving into the valley who have established their careers in other parts of the country and who come here for the lifestyle. Businesspeople in Whitefish feel that the arts are an important component in what atracts tourists here, so the town tends to be very supportive of the arts."

Essentials

Population: Kalispell, 27,000; Whitefish, 5,800; Bigfork, 3,500

Art Events: Flathead Artist of the Month Exhibition at Hockaday year-round, Whitefish Arts Festival in July, Bigfork Arts Festival and Huckleberry Music Festival in August, Watermedia Exhibition at Hockaday in September and October, Glacier Jazz Stampede in October

Art Spaces: Hockaday Center for the Arts, I. A. O'Shaughnessy Cultural Arts Center, Bigfork Art and Cultural Center, Bridge Street Gallery, Abbrescia Fine Art & Pottery Studio, Corbett Gallery, Whitefish Gallery & Jenson Studios, Artistic Touch, Sandpiper Gallery, Whitefish Times Coffeehouse, Ken Hansen Studio Gallery, Marshall Noice Gallery, Kootenai Gallery, Art Fusion, K. Fredericks Gallery, Montana Expressions, O'Keefe & Co.

Hangouts: Montana Coffee Traders, Paper Moon Coffeebar, Cappuccino Cowboy, Whitefish Times Coffeehouse

Bookstores: Books West, Bookworks, Electric Avenue Books, Village Bookshop, Waldenbooks, Bad Rock Books

Public Radio: KUFM FM 91.7

Chambers of Commerce: Kalispell Chamber of Commerce, 15 Depot Park, Kalispell, MT 59901, (406) 758-2800; Whitefish Chamber of Commerce, P.O. Box 1120, Whitefish, MT 59937, (406) 862-3548; Bigfork Chamber of Commerce, P.O. Box 237, Bigfork, MT 59911, (406) 837-5888

Tony Abbrescia,
Chain Saw Artist

On the streets of most small art towns you'll find the occasional artist painting a landscape or taking a photograph. But the fact remains that most artists work inside studios, and outdoor work takes up a small amount of their time.

Then there's Tony Abbrescia. Tony, "the Bear Guy," can be found nearly every day of the year, chain saw in hand, working at the intersection of Center Street and First Avenue West in the small art town of Kalispell, Montana. Tony says chain-saw art is his life's calling. He works outdoors almost every day of the year (provided the temperature is above 14 degrees), carving and slicing pine logs until he's turned them into bears.

"Basically I create sculpture that happens to be made with a chain saw, because the medium I like working with responds well to what a chain saw can do," Tony explains. "After a little bit of sanding, staining, and sealing, I can come up with a piece of art I'm happy with. I got into chain-saw sculpting three years ago because it looked to me like an art form that I could get results from without having to go through all the technical demands of bronze sculpture, and because from the first time I saw another artist doing it I saw people having fun watching the artist work.

"When I first started getting into this work there were a few other chain-saw artists in Kalispell doing bears, so I decided that if I was going to do bears then I'd come up with my own interpretation of what a chain-saw bear could look like. I went down to the hardware store and bought a $60 electric chain saw and went to work. The first piece I did turned out so bad I used it for firewood. But by the time I did my third bear I could feel I was getting the hang of it. . . . For me, the opportunity to work with just one form has been a great way to develop my style and refine my woodcutting techniques.

"Bears sell so well around here that I haven't seen any need to branch off into eagles or fish," Tony continues. "At this point in my career, I can do several styles of bears and get them right the first time, without wasting any of my chain time. I'm selling everything I make, and in three years I haven't lost one piece to a mistake.

Tony's bears range from two to four feet in height, and, selling at $85 to $220, his work is a bit less expensive than that of other chain-saw artists in town. "At first, I targeted the tourism market for my sales, because we get busloads of people coming through here from Memorial Day to mid-October," Tony says. "And while I do sell most of my work to tourists, what keeps me going in the winter months is my local

Profile

business. I have people who have bought three, four bears from me, and I have no idea what someone could be doing with that many bears around their home.

"Someday I'd like to work with larger logs and see how big a bear I could do. But getting good wood around here isn't as easy as you think it should be. My biggest competitors for logs are the firewood guys who have all the good places staked out. So each year I've got to drive further and further back into the forest to find the sort of dried, standing deadwood I like working with. My favorite trees are lodgepole pines and yellow pine. When I find a tree I like I just cut it down, drag it back into town, and turn it into bears. . . . The biggest problem I have with wood once I start carving it is when it develops cracks from drying out."

Tony explains that people like to watch him out on the corner—covered with sawdust and working on a piece. He says that customers like to talk with him before they buy. "I can really tell that for them part of the attraction of buying one of my bears is that they get to meet me and watch me working," he notes. "I've even had tourists buy half-finished pieces before they can see what the finished bear looks like."

Tony works with a gas-powered, diamond-tipped, quarter-pitch chain saw with a carving bar. "With that kind of equipment, I can just blaze right through a log," he says. "I don't tell people how much time it takes me to carve a bear because then they start feeling awkward about how much I earn for an hour's work. What I can tell you is that when I first started doing this kind of work it took me four tanks of gas to carve a bear. Now it only takes me one tank of gas, so you figure out how much I earn each hour.

"I enjoy what I'm doing, I like working outdoors and I like being an artist," Tony concludes. "I guess I've become a pretty good salesman, too. Everyone in town knows me. People honk and wave when they drive by, and for an artist that's a pretty great feeling to have so many people support the work you're doing."

Helena, Montana

The arts scene in Helena, a state capital with a decidedly small-town atmosphere, focuses on the needs of local residents rather than the whims of cultural tourists. In practice, that focus means limited sales opportunities for the community's talented group of visual artists, especially its world-class ceramicists. But it also means that the performing arts, art education, museums, and classical music are highly valued and widely applauded here. In recent years, both Lila Wallace and the NEA have invested significant amounts of grant money into Helena's exemplary home-grown arts scene.

Lifestyle

The challenge for artists living here is to find a spouse with a government job. Well, maybe things aren't quite that dicey, but certainly for most artists there's an edge-of-the-apocalypse aspect to carving out an existence here. Parts of the local economy are doing well, but Helena also has many residents living on fixed incomes or working in near minimum-wage positions.

Homes in the $75,000 range are spread nearly all over town, while fixer-uppers bottom out at substantially less. The community is a safe place for families and relocating retirees, but its brutal winters have kept incoming population figures down. Local schools are quite good, especially their art education programs and the Arts Plus program in dance and theater.

Arts Scene

One of the art world's most innovative teaching and residency centers, the Archie Bray Foundation, is headquartered here on a 26-acre facility. Quietly building an international reputation for its ceramics programs, the Archie Bray is every bit as amazing as Haystack, Penland, and Pilchuck. Offering a year-round program of adult and children's ceramics, as well as exhibition opportunities through its Warehouse and Bray Galleries, this facility wires Helena into the contemporary art world's mainstream and gives residents a better-than-average shot at developing their own careers in the arts.

Another facility that bridges the gap between Helena and the art world beyond is the Holter Museum of Art, a medium-size facility exhibiting local, regional, and national shows in its nearly 6,000 square feet of gallery space. Working to support the local arts scene, the Holter is fast to recognize emerging talent and makes substantial investments in one-artist and group exhibitions. It also serves the broader community through year-round art education programs for kids and adults, along with a series of art lectures.

Grandstreet Theatre, presenting a seven-play season of musical, comedy, and children's productions in its 200-seat converted Unitarian church facility, holds down one end of Helena's drama scene. The Carroll Theatre Department, performing in the Carroll College Old North Performing Arts Center, holds down the other end. The Myrna Loy Center, an old jailhouse that's been turned into a community arts center (why can't Jamestown do this for Lucy Ball?), is to Helena's art scene what Grand Central Station is to Manhattan's commuters. Its gallery space is Helena's best spot for contemporary art from

The three-story Children's Museum of Portsmouth offers art and science exhibits, activities, and performances geared toward kids and families. Strawberry Banke Museum presents exhibits on everything from Portsmouth's founding in the 1600s to the homes of Russian Jewish immigrant families to local corner groceries of the 1950s.

Ballet New England is based here, as are nine theater groups performing in such venues as the 900-seat Music Hall, built in 1878, and the 65-seat Players' Ring Theater, built in the early 1800s. National touring groups as well as local companies (such as New Hampshire Theatre Project and Pontine Movement Theatre) use these venues, while the Seacoast Repertory Theatre performs year-round in its own facility, a former brewery (what else?) in downtown's historic district. Seacoast Rep, an exemplary organization, presents main-stage and youth theater seasons (both running September to June) as well as young-actors' workshops, a summer performing arts camp, youth dance programs, and internship programs.

Art Talk

"Portsmouth, for many reasons, attracts a lot of experienced actors and theater professionals—people like myself and [my wife] Eileen, who have had exciting careers elsewhere and choose to live here for this area's quality of life," says Roy Rogosin, founder and producing artistic director of the Seacoast Repertory Theatre. "Running a professional, year-round theater is always a struggle, but we've made it through ten years, our budget tops $1 million, and most importantly, people here trust the integrity of what we're doing onstage. Portsmouth is seductive, filled with great restaurants, and right on the water—what more do you need?"

According to Kristin Sakai, manager of Gallery 33, "There's a market for visual art here, but it's on slightly shaky ground. We have artists here of all denominations, but most are struggling along and holding down other jobs. Tourism here is tremendous, just overwhelming. People come through and pick up a piece on weekends. New galleries open, some galleries close—anything that's high-end has difficulty right now, so we cater to mostly a crafts and prints market. Artists who paint New England and Portsmouth scenes seem to do best, while the more adventurous work is harder to sell. Portsmouth is a big draw for artists because it's charming and friendly. You don't have to make a whole lot of money to have a high quality of life."

Essentials

Population: 22,600
Art Events: Market Square Day in June, Bow Street Fair in July, Prescott Park Arts Festival in July and August, Blues Fest in September, Holiday Crafts Fair in November, First Night Portsmouth in December
Art Spaces: Open studio tours at the Button Factory, New Hampshire Art Association Gallery, Robert Lincoln Levy Gallery, Pierce Gallery, N.W. Barrett Gallery, Gallery 33

Hangouts: Dolphin Striker, Bagel Works, Cafe Brioche, Caffe Kilim, Cafe Mediterraneo
Bookstores: When Pigs Fly, G. Willikers!, Stroudwater Books & Cafe
Public Radio: WGBH FM 89.7
Chamber of Commerce: P.O. Box 239, Portsmouth, NH 03802, (603) 436-3988

Lambertville, New Jersey

This Delaware River art town is typical of many North American communities that have been reborn into arts hot spots. Decades ago, Lambertville was the unfashionable blue-collar counterpart to the long-standing arts community of New Hope, Pennsylvania, just across the river. But once artists and art-business owners noticed Lambertville's empty mill buildings and quaint row houses, the "uncool" town suddenly looked like a smart place to stake a claim. Today Lambertville has shed its ugly little sister image and blossomed into a homecoming queen. Nearly 20 fine-art galleries line its streets, and its artists' work has begun to sell year-round.

Lifestyle

Lambertville's main advantage over neighboring New Hope is the cost of real estate. The fashionable thing to do is to buy a millworker row house, pull off the aluminum siding, and restore the structure to its original beauty. Lots of artists who move here do exactly that, as do small business owners fleeing New York City and Philadelphia. The attractions are the area's high quality of life, low crime rates, and easy access to big-city art and business. Families can expect to pay $150,000 for an average-size home in respectable condition, while across the river in New Hope, the same home sells for nearly a quarter-million.

The entire town uses the Tow Path, a 30-mile gravel trail connecting Frenchtown with Trenton and running through Lambertville's riverfront. Bicycles, joggers, hikers, tourist, and families while away sunny afternoons here on weekends.

Arts Scene

The town has nearly 20 art galleries, and the advocacy group Arts Bridge is currently attempting to transform one of Lambertville's old mill buildings into a community arts center. Because of copious weekend cultural tourist traffic, galleries here make high-dollar sales to collectors from Philadelphia and New York. "Its not unheard of," one gallery owner said, "for someone to come into my gallery looking for a ceramic platter and wind up walking out of here with a $4,000 painting tucked under her arm."

Lambertville's Artist's Gallery cooperative represents the full spectrum of talents that have immigrated here in recent years, with work ranging from finely crafted home furnishings to minimalist constructions. Party because New Hope is one of the nation's oldest art colonies, landscape painting is especially strong in the region. But modernists have also made this area a prime summering destination, as witnessed by Lambertville's contemporary art gallery and the abstract sculpture installed on New Hope's riverfront.

The strength of the area's performing arts scene is in theater, with the Bucks County Playhouse presenting a six-month season of standards. The highly regarded New Hope Performing Arts Festival stages a national program of theater and popular and classical music for seven weeks in July and August. Some new work developed at the festival has gone on to be performed in New York City.

The local concert association presents classical music at Lambertville's Rescue Squad Hall during winter. The region's vibrant jazz scene is played out at the Ferry House, Villa

Capri, Jon & Peter's Place, and Lambertville Station. Home to a large gay community, New Hope also offers Havana and Club Zadar nightclubs, while Odette's Restaurant stages cabaret on weekends.

Art Talk

"Artists make a point of checking out what's going on in Lambertville's galleries," says Riverrun Gallery owner Grace Croteau. "It seems as if the local collectors buy all types of art, with visiting collectors honing in on the more expensive pieces. The entire area is filled with lots of painters, lots of potters and fine craftspeople, and recently a lot of sculptors who are building their own foundries. New Hope is a different scene than Lambertville. It's a place where personality counts for just as much as a person's talent. In Lambertville, artists tend to let their work do their talking for them. What this town really needs to develop a national reputation is an art center and working studio complex—something like Alexandria's Torpedo Factory but in one of our old mill buildings."

Martin Leyland, co-owner of A Mano galleries, says that while New Hope attracts more family visitors than Lambertville does, both communities benefit from cultural tourism: "People walk back and forth across this wonderful iron bridge connecting us over the Delaware River and go to art galleries, restaurants, and dozens of antique stores. There are a number of very good fine crafts artists, but what would really help this area would be an art center with artists' studios on its upper floors. New Hope wants an art center, and Lambertville wants an art center, so it will be interesting to see which community gets out in front on the issue."

Essentials

Population: 4,000

Art Events: Shad Festival Poster Auction in April, Arts Bridge Juried Exhibition in June & July, Pennsylvania Crafts Festival in September, Outdoor Arts Festival in October

Art Spaces: Adams Gallery, A Mano Galleries, Artful Eye, Artist's Gallery, Bell's Restaurant, Church Street Bistro, Coryell Gallery, Craftworks, The Ferry House, Golden Door Gallery, Greene & Greene Gallery, Haas Gallery, Harvey Gallery, Howard Mann, Jonsdottir Gallery, Lambertville Gallery of Fine Arts, Prufrock Coffeehouse, Riverrun Gallery, 7 North Gallery, Topeo Gallery, Ungerleider Studio, Zephyr

Hangouts: Church Street Bistro, Club Zadar, The Ferry House, Havana, Odette's, Villa Capri

Bookstores: Farley's Bookshop, Phoenix Books, Rivergate Books

Public Radio: WHYY FM 90.9

Chamber of Commerce: 4 South Union St., Lambertville, NJ 08530, (609) 397-0055

Red Bank, New Jersey

Just seven years ago, downtown Red Bank was an eyesore of empty storefronts with 1950s facades tacked onto historic buildings. Today this community has been completely reborn, and downtown's original facades have been restored. A special improvement program has filled downtown's Monmouth Street from end to end with live theater, performing arts, art galleries, and art-filled cafés. Along with the summer scene at beach towns like nearby Asbury Park, Red Bank has become central New Jersey's ("Exit 109" in localese) place to see, be seen, and have fun on weekends and at night.

Lifestyle

Historic downtown Red Bank is just minutes from some of the best beachfront in America—the kind of badlands local hero Bruce Springsteen memorialized and local residents turn into their nearly year-round playground. If people aren't surf-casting or sand castle-building, they're taking long walks bundled up against the wind or hunting shells and driftwood... as long as they're on the beach, everyone's favorite place. Red Bank's Navesink riverfront has been converted into parkland, and during summer every type of water sport, from powerboat racing to single-man rowing, takes place here. Average-size homes can cost $175,000, but they're hard to find.

Arts Scene

A few years ago, New Jersey Monthly magazine tagged Red Bank "The State's Hippest Town," and this community of 12,000 has never looked back. While many factors have led to the revival, much of the acclaim can be traced to the Count Basie Theatre, Red Bank's 1,435-seat performing arts hall named after the town's most famous native son. Touring theater, big-name rock bands, musicals, orchestras... the Basie holds all that as well as the Monmouth County Arts Council's offices.

Red Bank takes its arts future seriously enough to have converted its Monmouth Street police station into the Kids' Bridge Cultural Center, an interactive arts and cultural education center. A new gallery, Celebration, represents local and national cartoon artists, and in the past few years a number of top-name cartoonists have moved into town. Local artists run the Art Alliance Gallery in downtown Red Bank, while the community also supports several commercial galleries. Finally, many artists exhibit at alternative venues such as coffeehouses and restaurants.

Red Bank and the entire region are big on the performing arts. A few miles away, in West Long Branch, Monmouth University presents an October-to-April program of touring theater, dance, and classical and folk music at Pollak Auditorium. The Two River Theatre Company, currently presenting its four-play, September-to-May season at Lauren Woods Theatre in West Long Branch, is making plans for its own Red Bank performance space.

The biggest arts bombshell to hit Red Bank in the past couple of years is the RTG Theatre Company's construction of its own, 100-seat Royale Theatre on Monmouth Street downtown. This successful homegrown company does not rely on public funding or foundation grant money in presenting its season of located in a former school gymnasium. The way things are developing, Magdalena could become a prosperous arts community, provided a few key elements fall into place.

Art Talk

Fernando Mercado, artist-in-residence at the San Acacia Gallery, has survived five years selling the region's art. "There's not a week that goes by that an artist isn't in here asking me about where they can find a place to live and set up a studio," he says. "Magdalena's arts council has done a great job of encouraging the kinds of events that give a place an awareness about the arts. So far we've brought six artists into the gallery from Magdalena, and all of them sell well. There are still lots of vacant government buildings that can be converted to studios, so I expect what's happening in Magdalena to only get better."

Yvonne Magener, artist and owner of Scarabeo art gallery, wasn't planning on owning her own art space. "But Magdalena has all these wonderful old buildings that are perfect for turning into studios and galleries that I couldn't resist," she says. "I'm showing my work, my mother's work, and the work of a number of artists from this area. Magdalena has developed a good reputation as a friendly place that's affordable and welcoming to artists, and it's certainly a place that's moving forward. After all, we just got our streets paved, and that's progress, isn't it?"

Essentials

Population: 1,200
Art Events: Magdalena Spring Arts Festival in May, Old Timer's Reunion in July, Magdalena Fall Arts Festival in November
Art Spaces: Scarabeo, Blue Canyon Gallery, San Acacia Gallery, Magdalena Cafe, Magnolia Cafe, The Marketplace

Hangouts: Golden Spur, Magnolia Cafe
Bookstores: Magdalena Mountain Mail, Dana Books
Public Radio: KUNM FM 89.9
Chamber of Commerce: none

Yvonne Magener, Painted–Egg Artist

Some artists find their hometowns have turned into art towns. Others move to art towns after becoming fed up with the hassles of urban life. Still others decide to move somewhere and create an art town of their own. Yvonne Magener, who was born in South Africa, raised in Spain, and educated in Egypt, is one of the latter.

In the early 1990s, after a life spent searching the globe for creative inspiration, Magener found herself cruising through New Mexico on a trip to the small art town of Sedona, Arizona. Two hours out of Albuquerque, on a two-lane highway that skirted the edge of a rugged mountain range, Yvonne found a rusty and rustic ranching community named Magdalena. Today the town is one of New Mexico's emerging hotspots for artists seeking an alternative to the hustle and bustle and expense of Santa Fe and Taos.

Yvonne works in the out-of-the-ordinary area of egg decoration. She explains, "I decorate the eggs in geometric and religious patterns and sell them at retail from $185 to $500. Some of the people who buy them say the eggs remind them of Byzantine art or Greek art or early Roman art or even Egyptian art. I don't try to achieve any one specific religious style or reference in my work, but instead I just keep mixing up the metaphors to arrive at something everyone likes."

The road to this distinctive work began during Yvonne's childhood. "My parents are both artists, and when we were living in South Africa their business was designing these wild lamps and getting them into production," she says. "My mother always was doing something with her hands, and when she wasn't designing lamps she would sometimes be decorating ostrich eggs in a style she had learned as a young girl growing up in Germany. Those eggs were something she used to decorate the family home with during the holidays and were something special she would give to family and friends as Christmas gifts. Eventually she taught me how to decorate eggs, and so when we finally left South Africa and moved to Spain I was able to do my own egg designs without her supervision," she says.

"It was my father's idea to move to Spain, so we found ourselves living on the Costa del Sol in a lovely little village called Mijas. When we arrived the town was very quiet, very traditional, and a very beautiful place to live. There were some tourists coming through the area, so my parents, the artists, decided they wanted to open a little gift shop in the town of Fuengirola and make a lot of different things to sell in the store. So they started doing the lamps again, and branched out into things like T-shirts and paintings, and of course my mother and I were painting the local eggs. At the

Profile

time we moved there, the whole area was very lovely, but within a few years the pace of tourism began really picking up, and soon after that a huge real-estate development boom changed the character of the area forever.

"My parents stayed there 26 years, and I kept moving in and out of the area to go to school and take different jobs around the Middle East. But everytime I came back home I would decorate eggs. In 1982 my mother and I started a shop that we called Scarabeo, where we sold mostly decorated eggs, and everything was going very well until the tourism market crashed in the mid-1980s and we closed the shop.

Yvonne's mother had always wanted to live in New Mexico, so in 1995 the family took a trip to the Southwest. "We were driving to Sedona when we saw this beautiful straw-bale wall being built onto an adobe home in Magdalena, right along the side of the highway," Yvonne recalls. "We decided to stop and take a look at the construction techniques the workmen were using, and when we walked over, the owner of the house told us the place was for sale. Right on the spot my mother decided to buy the house and move there, so we went back to Spain, packed up our home, and headed to New Mexico."

"As it turned out," Yvonne continues, "New Mexico has these very large-scale commercial growers raising emu, ostrich, rhea, and geese, so we immediately contacted these growers and found out they were more than happy to let us buy the infertile eggs that these birds were laying. Now I'm completely involved with decorating eggs for a living.

"The eggs I buy are the ones that do not hatch after the farmers place them into incubators, which means the eggs were infertile, which also means that no living creatures were denied their lives in order for me to make a decorated egg. I buy these infertile eggs a couple of times each year after the farmers have blown out their yolks."

Yvonne explains that she has tried working with commercial chicken eggs, but their shells aren't as hard as the chicken eggs she used in Spain. "Instead, we use bisque eggs that are made here in the U.S., but our most popular decorated eggs are ostrich, emu, goose, rhea, and duck," she notes. "I'm also working with some hand-turned wooden eggs that I've started buying from an artist in New England who I found on the Internet. We sell the eggs on our Web site and in galleries in Taos, Santa Fe, Albuquerque, and Socorro." Yvonne's business has been so successful that she's bought a building in Magdalena and is now converting it into a studio/gallery/living space.

Ruidoso, New Mexico

Over the last decade, Ruidoso has developed an interesting counterpart to the arts scene in other New Mexico towns such as Santa Fe and Taos. Specifically, artists here respond less to collectors visiting from the coasts and more to the tastes of cultural tourists and wealthy art patrons from Texas. The state's cowboy heritage is quite evident in the art exhibited in Ruidoso's galleries and museum. But as the town has begun to prosper, its collector base has diversified. Today Ruidoso artists sell contemporary and figurative work, and even Santa Fe artists are trying to make inroads into the local gallery scene.

Lifestyle

Ruidoso is a beautiful place whose topography bears a resemblance to Santa Fe's. The town sits at 7,000 feet and near the 12,000-foot peak of Sierra Blanca and Ski Apache. The ski resort attracts a steady flow of winter visitors, who also keep Ruidoso's galleries, restaurants, and hotels busy.

Ruidoso's real estate market missed the late-80s spike that drove Santa Fe's housing prices into the stratosphere. Homes here are still quite affordable, with average prices in the $110,000 range.

As a mountain community, Ruidoso is surrounded by tall pines, spring-fed meadows, and open ranges laced with hiking, equestrian, and cross-country ski trails. Recreational access is right at everyone's fingertips. Collectors and artists fed up with Santa Fe's costs and crowding have found this town to be a supportive place to live and work.

Arts Scene

Ruidoso quietly chugged along as an art town until late 1997, when the $20 million Spencer Theatre for Performing Arts opened its doors and turned the local arts scene on its ear. With its 514-seat interior configuration and 700-seat exterior configuration, the Spencer serves as a regular venue for touring national and international theater, dance, and musical acts. The Spencer's lobby features three Dale Chihuly installations—which an art center can afford when it's backed by the financial clout of a person like heiress Jackie Spencer. The Spencer's initial season included a children's series and a mainstage series, and there's no limit to what this Antoine Predock–designed facility might accomplish in coming years.

On a visual arts level, Ruidoso is served by yet another outstanding institution, the Museum of the Horse. Despite its name, the museum nonetheless does a first-class job in providing a venue for juried invitational exhibitions and events such as art lectures and children's programs. Exhibits range from traditional Western equestrian crafts (the museum's original mission) to contemporary art, Western realism art, sculpture, and photography. Local hero Dave McGary—a sculptor whose representations of Native American historical figures are collected worldwide—has installed a massive bronze piece depicting seven larger-than-life galloping stallions at the museum's entrance.

There's a strong visual arts scene in the Ruidoso area, with a number of artists in the nearby towns of Nogal, White Oaks, and Capitan who sell work from their studio galleries.

Altogether there are more than two dozen galleries in the area, more than half of them in Ruidoso proper. Besides the Museum of the Horse and McGary's studio gallery, a must-stop in this area is the Hurd-La Rinconada Gallery in nearby San Patricio. The gallery is home to the New Mexico branch of the Wyeth family, one of America's premier artistic clans with roots in Pennsylvania and Maine.

Art Talk

Dave McGary, sculptor and gallery owner, notes that Ruidoso's appreciation of the arts has changed. "A lot of the growth we're seeing is from people who have done the Santa Fe and Taos thing and find Ruidoso to be where those places were 20 years ago," he says. "The Hurds and John Meigs built a foundation for what's happening today, and the art market that's developed here owes a lot to them. We could use more good galleries, but not the kind that sell paintings of whales and dolphins. If you're going to survive here as an artist, learn how to run yourself like a business and be prepared to find representation in Santa Fe, Taos, and Aspen."

Theta Smith, executive director of the Spencer Theatre for Performing Arts, says the impact of her facility spreads far beyond Ruidoso: "I don't think the people living around here realized how starved they were for quality performing arts until the Spencer opened its doors. A lot of our ticket buyers are coming in from Roswell and Alamogordo, which gives us the population base that can sell out our events. Our local audience is loaded with second-home owners, who tend to be very theater-wise and who want variety in their performing arts. Locally, we have to hold down our ticket prices to make the Spencer work for the people who live here year-round, but we have a generous endowment so there's not the pressure to sell out each and every performance."

Essentials

Population: 8,500
Art Events: Bluegrass Festival in June, Mescalero Apache Ceremonial Dances and Ruidoso Art Festival in July, Lincoln County Art Loop in July and December, Fall American Photography Exhibition, Fall American Art Show, AspenFest, Lincoln County Cowboy Symposium, and Carrizozo Arts Festival in October
Art Spaces: Museum of the Horse, Spencer Theatre for the Performing Arts, Galloping Tortoise, Fort Meigs, Hurd-La Rinconada Gallery, Crucis Art & Foundry, Benson Fine Art, McGary Studios & Gallery, La Couture Fine Arts, L.C. Mercantile, White Oaks Pottery Studio, Quemado Studio & Gallery, Western Trails Gallery, Wild Bunch Gallery, Red Rose Art Studio, Fenton's Gallery, Kindred Spirits Gallery

Hangouts: Bentley's Brewpub & Paw, Farley's Food, Fun & Pub, Galloping Tortoise, Marie Laveaux Nightclub, In-Espresso-Ble Caffe House
Bookstores: Aspen Bookstore, Great Southwest
Public Radio: KENW FM 89.5
Chamber of Commerce: P.O. Box 698, Ruidoso, NM 88345, (800) 253-2255

Santa Fe, New Mexico

L egendary for the strength of its art market, which takes a back seat only to New York's and L.A.'s, Santa Fe and its 200 or so galleries have carved out an enviable niche for themselves. Since this town of 63,000 first popped up on cultural-tourist radar screens back in the mid-1970s, "Let's take a vacation to Santa Fe and buy a painting" has become a familiar refrain—and has turned this small northern New Mexico community into a place where art fortunes can be made practically overnight.

Santa Fe's original artists were craftsmen who made religious art and home furnishings for the Spanish settlers who founded the town in the late 1500s. Through most of the twentieth century, Santa Fe's art scene was focused on Native American archival art, Spanish Colonial art, and elegant landscape paintings created by eastern artists who stumbled onto the place. It wasn't until the late 1970s, when the nation suddenly went gaga over the colorful and zany "southwestern art" created by Santa Fe's first wave of university-trained, urban-art-scene refugees, that things began popping for the local art market.

Today, Santa Fe's gallery scene has diversified into a matrix of lucrative niches, such as contemporary Latin American art, abstract Eastern European art, Australian Aboriginal art, and contemporary Native America photography. These styles have blended in galleries selling more traditional landscape painting, Western realism, bronze realist sculpture, and Spanish Colonial art to create a powerful arts scene that collectors from around the world find altogether irresistible.

Lifestyle

Because Santa Fe is the state capital of one of the nation's poorest states, the cost of living here hasn't reached the stratospheric levels of places like Aspen and Sun Valley. But if it weren't for the needs of the community's indigenous Hispanic population, Santa Fe could easily have turned into the kind of place where millionaires and billionaires jostle only each other for reservations at expensive restaurants.

As things are, Santa Fe is still reeling from a real-estate boom that tore through here in the late 1980s and early 1990s, sending average home prices above $200,000 and leaving longtime residents and retirees with unholy property tax burdens to pay for all the new roads, sewer lines, and city services needed by second-home owners. A recent spurt of city-subsidized "affordable housing" has given Santa Fe some $150,000 homes—though they're small and located in treeless subdivisions—while tumbling prices have torn a hole right through the guts of the "trophy home" market. In fact, the town is loaded with homes that just a few years ago commanded well over a million dollars but now have fallen nearly 50 percent in price. According to some, Santa Fe's years as a leader on the charts of cool and hip are a thing of the past, and urbanites in a desperate search of a zip code that will substantiate them as smart and interesting are bailing out no matter what the cost.

Nevertheless, this town remains an interesting place to live. There are great restaurants, coffee bars, bookstores, and flower shops, interesting people everywhere you turn, brewpubs, bakeries, and a perpetually strong art

Ithaca's many talented visual artists struggle to cope with a shortage of gallery space. The State of the Art co-op and the nonprofit Upstairs Gallery exhibit local art, as does Handwork, a gallery dedicated to fine crafts. Cornell's Johnson Museum of Art presents historical touring and contemporary exhibits in its I. M. Pei–designed facility, and the Handwerker Gallery at Ithaca College offers mostly touring contemporary shows.

Each June, the Ithaca Festival presents three days of arts, music, and other performances in two downtown parks. Other summer favorites include free concerts on the Commons, a huge farmer's market, and concerts at Taughannock Falls State Park.

Art Talk

"We're a community that loves everything from foreign films to experimental theater, a place that integrates its arts interests with those of the colleges," says arts administrator Richard Driscoll. "Most of Ithaca's arts organizations have their offices in the same downtown building, and we're trying to turn the Historic State Theatre into the sort of community performing arts center that Ithaca's actors, musicians, and dancers deserve. There's a great quality of life here—what other town this size supports three Thai, two Vietnamese, and three Indian restaurants?"

According to Lisa Bushlow, theater company education director, "Hangar Theatre presents a dozen programs that include mainstage and black-box seasons, touring performances throughout upstate, artist residency programs in schools, and drama education programs at all grade levels in Ithaca's public schools. This community supports all the arts, and during the summer months Ithaca attracts lots of tourists who come here for our theaters and restaurants. We're fortunate to have such an appreciative and educated audience."

Essentials

Population: 28,000 permanent residents; 20,000 students
Art Events: Ithaca Festival in June, Artists Market in August
Art Spaces: CAP Artspace, Corners Gallery, CSMA Gallery, Handwerker Gallery, Handwork, Hartell Gallery, Johnson Museum of Art, State of the Art Gallery, Stella's, Upstairs Gallery
Hangouts: ABC Cafe, Collegetown Bagels, Giovanni's, Groover's, The Haunt, Jasmine's, Key West, La Forza, Madeline Patisserie, Silverbird, Stella's

Bookstores: Autumn Leaves, The Bookery, Borealis Books, Corner Bookstore, Ithaca Books, Logos Bookstore Emporium, New Alexandrian Books, Triangle Bookshop
Public Radio: WSQG FM 90.9
Chamber of Commerce: 904 East Shore Dr., Ithaca, NY 14850, (607) 273-7080

Jamestown and Chautauqua Lake, New York

This part of western New York is home to some astonishing arts success stories as well as one of the nation's oldest arts-oriented communities, the Chautauqua Institution. Jamestown itself, its downtown loaded with brick buildings, is a classic example of a manufacturing town buffeted by economic forces. But through innovative public and private investments, the Arts Council for Chautauqua County has spearheaded Jamestown's revitalization.

The work started with the transformation of downtown's glorious vaudeville house into the Reg Lenna Civic Center—a 1,260-seat performance hall. The council also convinced members of 10,000 Maniacs, a local band turned national success, to convert several retail structures into artist live/work spaces and to invest in an upscale restaurant/art gallery. The town has also memorialized the legacy of its most famous native, Lucille Ball, with a Lucy-Desi Museum, the Lucille Ball Little Theatre, and an annual festival celebrating the legendary comedian's achievements.

Lifestyle

During summer months, the entire Chautauqua Lake region comes alive with arts, recreation, and everything else locals have not enjoyed since winter hit in mid-October. Real estate values here are absurdly low, with average-size houses selling in the $50,000 range and huge homes going for $100,000.

The region is home to several colleges with active exhibition venues, including Jamestown Community College's Forum Gallery and SUNY Fredonia's Rockefeller Arts Center. One of the nation's finest nature centers, the Roger Tory Peterson Institute of Natural History, is headquartered in Jamestown. The institute provides teacher training, hosts an international lecture series on environmental education, and contains a fine art gallery of touring and self-curated shows. It dovetails nicely with a 600-acre Audubon Nature Center on the edge of town that sponsors one of the National Audubon Society's most far-reaching community education projects.

Arts Scene

The region is well served by the performing arts, with the Reg Lenna Civic Center presenting year-round classical music, jazz, dance, and family events such as the Das Puppenspiel marionette theater. Fredonia's Rockefeller Arts Center offers a September-through-May season of drama, pops, and classical music, while a dynamic season of foreign cinema, drama, blues and folk music, children's theater, and classical music plays at the Fredonia Opera House, an elegantly restored, 400-seat performance hall built in 1891. The Jamestown Concert Association's classical music season takes place at The Commons, St. Luke's Episcopal Church, and the Reg Lenna. Chorale and chamber music fans enjoy the Community Music Project's four-concert season at the First Presbyterian Church.

The Chautauqua Institution offers nine weeks of national and international talent in classical music, theater, opera, popular music, and dance each summer. Set in an idyllic, turn-of-the-century village on the shores of Chautauqua Lake, the institution combines a resort atmosphere with a flood of art performances, classes, exhibitions, and lectures. For those staying on the institution's grounds, nearly all events are free, while the general public sometimes enjoys reduced-cost and free days.

During winter, about half the area's galleries close down, including the Chautauqua Center for Visual Arts, Logan Galleries, Winds of March Gallery, Gloria Plevin Gallery, and Pritz Gallery. However, off-season tourists can still visit Portage Hill Gallery (fine crafts), Suzanne H. Allen Gallery (visual arts and fine crafts), and Adams Art Gallery in Dunkirk (contemporary arts and fine crafts).

Art Talk

The Chautauqua Institution is "unique as a major summer festival because our programs focus on the idea of self-improvement through civil discourse and benefiting from the arts in our development as human beings," observes Marty Merkley, vice president and director of programming. "Our symphony is a tenured union orchestra that focuses on traditional chestnuts as well as contemporary music. Our opera tends to program on the conservative side, with at least one musical each season, and all of our programs are open to the region's broader communities. We provide an $80 million boost to the county's economy each summer and open our facility to local arts groups once our nine-week season is completed."

"When the summer rains come to chase people off their boats and indoors, all the galleries do well," says gallery owner Suzanne H. Allen. "In 15 years of business, we've seen more collectors interested in the local galleries—people from Cleveland, Buffalo, and Pittsburgh who are on summer vacation and who respond well to what this area's artists are creating. I keep a mix of contemporary and representational work in the gallery, with artists from the cities in a three-hour radius and local artists. The area's second-home owners are greatly interested in dimensional and textural work for their homes and not as interested in sweet, flat art as they once were."

Essentials

Population: 30,000
Art Events: Chautauqua Institution's summer season, Skyjam in August, Lucille Ball Festival in September, Art and the Animal and Dia de los Muertos Exhibitions at Adams Art Gallery in October
Art Spaces: Adams Art Gallery, Audubon Nature Center, Chautauqua Originals/Palace Gallery, Crawford Ceramics, Forum Gallery, Gloria Plevin Gallery, Good Morning Farm Gallery, Portage Hill Gallery, Prendergast Library Art Gallery, Pritz Gallery, Roger Tory Peterson Institute, Suzanne H. Allen Gallery, William Waite Gallery

Hangouts: Cherry Lounge, MacDuff's, Nellie's Deli, Stage Left Bistro
Bookstores: Chautauqua Bookstore, Paperback Exchange
Public Radio: WUBJ FM 88.1
Chamber of Commerce: 101 W. Fifth St., Jamestown, NY 14701, (716) 484-1101

Peekskill, New York

Peekskill is living proof that New York artists don't need to live in Brooklyn or SoHo to be part of the Big Apple's arts scene. This innovative art town, ingeniously using its vacant downtown factories as the foundation for an arts-based redevelopment project, has become a viable alternative for mid-career and emerging artists who want affordable living in an urban setting—less than an hour's commute from Chelsea's gallery district. In slightly less than a decade, Peekskill's 20,000 residents have attracted artists and created significant downtown development in several forms.

First is the mighty Paramount Center for the Arts, a 1,000-seat showcase offering visual arts, pop music, orchestral music, dance, and cinema. Then there's Westchester Community College's highly regarded Art Workshop program on downtown's North Division Street. The facility not only gives local artists employment and educational opportunities but also attracts graduates of WCC's computer-based graphic arts and design programs. And last but not at all least are the intrepid arts entrepreneurs and gallery owners who have invested their own business bucks into the town's ever-improving arts district.

Lifestyle

Peekskill retains much of the blue-collar flavor that characterized its light manufacturing days. Neighborhood taverns and brick commercial buildings abound. Real estate values have hovered for years in the $110,000 range for an average-size Victorian home—very affordable by regional standards. Artists raising families tend to move into neighborhood homes, while others occupy lofts over street-level coffeehouses and galleries downtown.

Using state funding, Peekskill has started building a $3.7 million studio and housing complex called ARTLOFT on the site of a former parking lot. The town has also received state grants to develop a waterfront park. Former mayor and current New York Governor George Pataki, a Peekskill native, oversaw the beginning of arts district redevelopment, and he's still a big supporter of the arts. But the real mastermind behind Peekskill's successful transition into a small art town is urban planning consultant Ralph DiBart, son of a former mayor.

Arts Scene

Artists from New York City provide Peekskill with its largest base of downtown loft dwellers, and in recent years painters, sculptors, graphic designers, and jewelers from suburban communities in Westchester and Putnam Counties have also moved here. Monthly open-studio tours not only have helped build a base of collectors of local works but also have attracted regional gallery owners hunting for new talent.

There are several art galleries downtown, as well as a successful revolving arts program that places local work in nearly two dozen Peekskill cafés, offices, and businesses. The Paramount's Upper Gallery, the Westchester Art Workshop Gallery, and Creative City Gallery at One Station Plaza are nonprofit art spaces known for their strong exhibitions.

If every small art town had its own Paramount Theatre Center for the Arts, we wouldn't have to fret about America's art future. Presenting everything from philharmonic orchestras to the Peekskill Rep, children's dance theater, touring blues musicians, and world music, the Paramount attracts over 54,000 ticket-buyers to its shows each year.

One Station Plaza Performance Space, a downtown free-form venue, presents the sort of alternatives that keep a local arts scene vibrant—open-mike poetry nights, jazz jam nights, local blues bands, and folk music. One of the community's most popular music events is the free Wednesday summer evening music series at Riverfront Green Park.

Art Talk

"One Station Plaza is a place for artists to try out new material and for established acts to perform for local audiences," says cofounder Nick Mottern. "We don't use public funding sources because we want to maintain a degree of creative independence—it's all from ticket sales, rentals, and volunteer work. Our space is in downtown Peekskill, seats 50, and is used every day. Rebuilding a downtown is a slow process, and lots of buildings still need renovating, but we're seeing more artists coming to town and more related economic activity from the tourists who follow them. One of the community's hottest issues is electric rates, which can equal the monthly rent payment for some of downtown's artists."

According to Ralph DiBart, urban planning consultant, "Downtown's never looked better in this, the sixth year of our ten-year game plan. There's a limited inventory of great living/working space downtown, especially for families, so the 50-unit ARTLOFT project is intended to attract the critical mass of artists needed to complete the arts district's cultural synergy and allow artists to buy in as property-owning members of the community. Westchester Community College's programs here are operating at full capacity and attracting a new wave of businesses and artists to town. Artists who live and work here can be as involved as they want in the community."

Essentials

Population: 20,000

Art Events: Monthly open studio tours, annual Off the Wall sculpture exhibition at Paramount's Upper Gallery, Super Studio & Jazz Festival in July, Arts, Crafts and Antiques Festival and Celtic Festival in September

Art Spaces: Gallerie JJENTH, Upper View Gallery, Driftwood Gallery, Flat Iron Gallery, Wallhangings, Etc., Hudson Valley Institute for Art & Photographic Resources, Paramount Upper Gallery, Creative City Gallery, Westchester Art Workshop Gallery

Hangouts: One Station Plaza, The Chocolate Tree, Susan's Restaurant, Jasmine's, Submarine Gallery

Bookstores: Driftwood Gallery, Bruised Apple Bookstore, Barnes & Noble

Public Radio: WNYC FM 93.9

Chamber of Commerce: One S. Division St., Peekskill, NY 10566, (914) 737-3600

Woodstock, New York

The legendary art community of Woodstock has attracted the nation's premier painters, sculptors, musicians, and writers since the early 1900s. Today this bucolic Catskill Mountains community has become a place where artists of every caliber— from international gallery stars to recent art-school grads struggling with rent payments—decide to settle in and work on their careers. For gallery owners, Woodstock's strong reputation and proximity to New York City mean that weekending collectors with bulging wallets can drop in at any time, returning to the city with thousands of dollars in impulsive art purchases. And who wouldn't love a place that has its own artists' cemetery?

Lifestyle

For nearly three decades, Woodstock has attracted people seeking a connection with the 1969 music festival that took place in nearby Bethel. But as was the case in Eugene, Taos, and Ann Arbor, "peace and love" energies have long since fallen short, and creative and entrepreneurial spirits have taken over.

Today Woodstock is an open-minded community that supports not only dozens of fine art galleries but also restaurants that exhibit local art, top-notch centers in visual arts and photography, a theater company, a local artists association, and summer performing arts festivals. There's great skiing nearby and boating on Ashokan Reservoir, and Woodstock itself is a gateway to Catskill State Park's trails and campgrounds.

Real estate prices are high because of the large numbers of second-home owners from New York City who spend their free time here. Average-size residences sell in the $225,000 range. More affordable living is found in nearby communities such as Kingston (home to several galleries and a performing arts center), where similar homes on a couple of acres run $135,000.

Arts Scene

Artists survive here mainly because of spending by cultural tourists from the city and by second-home owners looking to fill their "Woodstocky" homes with art. Many artists don't depend on the local market for their income. But for those who do, it's quite possible not only to build a career from Woodstock but also to be "discovered" by weekending gallery owners from SoHo, Bucks County, and elsewhere. The terms "hip" and "laid-back" fit Woodstock perfectly, and with so much interchange between local and big-city artists, nobody with a permanent Woodstock address need ever feel out of step with whatever trends are rippling through Chelsea or Madison Avenue galleries.

Visual artists and fine craftspeople who aren't in galleries exhibit on summer weekends at the Artisans Market in Playhouse Park. Local restaurants and cafés are filled with art. Year-round classes in many art disciplines take place at venues such as Town Hall and the Community Center, and the Woodstock Artists Association offers classes, art lectures, and an extensive exhibition schedule covering national juried shows, member shows, and an occasional blockbuster by the likes of Philip Guston. The Woodstock Guild promotes regional fine-craft artists through exhibitions at Kleinert/James Art Center.

One of the nation's premier education programs for mid-career and established artists is offered year-round by the Woodstock School of Art. The Center for Photography at Woodstock offers a five-month schedule of classes, lectures, and exhibitions by some of America's top photographers.

On the performing arts front, Byrdcliffe Theatre offers top-notch dance performances and classes; America's oldest chamber music festival, Maverick Concerts, takes place at the beautiful Maverick Hall; local rock musicians perform occasionally at Andy Lee Field; a summer concert series is held at Opus 40; Kleinert/James hosts classical music performances; and the Art Awareness space in nearby Lexington offers cutting-edge everything, from visual art to modern dance.

Art Talk

"Lots of serious collectors looking for well-known contemporary artists find their way to Woodstock," says gallery owner Elena Zang. "This town is fun, eclectic, and supportive of all the arts. We have year-round galleries showing local artists' work and several very good, very serious galleries showing international-level work. As someone living here, I can go out any night of the week and find something happening at an art center or café or city park—it's truly a magical place."

Woodstock School of Art's programs were once only summer affairs. But in recent years, according to Kate McGloghlin, the school's assistant director, demand has led to expanded programs. "We get artists from across the nation and overseas, with about two-thirds of the students being local artists," she says. "We have no entrance requirements, so in the same class you can have a college student, a vacationing artist, and someone who has had museum shows—all studying the same subject. There are lots of very good artists who come here to work on their chops, and artists who have put their careers on hold to raise families and are getting back into their careers. We put people up in a converted barnhouse, other artists' homes, B&Bs, and an RV park. There are 22 artists on our staff."

Essentials

Population: 2,000
Art Events: Renaissance Fair in May, Maverick Concerts and Bird-on-a-Cliff Shakespeare Festival in summer, Tibetan Summer Fair Chokhor Festival in August, Woodstock-New Paltz Arts & Crafts Fair in September
Art Spaces: Ann Leonard Gallery, Elena Zang Gallery, Center for Photography, Bearsville Gallery, Fletcher Gallery, Woodstock Artists Association, Hawthorn Gallery, Paradox Gallery, Kleinert/James Gallery, Art Awareness

Hangouts: Tinker Street Cafe, Joyous Lake, Jitters, Blue Mountain Bistro, Bear Cafe, Bread Alone Cafe, Maria's Bazaar
Bookstores: Golden Notebook, Mirabai Books, The Bookmark, KTD Tibetan Buddhist Bookstore
Public Radio: WAMC FM 90.9
Chamber of Commerce: P.O. Box 36, Woodstock, NY 12498, (914) 679-6234

Beaufort and Morehead City, North Carolina

Once, the primary arts focus in these adjoining Crystal Coast communities was on maritime crafts. Today artists in Beaufort and Morehead City have joined together with longtime locals, arts organizations, and an energetic group of urban retirees to promote access to the fine arts—with successful results.

Beaufort's historical association is a leading cultural group, overseeing preservation of the town's beautiful, eighteenth-century downtown. Nearby New Bern has a strong arts scene, including the Trent River Coffee Company for visual arts and music, plus a contemporary gallery and a nonprofit artists' gallery.

Lifestyle

As two of the nation's premier magnets for quality-of-life refugees, Beaufort and Morehead City have benefited greatly from a recent influx of monied retirees and lone eagle professionals who have bought into the area's hot real estate market. It's possible to buy a beachfront home here for about $150,000 or an in-town neighborhood home for $85,000.

The area's weather is mild. High temps in the mid-50s are common in January; midsummer days in the high 80s are cooled by steady ocean breezes. Windsurfing, hang gliding, and skim boarding are near-religions here, while those seeking gentler fun can golf on one of many fine seaside courses or surf cast. This is truly a retirement heaven—even for those who have to work for a living.

Arts Scene

There's no overstating the positive influence the Arts Council of Carteret County has exerted over this region's arts scene. It's an exemplary organization that works tirelessly to build coalitions. The council runs a visual arts gallery and an art education and workshop program, presents and cosponsors numerous theatrical and musical performances, and even finds time to help kids create fish prints at the annual Seafood Festival. In the past several years, the council has expanded its offices and exhibition space three times in order to serve the region's exploding arts needs.

The North Carolina Maritime Museum is the area's major cultural institution, exhibiting rotating art shows and hosting workshops in such traditional coastal crafts as decoy carving, model shipbuilding, oar making, boat building, and crab pot making. Additionally, more than a dozen commercial and nonprofit galleries, as well as several cafés and restaurants, exhibit local art in Beaufort and Morehead City.

The maritime museum's auditorium hosts the American Music Festival, a series of five yearly chamber concerts. Music lovers can also enjoy the Crystal Coast Choral Society performing at St. Peter's United Methodist Church and the North Carolina Symphony, which occasionally performs at the high school auditorium. The energetic, five-year-old Coastal Jazz Society has attracted loyal audiences to its regional and local performances at restaurants and community halls and has greatly improved Crystal Coast nightlife. The Down East Folk Arts Society brings national performers to venues such as the Crystal Coast Conference Center. Carteret Community Theatre stages its plays at Carteret Community College.

Arts education is widespread here. At the

Light Within, musicians teach workshops in everything from dulcimer playing to traditional Ocracoke music. Visual artists teach in home studios, through art council workshops, at galleries such as Life Forms Pottery, and through the community college's extensive evening programs.

Art Talk

Marjorie Hoachlander, founder and president of the Coastal Jazz Society, says the challenge for local jazz lovers is to keep building on the organization's successes: "People are demanding more jazz, and we're encouraging the sort of local musicians who can meet those needs, but we have to pay top dollar to bring in musicians from places like Raleigh, Greensboro, and elsewhere along the East Coast. We've convinced restaurants in the area that jazz is a great way to build their popularity, and there are at least three places that present live jazz on a regular basis. There are now 120 members in the jazz society, and we like to go out and have a good time in supporting the venues promoting our music."

The region's outpost of abstract art, Carteret Contemporary Gallery, appeals mostly to out-of-area collectors, according to gallery owner Charles Jones. "Second-home owners are big buyers at all levels of the market, and after that there are city people who come down to the area visiting and are surprised to find a contemporary art gallery here," Jones says. "The Raleigh/Durham/ Chapel Hill collectors are corporate types with sophisticated art tastes, and we see lots of them. This gallery has survived six years, with two of those being my dues-paying years. But now the summers and shoulder seasons are quite strong, and we have to rotate our exhibitions every three weeks during the busy season."

Essentials

Population: Beaufort, 3,900; Morehead City, 7,600
Art Events: Cinco de Mayo (New Bern) in May, Summer Jazz Festival in August, Seafood Festival in October, Candlelight Art Tour in November
Art Spaces: Carolina Artists Studio Gallery, Carteret Contemporary Gallery, Circle 10 Gallery, Down East Gallery, Guppy's Gallery, Handscapes Gallery, LaVaughn's, Life Forms Pottery, Mattie King Davis Gallery, North Carolina Maritime Museum, Stepping Stones Gallery, Turner Street Gallery, Upstairs Gallery, Windward Gallery

Hangouts: Clawson's, The Plant, Trent River Coffee Company, West Side Cafe
Bookstores: Back Road Books, Beach Bookmart, City News, Dee Gee's Books & Gifts, Light Within
Public Radio: WTEB FM 89.3
Chamber of Commerce: P.O. Box 1406, Morehead City, NC 28557, (919) 726-6350

Chapel Hill, North Carolina

This bastion of liberalism in one of the South's most conservative states supports a broad-based arts scene whose greatest strengths are in music and performance. Home to the University of North Carolina and its 24,000 students, Chapel Hill and its 45,000 residents are strongly influenced, if not overrun, by this prestigious institution's arts programming. Little town versus gown enmity exists, and even Chapel Hill's recent refugees from the Northeast gladly toss aside their dour wardrobes for closets full of Carolina blue. The neighboring community of Carrboro, once considered an unfashionable mill town, provides the perfect balance to Chapel Hill's steadily escalating real estate market . . . and is anxious to enjoy the fruits of an arts-based economic revival.

Lifestyle

Since the mid-1980s, Chapel Hill has been a favored destination both for retirees and families departing the Northeast's gloom and economic stagnation. Downtown's Franklin Street contains many of the community's art galleries and restaurants. From there, it's an easy walk to UNC performance venues in Memorial, Person, and Hill Halls.

The community's gorgeous, tree-lined neighborhoods on winding roads are the sort of fabled real estate investment people dream about—but with prices escalating steadily. Chapel Hill is home to the $200,000 "starter" house, and though lower priced fixer-uppers are available, many newcomers seek affordable housing nearby in Cary or increasingly gentrified Durham.

Arts Scene

Chapel Hill offers easy access not only to the local art scene but also to the increasingly sophisticated offerings in nearby Raleigh (which has a resurgent gallery, studio, and theater district) and Durham (a national center for contemporary dance and jazz). While Chapel Hill itself offers some worthy jazz, the ArtsCenter in Carrboro functions as the dynamic center of the off-campus arts scene. The center uses its exhibition area for contemporary shows and installations by local, regional, and national artists, while also hosting a nonstop calendar of jazz, theater, dance, world music, and children's performances in its 300-seat theater.

Opera diva Leontyne Price, European orchestras, and New York contemporary dance companies have all played the 1,600-seat Memorial Hall as part of UNC's very strong Carolina Union Performing Arts Series. The North Carolina Symphony also uses the hall for performances. Meanwhile, the university's well-funded music department schedules the exhaustive Newman Series of recitals and performances by student, faculty, and national artists at Person and Hill Halls.

While local theater companies such as the experimental Sonambulist, Mojo, and ACTER perform at the ArtsCenter or the high school, Playmakers Repertory, part of the UNC drama department, uses the Paul Green Theatre during its September through April season. Playmakers' three in-house resident companies present main-stage standards, while student and graduate actors and playwrights appreciate the anything-goes atmosphere of the company's black-box Lab Theatre. Last year, a new

American opera premiered at Chapel Hill High School, reflecting the fact that here, anything's possible.

The area lacks a museum of contemporary art (though the North Carolina Art Museum is improving in this regard), so such Chapel Hill venues as the ArtsCenter and Hanes Art Center's Allcott Gallery are critical to local artists. Outside of coffee bars, cafés, and a few highly regarded commercial galleries, these centers offer the only available wall space. Chapel Hill's Ackland Art Museum primarily focuses on its own collection of traditional and historical work, but it does sponsor occasional contemporary regional shows.

Chapel Hill has some decent nightlife, with local independent and alternative bands at Lizard & Snakes, Local 506, and The Cave. Cat's Cradle in Carrboro is also a very active venue, presenting name acts such as John Cale and Leo Kottke, as well as touring jazz and folk musicians. Fusion's New World Cuisine doubles as the community's favorite jazz bar.

Art Talk

Joe Rowand, owner of Sommerhill Gallery, finds the region's collector base to be large and diverse: "The Triad [Chapel Hill-Raleigh-Durham] area brings in lots of relocating corporate people and visiting parents—people who like to collect art. People expect to find a cultural scene in Chapel Hill, and between the galleries, nightclubs, and performances, it's all here for them. Cultural tourism is in a surprising growth stage, and we're seeing more travelers coming to Chapel Hill for a look through the galleries."

"Many of our programs are experimental, especially in our theater," says Eileen Helton, executive director of the ArtsCenter. "We've presented plays by touring small companies, new works by Czech playwrights, and have provided an incubator for local companies like Sonambulist. Lila Wallace Reader's Digest Fund selected us for their jazz program, and through that support we've been able to present a performance series here and an outreach jazz education series to regional schools. Our performance series concentrates on talents on their way up, and in 1989 we did a Garth Brooks show that drew all of 70 people. Our visual arts gallery is run by center/gallery, whose presentations are mostly by local contemporary artists."

Essentials

Population: 45,000

Art Events: Apple Chill Festival in April, Bull Durham Blues Festival in September, Festifall in October

Art Spaces: Ackland Art Museum, Allcott Gallery, ArtsCenter, Chapellier Fine Art, Horace Williams House, Minata Gallery, North Carolina Arts Gallery, North Carolina Crafts Gallery, Sommerhill Gallery, Steinway Gallery

Hangouts: Caffe Driade, Carolina Brewery, Fusion's New World Cuisine, West End Wine Bar

Bookstores: The Bookshop, Carolina Bookshop, Dancing Moon Books, Intimate Bookshop, Waldenbooks

Public Radio: WUNC FM 91.5

Chamber of Commerce: P.O. Box 2897, Chapel Hill, NC 27515, (919) 967-7075

Wilmington, North Carolina

An art scene supported by Wilmington's film industry and thousands of University of North Carolina-Wilmington students has given this laid-back, mid–Atlantic Coast outpost a strong reputation as a great place to live, work, or retire. Wilmington's is a well-balanced arts scene, with enough diversity to address the entire community's needs for visual arts, performing arts, and music . . . but without one dominant art form soaking up the lion's share of funding or media attention. Cultural tourists and art collectors are still discovering this place, usually while they're in the region vacationing or working on a shoot. Wilmington's future looks bright—each year the town becomes a better place to live, attracting more artists and developing a broader range of creative events.

Lifestyle

Surf's always up along the nearby shore. Wrightsville Beach and Carolina Beach are magnets for artists needing anything from a few hours tossing around in six-foot waves to a few days of sun-fueled inspiration. Real estate prices have risen steadily here, especially in Wilmington's large and beautiful historic district, where rehabbed places start at $200,000. Overbuilding in outlying areas has created a buyer's market (nice homes run $125,000) for residences close to golf courses, beaches, and malls.

Though Wilmington earned its reputation as blockade runner's haven during the Civil War (rumrunners and drug smugglers have also plied this coast), in recent years the town has become Hollywood East, with several studios establishing production facilities on the edge of town and renting office space in the heart of downtown. Michael Jordan was born here, which is why Cape Fear Museum now has a Michael Jordan Discovery Gallery. And don't forget to feed a Venus's flytrap; they grow wild here.

Arts Scene

While UNCW exerts an undeniably huge influence over Wilmington's art scene, Wilmington has also benefited from an influx of refugee artists and musicians—people who place a priority on living near the ocean. The downtown streets closest to the Cape Fear River waterfront (Water, Front, Second, and Third Streets) hold most of the community's art galleries, live music venues, and alternative exhibition spaces in coffee bars and restaurants. Each passing year brings at least two new galleries or exhibition venues to town.

St. John's Museum of Art is Wilmington's most influential visual arts presence, with a strong focus on historical Carolina masterworks, rotating shows by living regional, local, and national artists, and local art sales through its Collectors Gallery. The Cape Fear Museum features science and ecological art, while the University Union on campus exhibits student works.

The region's premier performing arts program is UNCW's Arts in Action series, which presents contemporary dance, new music, and avant-garde performances at Kenan Auditorium. Wilmington Symphony also performs its season at Kenan Auditorium, while Wilmington Choral Society's concert season is staged at churches and community halls. Wilmington also has an active chamber music society that presents visiting artists for Friday afternoon concerts at St. James Church and headline performers at the Thalian Hall Center for the Performing Arts Ballroom. The well-supported concert association pulls in national music and dance stars for its November-to-April season at Kenan.

The town is home to a thriving theater community, fueled by professionals who work on local film shoots for rent money and produce local shows to feed their creative souls. Thalian Hall's main-stage and studio theater continually burst with rehearsals and performances by companies such as Minerva, Thalian, Opera House, and Big Dawg, which present a lot of locally created pieces and the regular dramatic fare. The Community Art Center, Bessie's, and Scottish Rite Theatre are other key theater venues.

Strong jazz, alternative, and rock venues are concentrated downtown and give Wilmington a respectable nightlife. Touring national acts play the River Club and Rockits, while local bands gig at the Ice House, Water Street, and Crooks.

Art Talk

"We do some shows that bring complaints from local pastors," says John Malejan, owner of the Deluxe Cafe, an alternative art exhibition space. "But what we like is work that's odd, and we keep it changing every six weeks. Local second-home owners and visiting film people buy lots of the paintings. We can do multiple artist shows with as many as 50 paintings on the walls, and we try to work with mostly local artists as a way of picking up some of the slack in Wilmington's commercial gallery scene. NoFo Gallery hangs the work. Downtown Wilmington has dozens of bars with live music on weekends—jazz, blues, rock, and anything you can think of."

Star Sosa, owner of Spectrum Gallery, says Wilmington is a "magical and growing place. My gallery has 1,200 square feet, 24-foot-tall ceilings, and brick walls, and it's affordable! Retirees are buying lots of art for their new homes, and they want local work. There's tremendous local talent working in glass, painting, jewelry, and fine crafts. Acme Art, a studio warehouse space, has an incredible level of creative energy, and all the artists are easy to work with."

Essentials

Population: 65,000
Art Events: Artists of Southeastern North Carolina show in June, Cape Fear Blues Festival in July, Piney Woods Cultural Heritage Festival in August, Jazz Festival in September, Riverfest in October
Art Spaces: St. John's Museum of Art, Deluxe Cafe, Cyber Perk, Crooks, Faded Rose, WHQR-FM, Airlie Moon, Golden Gallery, Spectrum Gallery, NoFo Gallery, Creative Resource, Makado Gallery, Acme Art, Griffith Gallery, New Elements Gallery, American Pie, Fidler's Gallery

Hangouts: Firenze Caffe, Peace & Plenty, Delux Cafe, Crooks, Ice House, Water Street Restaurant
Bookstores: Books a Million, Barnes & Noble, Waldenbooks, Bristol Books, Two Sisters Books, Little Professor, B. Dalton, Seahawk Books
Public Radio: WHQR FM 91.3
Chamber of Commerce: 24 N. Third St., Wilmington, NC 28401, (910) 341-4030

Raoul Sosa, Jeweler

The competitive field of high-end jewelry making isn't for the faint of heart. Working with tiny precious stones worth thousands of dollars, the lapidarist jeweler is under constant, intense pressure. Minuscule errors can instantly turn a $3,000 stone into a handful of dust.

Raoul Sosa, one of the nation's most accomplished lapidarist jewelers, specializes in an ancient technique known as inlay. He lives in the small art town of Wilmington, an oceanside paradise attracting a new generation of creative residents. Sosa, whose career has taken him from San Francisco to the small art towns of Mill Valley and Santa Fe, says nothing gives him greater pleasure than putting in a hard day's work in his busy studio, then heading out to enjoy the sunset at a Wilmington-area beach. His finished pieces sell from $500 to $12,000 and are available in galleries in Laguna Beach, Santa Fe, Vail and Wilmington.

"I don't just cut stones," Sosa notes. "I have an obligation to bring out the beauty and intricate coloring inherent in a stone. But what I do as a lapidarist jeweler involves much more than simply placing stones into precious metal settings. I see my lapidarist jeweler's work as more of an art and a fine craft than what your average jeweler does. Mass production doesn't interest me. It's those individual pieces that commercial production techniques could never hope to achieve that are my specialty, the creation of soulful pieces of jewelry that can only be accomplished by a person who loves what they do, working one-on-one to create something spectacular.

"I know that I love what I'm doing when I'm in the middle of working on a piece and it suddenly starts to come together and take on a type of beauty that's truly uplifting, a level of beauty that shimmers. To get something to achieve that sort of beauty, there has to be a complete attention and commitment to the design, craftsmanship, and detail work necessary to completing that piece, and you have to be willing to do everything you can to find and use the best materials you can get your hands on."

Sosa explains that many jewelers are content to work with low-grade stones—but his standards are high. "Sometimes I wish I wasn't driven to use A-grade stones and could just put together pieces without being so demanding on myself," he says. "But the whole reason I got into lapidarist jewelry was to create pieces that are as beautiful as a spectacular sunset, and to have that event happen, things have to be just right with nature, which is the same way I feel about my work.

"Its my training that's led me to be so demanding in my work. I was always the sort of kid who was good at working with his hands, and I remember admiring a relative of mine because he was a dental technician and had a profession where he

Profile

created things with his hands. This desire I had to shape and form things led me to go to work for a taxidermist when I was 22, and he turned out to be a very influential person in my development when he started giving me pieces of ivory and telling me I should carve those pieces into something. Hunters who came into the shop started buying those early pieces, and within a few years I was confident enough to strike out on my own. Ivory had a great popularity in the 1980s. But then, because of a lot of misperceptions, people stopped buying ivory, and I had to find something else I could do with my hands."

Sosa had always admired the inlay jewelry work of Native American artists of the Southwest, especially Charles Loloma. "[I] decided that if I could accomplish something new in my life, it would be to create work that was inspired by theirs," he recalls. "I didn't want to leave ivory, because it's a wonderful material to work with. But I had to make a living, so I decided just to set my goals on working with stones. Inlay work is so appealing. It's so sculptural and so dramatic that I immediately took to the intricacy and challenge of the work. For me, the whole process of learning a new medium was like being a kid and learning a new sport. I just loved it from day one."

Sosa notes that his work involves a time commitment combined with experience and high standards. "Time is one of the biggest issues someone in my field has to deal with," he explains. "There's a decision you have to make about how much time you'll need to put into a piece...and for me that means anywhere from 20 to 40 hours of work to create something wonderful. I'll spread those hours out over the course of two weeks, but since I really don't like leaving a lot of projects half-done, I tend to dedicate the time that's required as soon as I can focus my attention to a project. As soon as I get a casting back from my caster, I'm like an artist who has just been given a framed canvas . . . I want to just start creating.

"Selecting good materials is one of the most critical aspects of my process, and I have to invest a lot of hours just to find stones I want to work with," Sosa adds. "It's a process called 'reading' the stone, and it takes years of practice to estimate the potential that's locked away inside an uncut piece of stone you pick up at a gem show. Then, you've got to be able to properly cut that stone so as to develop its maximum yield as a precious stone. If everything goes right, you're lucky to end up with a cut stone that's 25 percent the weight of the uncut stone you started with. Every stone handles differently, every stone has its own set of angles and fracture lines that you've got to work with. To me, this is a hands-on field that you get into for the simple reason that it's your life's work and you want to create beautiful things."

Athens, Ohio

The historic college town of Athens was included in this book's first edition and returns largely on the strength of Ohio University's increased commitment to the arts. A multimillion-dollar renovation has turned Templeton-Blackburn Alumni Memorial Auditorium into a state-of-the-art performing arts center. The university has also opened the impressive Kennedy Museum of American Art, a first-rate institution exhibiting contemporary and historical works, as well as one of the world's premier collections of Native American ceremonial textiles. Athens has another leg up on the arts scene thanks to the broad range of programs offered by the 7,000-square-foot Dairy Barn Cultural Arts Center. Another college-town perk is a wonderful music scene, played out in a variety of nightclubs, jazz bars, and coffeehouses.

Lifestyle

Like some other midwestern college towns, Athens retains its countercultural roots through a liberal local government, a plethora of head shops and body piercing joints, more than a few bars packed during weeknight happy hours, and events such as the Halloween bash downtown. But college-inspired looniness aside, Athens is an isolated community proud of its historic roots. . . a can-do sort of place that's clean, safe, and family-friendly.

The town is linked to other communities along the Hocking River by the Hocking Bikeway and is surrounded by state parks, farmlands, and national forests that provide both beauty and inspiration. Average Athens homes cost about $110,000, while residences in nearby towns run as low as $50,000.

Arts Scene

When the Kennedy Museum of Art opened in 1997, community awareness of the visual arts took an enormous leap forward. This institution manages an intriguing mix of contemporary and historical arts, while providing important and quickly expanding educational programs for schoolkids, adults, and seniors. While the Kennedy has not eclipsed the Dairy Barn as the heart and soul of Athens's creative community, it has contributed a sorely needed level of support for the town's arts scene.

While the Kennedy's exhibitions tend to focus on artists from outside the region, the Dairy Barn's shows are primarily local, or have a strong Ohio connection. The Dairy Barn also offers year-round art classes and hosts the Quilt National, a juried exhibition of top national fiber artists that draws national art dealers.

On campus, the OU Art Gallery and Trisolini Gallery exhibit mostly student and faculty work. Many commercial spaces, such as Lamborn's Studio and Court Street Collection, tend to combine crafts, framing, gifts, and art. Other exhibition spaces are found inside restaurants, cafés, and coffee bars.

OU's October through April Performing Arts Series is strong and varied, covering theater, classical music, world music, chamber, and gospel. A free Concerts Under the Stars series provides classical music on summer Wednesday nights, while a winter chamber music series takes place at the First United Methodist Church. For nine months of the year, OU's Music Building hosts faculty, student, and guest artist recitals.

The OU theater season consists of eight

plays staged in the Baker, Forum, and Hahne Theaters during the school year. The Ohio Valley Summer Theatre's eight-week season also takes to the boards in Baker Theater. Meanwhile, in neighboring Nelsonville, the resident drama company at the restored Stuart's Opera House stages monthly plays. Cinema fans can enjoy Athens's film and video festival each spring.

The area's broad nightclub scene caters both to OU's 6,000 students and to local tastes in jazz, reggae, and blues. Main venues include the Smiling Skull Saloon, Casa Cantina, Night Court, and The Pub.

Art Talk

Local artist Katryn Meadows notes, "Athens is a fairly good place for an artist to live, as long as you realize it's a college town and a homey type of place. Most local artists create work that has a strong local feel if they're interested in selling around here. If you're good at what you do, you tend to get lots of custom orders, and you wait for the big art fairs in summer and the chance to sell direct to people. Alumni weekends and bicycle races are the best sales times."

Shirley Brown, owner of the Futon Gallery, says her business approach is simple: "Futons are becoming an upscale sort of furnishing, and the type of people buying them are also the same people who buy art. We show everything from watercolors to sculpture, mixed-media works, and oil paintings—and I'm surprised at how much of it sells. Athens has a huge community of very talented artists, and they come in here all the time looking for opportunities to show. I only take a 20-percent commission on sales, most of which are in the under-$250 category, but occasionally a piece will bring $500 or so. Our downtown Art Walks [bring] lots of people into downtown every other month, and slowly but surely this little town is sprucing itself up."

Essentials

Population: 22,000
Art Events: Bob Marley Day Festival in May, Poston Lake Bluegrass Festival in June, Quilt National in summer, Barn Raisin' Community Arts Festival in September, Paul Bunyan Chainsaw Art Show in October, Halloween Street Party in November
Art Spaces: Casa Cantina, Dairy Barn Cultural Arts Center, Futon Shop & Gallery, Kennedy Museum of American Art, Learning Resource Center at Hocking College, Nine Moons, Ohio University Art Gallery, Perk's Coffeehouse, Trisolini Gallery

Hangouts: Casa Cantina, Front Room Coffeehouse, O'Hooley's Pub & Brewery
Bookstores: Athens Bookcenter, Follett's University Bookstore, Little Professor Books, Specialty Books, The Story Shop
Public Radio: WOUB FM 91.3
Chamber of Commerce: P.O. Box 238, Athens, OH 45701, (614) 594-2251

Yellow Springs, Ohio

A former spa community less than 30 minutes from downtown Dayton, this small art town of 4,000 residents is also home to Antioch University and longstanding traditions of liberalism in politics and tolerance for alternative lifestyles. Mark Cramer, author of *Funkytowns, USA,* calls this place Mellow Springs, which just may say it all.

Yellow Springs works as an art town because of its homegrown art gallery, café, and performing arts scenes, and also because it's close to the art action in nearby Dayton and Springfield (home to a $15 million performing arts center). In recent years, as these neighboring population centers have expanded, 2.5-square-mile Yellow Springs has come under extraordinary growth pressure. The community now has its first KFC franchise, as well as busloads of day-tripping weekend tourists, most of them prowling the town in search of ice cream cones and T-shirts.

Yellow Springs is also the northern terminus of the Little Miami Scenic Bike Trail (a 60-mile paved pathway). That too is a magnet for weekenders from nearby cities (and to some local folks the traffic has been nothing but a headache).

Lifestyle

The local real estate market has climbed steadily in recent years, as urbanites not anchored to the idea of living within sight of shopping malls have opted for Yellow Springs' safety and hometown friendliness. Add to that the well-paid staff and faculty of Antioch College (600 students) and a steady trickle of relocating artists, and what you get are average home costs in the $120,000 range, with considerably less-expensive housing in such neighboring communities as historic Clifton.

Arts Scene

Walkable, historic, downtown Yellow Springs holds nearly 20 art galleries, most selling local and regional work. Several fine bookstores complement a small community of bookbinders working for national clienteles. In the middle of downtown are a hardware store and drugstore, both in business since FDR's presidency.

During the community's twice-yearly Arts Stroll, the galleries all stay open late. The local arts council organizes classes year-round at the John Bryan Community Center, which is also home to the town's most active visual arts exhibition gallery.

The town's premier performing arts event, the five-concert Chamber Music Yellow Springs season, takes place at the First Presbyterian Church, with national performers such as the St. Petersburg and Brentano String Quartets. There are folk and jazz performances at Sam & Eddie's Open Books, world music at the WEB Coffeehouse, and rockin' blues on weekends at the Southside Sports Palace. A community drama group, Center Stage, presents plays year-round, and a first-run movie house specializes in art flicks, indie and foreign films, and documentaries . . . heady stuff, but quite popular here.

Nearby Dayton is home to one of the nation's most outstanding performing arts events, the 12-concert season presented by CityFolk, an organization dedicated to contemporary

American folk music, jazz, and world folk music. Concerts are staged in venues such as the Canal Street Tavern, Dayton Art Institute, and beautifully restored Victoria Theatre.

Art Talk

Luan Heit, director of the Bryan Center Gallery, says Yellow Springs' Art Strolls are important community events. "The Art Strolls bring out two kinds of people: visitors from Dayton and Springfield who are interested in the arts, and local people who enjoy an evening of socializing with their neighbors," Heit says. "We're a small town with the sort of atmosphere artists love—the kind of place they're attracted to. At the Bryan Center Gallery, we haven't had to look outside Yellow Springs and the immediate area to find the quality work we need for our exhibitions, and it's all here—from abstract painting to pastel landscapes to ceramics and glass. Our talent is what I call eclectic. The art association holds classes each quarter of the year at Bryan Center, with everything from tai chi to bodywork, sculpture, writing, and painting—all taught by volunteers."

Artist Anna Arbor wants local artists to have better studio spaces. She says: "My husband and I bought the old Union Schoolhouse two years ago ,and we're converting it to a studio and museum facility for local artists and their art. Right now, even though the building is only partly done, we have five painters, two massage therapists, one hypnotist, and an Akido instructor using the space. . . . This town has a number of fine-craft artists who travel on the national craft-show circuit and artists who exhibit their work worldwide. To me, this is a town filled with both artists and art appreciators."

Essentials

Population: 4,000
Art Events: National Folk Festival in June, Yellow Springs Art Stroll in June and October, Bluesfest in September, James Rose Puppets
Art Spaces: Gemini Gallery, Bryan Community Center Gallery, WEB Retail Gallery, Oten Glass & Studio, Art Studio Workshop, Catalpa Lane Pottery, Galingale's, From the Four Directions, Glen Street Gallery, Henderson Gallery, Bonadies Glass Studio, Rita Caz Gallery, Hudson Sculpture, Joseph Williams Studio, Village Artisans, Yellow Springs Pottery, Angel Rain, "would you, could you" In A Frame, Herndon Gallery at Antioch College

Hangouts: Sunrise Cafe, Ye Olde Trail Tavern & Restaurant, Winds Cafe, Dayton Street Gulch, The Emporium, Coffee Cantata
Bookstores: Sam & Eddie's Open Books, Dark Star Bookstore, Epic Bookstore
Public Radio: WYSO FM 91.3
Chamber of Commerce: 108 Dayton St., Yellow Springs, OH 45387, (937) 767-2686

Niagara-on-the-Lake, Ontario

The heart of Ontario's wine country is also home to one of North America's largest summer theater festivals—the Shaw Festival—staged from early April through October in the waterfront art town of Niagara-on-the-Lake. This massive event, which for 35 seasons has been a highlight of Canada's arts calendar, takes place in three beautiful playhouses sprinkled around this historic arts community. The festival includes not only a main-stage season of George Bernard Shaw's works but also a reading series of classical theater pieces, revivals of plays from the 1920s, '30s, and '40s, and turn-of-the-century pieces that few, if any, other theater companies have the guts or talent to present.

The Shaw Festival has spawned a vibrant and multifaceted arts scene both in Niagara-on-the-Lake and in nearby places such as St. Catharines. Vineyard tours and wine festivals also attract high-spending cultural tourists from all over North America. The powerful tourism magnet of wine, theater, and art has brought economic prosperity to this hamlet just an hour's drive north of Buffalo, New York.

Lifestyle

Life in Niagara-on-the-Lake centers around its spectacular Lake Ontario waterfront. Most tourist draws are located in the town's Heritage District. Nearby St. Catharines also has a high level of arts appreciation, influenced in no small part by Brock University and its performing arts series presented in the Shawn O'Sullivan Theater.

Located in the southernmost reaches of Ontario, Niagara-on-the-Lake appeals to relocating retirees and professionals who want moderate weather patterns, along with easy access to the arts and nearby metro areas of Buffalo and Toronto. To many, this small art town represents the best of all worlds. The city remains a safe and beautiful place where an average home sells in the $150,000 U.S. range.

Arts Scene

Not only does the Shaw Festival stage 12 magnificent productions during its seven-month season but it also presents experimental theater through its Theatre Beyond Words company, which performs at a local school. The festival also hosts annual events such as the juried Shaw Guild Arts & Crafts Festival and the Village Fair & Fête.

The region's summer arts scene kicks off the Folk Arts Festival, staged in St. Catharines in May, and wraps up with the Niagara Grape & Wine Festival in September, a rollicking week of madness that spills out of both Niagara-on-the-Lake and St. Catharines and into the dozens of vineyards spread throughout the region. Hillebrand Estates Winery, located right in town, uses its beautiful grounds for a schedule of summer events such as the Vineyard Strings Festival in June, Vineyard Jazz Festival in July, and Vineyard Blues Festival in August. Niagara Symphony, a 55-member orchestra performing nine concerts during its eight-month season, occasionally uses the Shaw's Festival Theatre for its performances.

Despite these impressive offerings, the town could use a visual arts center, a place that would help round out the cultural experience for the Shaw's primary audience of monied tourists. For now, Niagara-on-the Lake's half-dozen or so commercial galleries have to fend for themselves, without much organized community support. Increasingly, cultural tourists drive into nearby St. Catharines to attend exhibitions at venues such as the Niagara Artists' Company, Rodman Hall Arts Centre, and Brock University's Centre for the Arts—or to Queenston to visit the Weir Collection Library of Art.

Art Talk

Odette Yazbeck, senior communications manager at the Shaw Festival, says Niagara-on-the-Lake is a perfect place for a theater festival. "This is an historic and artistic community," Yazbeck explains, "the kind of place where actors, writers, and artists from Toronto have weekend homes. Our company is the only one in the world dedicated to Shaw's work, and by being specialists of plays written in the 1856 to 1950 era, we've built an international audience for what we do. More than 300,000 people attend the festival's plays each season, and our draw from Ohio, New York, Michigan, and Massachusetts audiences is very strong."

Wendy Badger, special events director for Hillebrand Estates Winery, says there's substantial crossover between her winery's visitors and the Shaw Festival's cultural tourists: "Wine drinkers like art, they like jazz, and they like events that combine food and wine with the arts. I think there's a very positive benefit for all of the area's organizations that comes from having each of us pull our audiences in from Toronto, Buffalo, and elsewhere. The winery is located on a beautiful escarpment just 15 minutes outside of town, and people love coming here year-round for events, but especially in the summer for our vineyard music and arts weekends."

Essentials

Population: 14,000
Art Events: Folk Arts Festival in May, Vineyard Jazz Festival and Artistry by the Lake in July, Peach Celebration and Shaw Guild Juried Arts & Crafts Show in August, Niagara Grape & Wine Festival in September
Art Venues: Doug Forsythe Gallery, Preservation Fine Art Gallery, Astor Gallery, Moggridge Studio, Ninavik Gallery, Victoria Gallery, Niagra Pumphouse Visual Art Centre, Rodman Hall Art Centre & Gallery, Masters Art Gallery, Short Hills Art Gallery, Tintern Island Gallery

Hangouts: Moffat Pub, Vineyard Café, Queen's Landing Inn, Quasi Café, Old Bakery Restaurant, Issac's Pub
Bookstores: Joan Draper Bookseller, Old Niagara Bookshop
Public Radio: CBC 740 AM
Chamber of Commerce: P.O. Box 1043, Niagara-on-the-Lake, Ontario, Canada, LOS1JO, (905) 468-4263

Stratford, Ontario

This beautiful town in southern Ontario, home to more than 1,000 acres of municipal parkland and built along the meandering banks of the Avon River, offers one of the richest art scenes in North America. The early May to mid-November Stratford Festival, a celebration of the works of Shakespeare and other great playwrights, attracts astounding numbers of cultural tourists from all over the world. The festival's three theaters are scattered around Stratford's Elizabethan downtown, an eminently walkable community loaded with nearly two dozen art galleries and at least twice that many superb restaurants. Surrounding the downtown are spotless neighborhoods filled with wood-frame homes and tree-lined streets.

Lifestyle

An hour and a half from Toronto, Stratford has masterfully capitalized on its carefully honed reputation as a weekend destination for frazzled urbanites. It is a soothing and interesting place to recuperate in a romantic B&B, toss around the plastic, have a great meal or two, and rebuild that urban warrior armor. A reputation like that is money in the bank, and Stratford's art business owners have one person the thank for their bounty: Tom Patterson, the visionary who landed here in 1953 and said "Let's put on a play!"

Real estate prices are still absurdly low in Stratford, with an average home selling in the $125,000 U.S. range. What you buy into is a safe place with great schools and an extremely arts-oriented community. During summer, Stratford is a verdant paradise that's home to swans, butterflies, and migratory birds. In winter . . . well, let's skip that season.

Arts Scene

The Stratford Festival is a powerful force in the theater world. It serves both as a platform for experienced theater professionals at the height of their careers as well as a training ground for university students. In an average year, from four to six Shakespeare plays highlight the festival's eight-month, 12-play calendar. Other works range from Greek tragedy to classics of twentieth-century theater to the occasional comedy. The festival also presents a Celebrated Writers Series in summer, a season-long program of pre- and post-performance lectures with actors and theater scholars, and educational programs for drama teachers and aspiring actors.

A number of actors and tech experts drawn here by the festival have stayed on as permanent residents. In the off-season, many commute to Toronto to work in professional theater. Others sign on for stints with London's Grand Theatre in winter or the Blyth Festival of Canadian plays in summer. In addition, a local comedic company called Foolscap performs at venues such as the Gallery/Stratford, City Hall Auditorium, and the Victorian Inn.

While the closest symphony orchestra performs at Center in the Square in nearby Kitchener, Stratford does have its own concert choir, which performs at Knox Presbyterian Church. During summer, some of Stratford's most popular evening events are ragtime performances staged on a barge on the Avon River. The Stratford Concert Band plays at the bandshell in Upper Queens Park, while jazz bands perform free in another park. The Stratford Folk Guild stages year-round concerts by contemporary folk musicians at a high school auditorium.

Stratford's nonprofit visual arts exhibition and education center, the Gallery/Stratford, organizes local and regional art exhibits, as well as art education classes and occasional chamber music concerts. Throughout summer, a juried Art in the Park show takes place thrice weekly along Lakeside Drive. The show is an important sales venue for local artists, as is the annual Artists' Studio Tour weekend.

Art Talk

Mary Hill, community development officer for the Gallery/Stratford, says that Stratford is never boring. "When you sit down at a café, the person at the next table is likely to be an opera singer, a costume designer, or a book illustrator," she explains. "This town is filled with people who have done interesting things in their lives and continue to do them all over the world, but who choose to live here. The Gallery/Stratford is able to mount everything from touring national exhibitions to shows by local artists, and we sell local art as well, because most of the commercial galleries in town exhibit work by artists from outside the area."

Karen Harmer, media relations manager for the Stratford Festival, says the town is increasingly turning into a year-round residence for artists: "Just the past couple of years have seen a new performing arts group get established, more restaurants keeping their doors open in winter, and more artists associated with the festival choosing Stratford as a place to live. Summer months are wonderful here. The town is filled with tourists, the shops along York Street are filled with buyers, the restaurants are packed, and there's even a nightlife. And everything is within walking distance, so once people get here they just park their cars and forget about them."

Essentials

Population: 28,000

Art Events: Art in the Park from May to September, Gala Summer Opening at the Gallery/Stratford and Artists Studio Tour in June, Concerts in the Park from June to September, Dragon Boat Festival in September

Art Spaces: Gallery/Stratford, Canadian Clay & Glass, Pottery 5, Gallery Indigena, The Amulet & Originals, Swann Gallery, Crescent Hill Gallery, Gerard Brender à Brandis, Colorful Dreams, Gallery 96, Classic Art, Be Mused

Hangouts: The Boar's Head, The Belfry, Bentley's Bar, Down the Street Bar, Balzac's Coffee Roastery, Festival Bakery & Cafe, Fellini's Caffé, Buzz Stop

Bookstores: Fanfare Books, Book Stage, Book Vault, Callan Books, Cole's Books

Public Radio: CJCF AM 1240

Chamber of Commerce: 121 Ontario St., Stratford, Ontario, Canada N5A3H1, (519) 273-5250

Ashland, Oregon

A warm climate, lots of sunshine, moderate rainfall, and a two-hour drive to Pacific Ocean beaches make Ashland one of Oregon's fastest-growing communities. Retirees love its climate and arts access, families love its moderate cost of living and safe neighborhoods, and artists love its wealth of opportunities in theater, music, and the visual arts.

Shakespeare and Ashland were first linked in 1935 with the Oregon Shakespeare Festival, a partnership that's gone a long way toward making Ashland and neighboring Medford the prosperous communities they are today. The marriage has created progeny in the form of a dynamic live theater scene and has contributed to the success of the Britt Festival, a summer-long popular and classical music series presented in a spectacular amphitheater in nearby Jacksonville.

Lifestyle

Ashland is 20 minutes from an alpine ski resort, 30 minutes from two of the continent's best white-water rivers, 50 minutes from a national park, and two hours from the coast. The region is filled with fruit orchards, and its summer climate bears more than a passing resemblance to the desert Southwest.

Homes in town average $175,000, while spreads with a bit of land on the outskirts of Ashland run in the $235,000 range. There are ways to beat the high prices, namely by moving into Medford or the historic gold rush town of Jacksonville. But Oregon's political turmoil has decimated the state's once-strong support for the arts and art education. So, for many families, Ashland's many nonprofit arts organizations and programs are a major reason for staying within city limits.

Arts Scene

For theater and music professionals who want small-town life and decent job opportunities, Ashland can't be beat. However, some theater people live but don't work here—instead traveling to film or theater jobs in Hollywood or other West Coast cities.

The Oregon Shakespeare Festival is one of the nation's most prominent presenters of the Bard's works. Over the years, the festival has widened the scope of its productions to include a main-stage season of plays by the theater world's biggest names and an experimental season of new works presented in a black-box setting. The festival's three theaters offer their works in repertory during summer, with main-stage performances in the 1,200-seat Elizabethan Theater as well as the "Globe-esque" Allen Pavillion. New plays are presented at the Black Swan Theater.

OSF's success has paved the way for complementary companies such as the Oregon Cabaret Theatre, Innersource, Rogue Valley Playback, and the Actor's Theater—groups that are highly regarded for the quality of their work and their willingness to present new pieces by local and national playwrights. Southern Oregon University's theater department presents its six-production season in the black-box Center Square

Theatre and the main-stage Center Theatre, while Ashland Community Theatre uses Town Hall for its season of musicals and comedies.

Recently, an old movie palace has undergone a multimillion dollar renovation. The resulting 750-seat, state-of-the-art performance space is now called the Ginger Rogers Theater. Touring national theater, dance, and musical acts that used to bypass Ashland on their journeys between San Francisco and Portland now stop and play a night at the Craterian. SOU's One World Series stages its six performances by international music groups at the Music Recital Hall. The Rogue Valley Symphony and Rogue Valley Opera stage their performances during winter.

The Britt Festival's Classical Music Series, under the direction of Peter Bay, is the highlight of southern Oregon's music scene. Staged in a 2,200-seat amphitheatre overlooking the Rogue River Valley, the festival's three-week classical music season is preceded by a month-long popular music season that has featured the likes of Little Richard, John McLaughlin, and Ani DiFranco.

Schneider Art Museum presents a year-round schedule of exhibitions by leading national contemporary artists in its Heiter and Tree Haven Galleries, as well as kids' art workshops. The Rogue Gallery and Art Center in Medford exhibits local and regional artists and also offers year-round art classes for kids. Monthly First Friday Art Walks take visitors through the dozen or so commercial galleries clustered in downtown Ashland.

Art Talk

Jeff Jones, founder of the Ashland Chalk Drawing Festival, says local artists go out of their way to support Ashland's arts scene. "Our event, even though it's only a year old, was able to attract lots of support from local artists, and by the time it was over we had over 200 participating over a weekend," notes Jones. "Artists saw it as a great way to get their work out in front of the public, and we used the event as a way to raise money for our natural history museum. In '98, what we're wanting to do is expand the event to three weekends and use it as a fund-raiser for the arts council—to help support the programs they do for young people."

Heidi Grossman, owner of Living Gallery, says the visual arts market potential in Ashland is unlimited. "All the pieces are in place," Grossman says. "We have great restaurants, a world-class Shakespeare festival, and very good performing arts, so what I'm trying to do is develop a high-end art market in Ashland. We have a number of very good galleries already here, and there are cultural tourists coming through town nine months out of the year who can and do buy expensive art. In my gallery, the most expensive pieces are the ones that sell first, and that tells me there's a market here for quality work that's fresh and new. I'm a block from Shakespeare and just a half-block off Main Street, and I am completely in favor of doing whatever we can do as a gallery association to build the local art market."

Mitchell Powell, gallery owner, art furniture craftsman, and president of the Ashland Gallery Association, says that Ashland's transition into a thriving art community has been guided by careful growth controls. He explains: "Because our downtown is small and intimate, and because we have effective municipal planning, Ashland has developed into a haven for fine arts of every variety. People here are aware that there's a danger we could become "Carmelized" through real estate appreciation, but we have a number of builders creating affordable homes for mid-income people, and there's a respect for maintaining the integrity of Ashland's long-range growth plan. There are 18 galleries in the gallery association, and there's a lot of art product hanging on the walls of these businesses. Summers are by far the best times to sell, and one of the things we're all trying to work on is promoting Ashland's off-season as a great time to come into town and purchase art. One of the events that's been very successful toward this end is the Taste of Ashland, which teams galleries with restaurants, wineries, and brewpubs on an April weekend. We sold 700 tickets to the Taste in '98 at $22.50 apiece, with the income targeted toward the gallery association and local charity organizations working with youth art programs. The Taste of Ashland is developing a nice arts focus and has branched out into associated events related to promoting the arts. There is a lot of interest in developing an arts district in a part of town adjacent to a closed lumber mill, and in the past year I've taken a 40,000-square-foot building and have converted it into a sales gallery and workshop for my art furniture business. The eventual plans are to start a bistro on one end of the building and create a performing arts space that seats a couple of hundred people. On the building's top floor we want to put in live/work spaces for artists. It's a project Ashland's ready for and one that will take us yet another step in the direction of being an arts destination."

Ann Seltzer, marketing manager for the Oregon Shakespeare Festival, says her organization's fast growth rate has been the result of planning and location. "We're lucky to have a director who can guide us into the future and anticipate problems before they arrive, and we're fortunate to be located in a charming community that's walkable from one end of town to the other," Seltzer says. "Eighty percent of our budget is raised through ticket sales, and last year we had about 350,000 tickets sold to what we estimate as being 100,000 buyers. Fourteen percent of our ticket buyers are from the surrounding area, 37 percent from elsewhere in Oregon, 43 percent from California, and 12 percent from Washington. Our smallest theater, the Black Swan, is so popular that we either need to expand its 143-seat capacity or build a new, 220-seat facility. . . . Ashland is a very strong theater town, and there's a lot of cooperation between the theater companies—through everything from shared costumes to the use of guest directors. The local high school has an outstanding internship program that places students into positions with the theater companies in the technical and acting departments, and there's a festival of new plays each March that encourages the community's young talent to have their works performed."

Lupine, president of the Ashland Folk Music Club, says the community's changing demographics are opening up new opportunities for music promoters: "We have a lot of retirees coming in from the Bay Area and a lot of young professionals moving in from Portland and Seattle. Between these two groups there are hundreds of new people in town who are ready to support organizations like the Ashland Folk Music Club as ticket buyers. We have sold as many as 300 tickets for our individual shows, but our average audience is more in the 100 range. With the Britt Festival, the Ginger Rogers Theater, and the college all programming more events, that's made it important for us to be able to compete for the audience that's out there. We have a lot of audience interest in Celtic music and dance, and contra dance remains one of our primary focal points. Ashland is fortunate to be on the highway that runs between Seattle and San Francisco, which allows us to snag unusually high-quality bands for a town this size and get them in here for a show. These days, there isn't a weekend night that goes by when there aren't several musical events to choose from, and that's a huge change from what Ashland was like when I moved here a few years ago."

Essentials

Population: 17,300

Art Events: First Friday Art Walks, monthly Ashland Folk Music Club concerts, New Chautauqua Series literary lectures year-round, Chalk Drawing Festival in June, ballet concerts in Lithia Park in July and August, Celebrate the Arts in August, Experience the Arts in September, Medford Jazz Jubilee in October

Art Spaces: Schneider Museum of Art, SOU Central Art Gallery, Rogue Community College Wiseman Gallery, Rogue Gallery and Art Center, Blue Heron Gallery, Living Gallery, Mitchell Powell Furnishings and Gallery, FireHouse Gallery, GeBzz the Gallery, Graven Images Gallery, 4th Street Gallery, Hansen Howard Gallery, JEGA Gallery and Sculpture Garden, On the Gallery Wall, Siskiyou Woodcraft and Gallery, Valley Art Gallery, Arts Council of Southern Oregon Gallery

Hangouts: Mark Antony Lounge, Ashland Creek Bar & Grill, Evo's Java House, Callahan's, Primavera, The Beanery, Standing Stone Brewing Company, Siskiyou Micro-Pub

Bookstores: Bloomsbury Bookshop, Blue Dragon Bookshop, Shakespeare & Co., Ashland Books & Music, Travel Essentials, Barnes & Noble, Shot in the Dark, Soundpeace

Public Radio: KSRG FM 88.3, KSMF FM 89.1, KSOR FM 90.1, KSJK AM 1230

Chamber of Commerce: P.O. Box 1360, Ashland, OR 97520, (541) 482-3486

Cannon Beach, Oregon

annon Beach's success as a small art town has as much to do with the community's spectacular, 9-mile stretch of Pacific coastline as it does with the flourishing group of artists and retirees who have settled there. Haystack Rock, a towering, 235-foot monolith that juts out of the ocean just behind Cannon Beach's quaint downtown, is precisely the sort of inspirational jaw-dropper artists can spend days, months, and even years painting. In fact, most of the seashore along this stretch of Oregon's coast looks as if some celestial giant spilled a sackful of rocks into the cold waters. The amazing landscape is forever serving as a backdrop for car commercials, Hollywood romances, state travel literature, and, of course, Cannon Beach's eternally grateful arts community.

Lifestyle

Raked by frequent storms and soaked by winter's incessant rains, Cannon Beach may not fit everyone's concept of a beach town. The weather fills newcomers with second thoughts about long-term prospects for surviving life here . . . but that just makes northwesterners love the place even more. Actually, one of the coast's best-kept secrets is a northwestern oddity called the "sun break," which is a blue hole punched through the day's cloud cover. Sun breaks occur fairly regularly along the coast and bring anything from a few minutes to several hours of respite from the overcast and drizzle—times when locals squeeze in their bike rides, dog walks, and beach strolls.

Cannon Beach is just 90 minutes from Portland, which means it's close enough to be prime second-home territory, and this proximity has pushed the average cost of a home into the $200,000 range. Just a few minutes up the coast in Seaside, however, homes average $120,000, which explains why increasing numbers of artists and retirees are finding that Seaside suits them just fine.

Arts Scene

Even if you don't care too much for the preponderance of seascapes, seagulls, Haystack Rock scenes, and sand dune landscapes filling the walls of most Cannon Beach galleries, you've got to admit there's a helluva lot of it—which means someone's buying the work. Actually, Cannon Beach is one of those rare places where artists can make a decent living selling into the local cultural tourism market—provided they're selling through their own studio/galleries and have the smarts to run their lives like a business. Contemporary art that has any resemblance to the abstract, non-objective work sold in urban galleries has a hard time fining buyers here, though more than a few art dealers have made valiant efforts over the years to carve out a contemporary-art niche. The bottom line is, almost all tourists come to Cannon Beach to buy the art equivalent of a beach souvenir, and second-home owners who want contemporary art usually buy it in the city instead.

The best gallery in town is the nonprofit exhibition space run by the Cannon Beach Arts Association, which shows contemporary work that in most cases isn't found in the galleries. The most consistent contemporary statements are being made in studio glass and bronze sculpture. In the past few years, several galleries have popped up in Seaside, a bit farther north in Astoria, and across the Columbia River in Ilwaco.

The pride of Cannon Beach is the Coaster Theater Playhouse, home to seven productions staged from October to August, with the focus on comedies, light dramas, and musicals. Astoria is home to Clatsop Community College's Performing Arts Center, a venue for local and touring theater, music, and dance.

Art Talk

Joyce Lincoln, coowner of Northwest by Northwest Gallery, says the local art market is strong: "There are not a lot of artists living in Cannon Beach anymore because it's turned into an expensive place to live, but what we do have are a lot of second-home owners building in the area and buying art in Cannon Beach galleries for their homes, and a whole lot of Seattle weekend visitors. Seattle is our strongest base of collectors for two reasons: they love visiting this beautiful place and they like buying art in a state that doesn't have a sales tax."

Patricia Shannon, owner of the Ricciardi Gallery, says Astoria is developing a strong arts identity: "We're not interested in being as tourist-oriented as Cannon Beach, but what we're finding is that a lot of collectors who used to make all their purchases in Cannon Beach galleries are coming up to Astoria for the more contemporary and more affordable art that's being shown here. Portland collectors are a big part of our business. My gallery has three exhibition areas, spaces I'm constantly changing out because there's so much talent here deserving exhibitions and so much collector traffic stopping in to see what's up on our walls and new. This is a very exciting time to be moving here and starting an art business here, and it's still very affordable."

Essentials

Population: 1,400

Art Events: Puffin Kite Festival in April, Sandcastle Contest in June, Summer Concerts at Quatat Park in July and August, Stormy Weather Arts Festival in November

Art Spaces: Cannon Beach Art Association Gallery, Northwest by Northwest Gallery, Bronze Coast Gallery, Pavilion, Valley Bronze of Oregon, ExposureArt, Windridge, White Bird Gallery, Art Reigns, Ray Watkins Watercolors, Heart of Glass, Rare Discovery, Ricciardi Gallery, Oregon Gallery, Arabella Gallery, Jeffrey Hull Gallery, Michael's Gallery, Icefire Glassworks, Gallery Marquilly, Hershey Studios, Showalter Cove Gallery, Haystack Gallery, Norvell Studio Gallery, Bubba's Pizza, The Blue Door, Greaver Gallery, Ballentye & Douglass, Steidel's Art, Nature Art & Sounds

Hangouts: Midtown Cafe, Relief Pitcher, Coffee Cabaña, Wet Dog Cafe & Brewpub, Bill's Tavern, Ricciardi Gallery Cafe

Bookstores: Cannon Beach Book Co., Ecola Square Books, Parnassus Books, Brass Pelican Books, Charlie's Turnaround Bookstore

Public Radio: KMUN FM 91.9

Chamber of Commerce: P.O. Box 64, Cannon Beach, OR 97110, (503) 436-2623

Joseph and Enterprise, Oregon

Northeast Oregon is the end of the trail—a place where two-lane highways dead-end at the foot of towering mountain ranges and the rims of gaping canyons, which is precisely why a vibrant, hardworking, and successful arts community has emerged in this corner of paradise. With each passing year, more artists working in a range of creative media—but primarily the hot-ticket realm of realistic bronze sculpture— find their way to the Wallowa Valley and settle in for the long haul. Savvy art collectors and cultural tourists from across the Pacific Northwest make pilgrimages to the valley part of their annual art-buying itineraries, lending the local arts scene an air of integrity and laid-back prosperity.

Lifestyle

Hunting, fishing, horseback forays into the Wallowa Mountains, alpine skiing, and even a small-scale version of yachting are all part of the valley's lifestyle. These activities are right at the fingertips of local residents—in many instances no more than a ten-minute drive from the doors of artist studios.

When the notion of friendly and safe communities comes to mind, Joseph and Enterprise should be right at the top of everyone's list. Local crime is more along the line of high school pranks than the drug-induced mayhem common in urban areas—though a double homicide last year sent shock waves through the county.

After economic downturn, the lumber mills in Joseph and Enterprise are back in operation, bringing a wider sense of economic security to the area, though Enterprise is still working its way out of the doldrums. An average home in Joseph is a bargain in the $90,000 range, while Enterprise's prices are even lower.

Arts Scene

Joseph earns its reputation as a great small art town because it is a national center for the creation of bronze sculpture. Artists from across the continent have been sending their clay sculpture models here for several years—into the hands of Joseph's expert foundry operators, who turn those models into exquisite bronze sculptures that are sold in galleries from Boca Raton to Santa Fe. Three full-fledged foundry operations form the base of Joseph's arts scene and employ dozens of skilled artisans, who do everything from the enlarging of clay models to molding sculpture casts, welding, patina application, and the crating of finished works. In some places, three businesses specializing in the same process would lead to cutthroat competition, but in Joseph there's more than enough work pouring into the foundries from artists around the nation. Everyone is too busy to battle for bucks, and instead foundries and artisans assist each other in a supportive climate.

Each of the foundries operates its own gallery, with Richard Manuel's taking the "eclectia" prize for combining the foundry site with a barbecue joint, museum, and theater. Some area sculptors have opened up their own galleries. One of the strongest elements in Joseph's arts scene is the Joseph Art School, a facility offering classes in painting, wood carving, and sculpture from May to October.

The Wallowa Valley Arts Council organizes

a series of summer art festivals and presents a year-round slate of eight performances at the OK Theatre, a 300-seat playhouse in downtown Enterprise. During summer, Joseph hosts a Chamber Music Festival, and Whitman College stages a repertory theater program from June to August at Joseph's outdoor stage. The Elgin Opera House, just west of the Wallowa Valley in Elgin, is another area performance venue, used by groups including the Elgin Community Theatre. LaGrande, 70 miles west of the valley, is home to Eastern Oregon University, whose art department operates the Nightingale Gallery and whose music department provides many of the players comprising the Grande Ronde Symphony.

Art Talk

David Jackman, owner of Valley Bronze of Oregon, says the valley's economy continues to diversify: "Sculptors and painters continue moving into this area because it offers them more by way of outdoor activities than other places and still is a very affordable place to live. If you want hunting and fishing, snowmobiling and skiing, riding and hiking, all of its right here.

I've seen at least a 30-percent growth in the number of retail establishments here in the valley in the past couple of years, and we're still the oldest and largest foundry in town, but more foundry operations are starting up and doing very well. That shows you that people here know how to make a business succeed, and artists understand that having ther work cast in Joseph means it will be done properly and professionally."

"We're fortunate to have excellent art instructors right here, but I'm finding that with more students coming into Joseph for art classes from other parts of the country, having a national group of art instructors makes good sense," says Jessica Henry, owner of the Joseph Art School. "The typical student is in the 45 to 55 age bracket and comes from anywhere in the Northwest, but we're also popular with people from British Columbia, New York, and Texas. The valley's reputation as an arts center is what attracts people here at first, and when they find out that we're a small town with great galleries, beautiful campgrounds, and inspiring scenery, that's what keeps them coming back."

Essentials

Population: Enterprise, 2,000; Joseph, 1,250
Art Events: Old Time Fiddlers' Contest in April, Youth Art Festival in May, Wallowa Valley Festival of the Arts in June, Fishtrap Writers' Conference and Wallowa Band Nez Perce Pow Wow and Friendship Feast in July, Wallowa Lake Chamber Music Festival in August, Nez Perce Art Show in September
Art Spaces: Valley Bronze of Oregon, Manuel Museum, Joseph Bronze, Wild Horse Gallery, Bronze Gallery of Joseph, Wallowa Lake Gallery, Skylight Gallery, Gene Hays Gallery

Hangouts: Embers Brewhouse, The Hydrant, Renee's Gourmet Coffee, The Book Loft
Bookstores: Book Corner, The Book Loft, Paper Museum and Bookstore, Sunflower Books
Public Radio: KPBX FM 89.5
Chamber of Commerce: P.O. Box 427, Enterprise, OR 97829, (541) 426-4622

Easton, Pennsylvania

Since the opening of the Crayola Factory, an interactive children's science and art education center sponsored by Binney & Smith (also makers of Silly Putty), this Delaware River community has seen up to 1,800 visitors daily crowding into its resurgent downtown. Part of the Two Rivers Landing redevelopment district, the Crayola Factory shares space with the National Canal Museum, which offers canal boat rides on the nearby restored Lehigh Canal. An easy drive from New York City and Philadelphia, Easton has—practically overnight—become a favorite day-trip destination, and the visitors have given a boost to the area's restaurants, art galleries, and artists.

Lifestyle

This one-time manufacturing center presents two very different, yet quite affordable, housing choices for artists. Those raising families gravitate toward the large inventory of Victorian and colonial homes in tree-lined neighborhoods. A favorite is the historic district adjacent to Lafayette College. Other artists prefer downtown Easton's industrial loft space. The leader of Easton's downtown arts revival, sculptor Karl Stirner, has turned his studio complex at 230 Ferry Street into a dream space that would be out of reach in most American and Canadian cities. Average neighborhood homes sell in the $100,000 range, with medium-size lofts costing $65,000.

Arts Scene

A few years ago, Easton's 1,500-seat State Theatre Center for the Arts endured some rocky financial times. But, snatching victory from the jaws of defeat, executive director Shelley Brown has injected new life into this historic structure through an ambitious September-through-May calendar of blues, pop, musicals, comedy, and light opera. Higher-brow offerings can be found September through April at Lafayette College's Williams Center, a 400-seat venue presenting new music, jazz, modern dance, classical music, theater, and chamber music.

The Williams Center also houses Easton's premier visual arts gallery, which offers national, touring, and regional contemporary art exhibitions. One of Easton's finest commercial art spaces, ConneXions Gallery, exhibits work by Lehigh Valley artists and their national peers. De Arte Magick, the latest addition to downtown's developing arts scene, specializes in contemporary work.

In nearby Bethlehem, SoLé Arts District (a revitalized industrial area) boasts the Banana Factory, a former food warehouse turned artist's studio complex, contemporary art gallery, and community cultural center focused on art education for kids. Its neighbor, the tiny Touchstone Theatre, has carved out a strong reputation for new works, one-artist performances, and touring shows. Another Bethlehem gem is Godfrey Daniels, a nightclub that presents new acts and folk music stars. Bethlehem residents anxiously await the completion of Lehigh University's $33-million arts center and two top-rate contemporary galleries.

For nine days in August, the Bethlehem region pumps up the volume with Musikfest (presented by the same folks who put on Christkindlmarkt in December). This festival somehow manages to pull together rock bands, visual artists, classical orchestras, gardeners, fine craftspeople, street musicians, blues artists, reggae bands, kids' theater, chorale groups, pop performers, and chamber music groups.

Art Talk

Dave Fry, artistic director and founder of Godfrey Daniels (named after a W. C. Fields punchline), describes his "listening room" folk music club: "We don't have a liquor license, but we have a great coffee bar and a BYOB policy, which attracts lots of families and an audience mostly in the 30-to-50 age range. Musicians love playing here because we treat them well, have great sound, and offer an atmosphere where they can connect with our audience. John Hartford, Chubby Carrier, John Gorka, Fairport Convention, Steve Riley, and the Mamou Playboys—acts on that level are what we specialize in. We have national acts three or four nights a week, local acts one or two nights a week, poetry readings, open mike nights, Celtic music jams, you name it. You just don't find music clubs like this anymore in the big cities, especially clubs where an entire family can come in, enjoy themselves, and catch a great touring act."

Sculptor Karl Stirner, who lives in a downtown Easton industrial loft, says the Crayola Factory has "created a huge change in downtown, where we had 62 new businesses start in the past year. They're telling us that 300,000 new visitors (called 'yellow baggers' for the color of their Crayola shopping bags) are coming here each year and spending an average of $13 per head when they visit. The city is altering parts of downtown to accommodate the influx of buses and tour trolleys, and there are new restaurants, new shops—everything is looking better. We have two new galleries in town representing local artists and beyond. There are more loft spaces coming available, priced around $2 a foot, which is attracting lots of interest from artists. With some luck, we may even have a culinary school coming into downtown in an old hotel building."

Essentials

Population: 26,000

Art Events: Canal Festival in June, Riverside Amphitheater Music Series in summer, Musikfest in August, State Theatre Center for the Arts performance series September through May, Celebration of the Arts Festival in September

Art Spaces: ConneXions Gallery, De Arte Magick Gallerias, The Gallery at Williams Center, White Birch Gallery

Hangouts: Cafe Tashie, O'Neill's Espresso, Pearly Baker's Ale House, Quadrant Book Mart & Coffeehouse

Bookstores: Quadrant Book Mart & Coffeehouse

Public Radio: WDIY FM 88.1

Chamber of Commerce: P.O. Box 637, Easton, PA 18044, (610) 253-4211

Baie St. Paul, Quebec

This beautiful community along the St. Lawrence River has one of North America's highest concentrations of art galleries, art museums, and working artists. Baie St. Paul, an hour's drive northeast of Quebec City, is a Canadian counterpart to legendary U.S. art towns such as Taos, Carmel, and Provincetown.

Since the late nineteenth century, the town has captivated the imagination of Canada's most successful artists. Baie St. Paul not only spawned its own school of Charlevoix landscape painters also but sustains them through a cultural tourism-based economy that has made the town one of the art world's top success stories.

Lifestyle

If you visit in winter, bring downhill skis and a motoneige (snowmobile), because without them you'll be marooned on Baie St. Paul's thick blanket of snow (which explains why some local artists spend their winters on Mexico's Pacific coast). Le Massif, a ski mountain, skirts the town's southern edge and is Baie St. Paul's winter place to see and be seen.

Cultural tourists start trickling into town in early May, which is also when many local businesses reopen their doors. The Charlevoix region turns into a fabulous summer playground, characterized by art festivals, high-dollar art sales, and busy restaurants. Visitors can go salmon fishing on the Rivière du Gouffre, which cuts right through the heart of town, and whale watching for the nine species of whales that live in the St. Lawrence River right off downtown.

Arts Scene

Clarence Gagnon may not have been the first painter captivated by Baie St. Paul's beauty but he certainly was the most influential artist in the town's history. Mesmerized by the Charlevoix's rose-hued, transitional winter light and its "Garden of Eden–esque" summers, other artists flocked here in the wake of Gagnon's success and formed the Groupe des Sept and other art colonies. Soon, art collectors from Montreal and Quebec City started dropping in, and the race was on.

Today Baie St. Paul is stacked with more than three dozen galleries, and even neighboring communities such as Les Éboulements, Pointe-au-Pic, and the tiny villages rimming Île aux Coudres are loaded with seasonal galleries and the homes of many of Canada's most outstanding artists. Two institutions serve as the premier exhibition locales in Baie St. Paul, with a third, the Musée de Charlevoix, located 25 miles away in Pointe-au-Pic. Centre d'Art de Baie St. Paul exhibits works ranging from traditional Charlevoix landscapes to fine crafts, contemporary local art, and touring exhibitions from across Canada. The Centre d'Art also offers art classes throughout the year and organizes the successful yearly exhibition and forum Symposium de la Nouvelle Peinture au Canada, an event so large it takes over the sacred ground of Baie St. Paul's hockey arena for all of August. Centre d'Exposition de Baie St. Paul is more tightly focused on the contemporary art world, mounting year-round, one-artist installations and invitational juried shows and hosting touring national and international contemporary exhibitions. Its sprawling, three-story exhibition facility is located in downtown Baie St. Paul—an eminently walkable place ideally suited for gallery jaunts.

With the exception of Rêves d'Automne, a two-week blowout that brings top-name entertainers into town for shows at nightclubs and dance halls, performing arts tend to be stronger in outlying communites than they are in Baie St. Paul. Théâtre Chantant performs a summer musical on Île aux Coudres, the enormous Manor Richelieu in Pointe-au-Pic stages a summer comedy, and Baie St. Paul has recently started the Festival du Théâtre Amateur in May.

The best news to hit the area's performing arts scene was the 1996 opening of the impressive, 600-seat Salle Françoys-Bernier concert facility at Le Domaine Forget in Saint Irénée, just a short drive northeast of Baie St. Paul on the St. Lawrence River. This site now hosts the Festival International du Domaine Forget, a 30-concert extravaganza of jazz, orchestral, and virtuoso performances by a distinguished list of music professionals, and a May-to-August academy for musicians of all ages that, like the Festival at Round Top, plugs the pros into a learning environment with students.

Art Talk

Painter Pierre Bédard says that local artists feel they're part of an important tradition: "I know that when I travel to Calgary or to Toronto, people look to me as a painter working in the Charlevoix style of art, and this type of recognition gives all the artists living in Baie St. Paul a sense of responsibility for living up to the community's reputation. This is a good place, a unique place, and a place where younger artists can come to build their careers. It's also a place with a lot of competition among the artists for making sales, yet if you fail to concentrate on the quality and individuality of the art you create, then there won't be as many sales as you would like."

Gilles Bédard, also a painter, says the local art scene is more open minded than people realize. "Certainly there's a strong sense of this place's traditions among the artists," Bédard says. "But I've noticed a lot of talent moving here from Montreal and Quebec City who are pursuing very different careers focused on contemporary art. For me, Baie St. Paul has been a wonderful place to paint, to be inspired by the landscape, the flowers, and the mountains. I've worked here for 25 years and have always had strong sales of my paintings, sometimes right off my easel before the work is half-finished. The artists here are independent of each other yet are also part of a close community. I like to think that right now is the golden era of Baie St. Paul as an artists' community."

Essentials

Population: 6,700

Art Events: Symposium de la Nouvelle Peinture au Canada, Rêves d'Automne, Festival du Théâtre Amateur, Festival International du Domaine Forget

Art Spaces: Centre d'Art de Baie St. Paul, Centre d'Exposition de Baie St. Paul, Musée René Richard, Galerie d'Art Iris, Galerie d'Art Clarence Gagnon, Atelier-Galerie Moisson d'Art, Galerie d'Art Yvon Desgagnés, Galerie d'Art Chez Moi, Galerie d'Art de la Baie, Les Artistes Bourbeau, Atelier-Galerie Daniel Froment, Atelier-Galerie Marie Joncas

Hangouts: Le Café des Artistes, Scénario Pub, Au Café des Rêveurs (seasonal)

Bookstore: La Librairie

Public Radio: CBC FM 103.1

Chamber of Commerce: 11 St. Jean Baptiste, Baie St. Paul, Quebec, Canada, GOA IBO, (418) 435-6187

Beaufort and Hilton Head, South Carolina

The arts-rich communities of Hilton Head and Beaufort on South Carolina's coast are only 45 minutes apart, and each offers a surprisingly strong local arts scene attuned to residents' needs and the expectations of cultural tourists. Hilton Head, a resort community of 27,000, splashed onto the cultural scene when its $10-million Self Family Arts Center, largely funded by a wealthy South Carolina family, opened in 1996. Home to a resident theater company, a visual arts gallery, a performing arts series, and year-round art education programs, SFAC has catalyzed Hilton Head's explosive growth as an arts town. Gorgeous Beaufort, whose historic downtown borders the picturesque Intracoastal Waterway, has cultivated its own performing arts scene at venues such as the Shed at Port Royal and the University of South Carolina-Beaufort Performing Arts Center. While fostering the careers of local artists, Beaufort's downtown gallery district has developed a strong reputation as a day-trip destination for cultural tourists from Charleston and Savannah.

Lifestyle

Beaufort has long attracted retired U.S. Marines from nearby Parris Island, while Hilton Head became popular as a weekend destination for Atlanta urbanites. Both communities have grown and prospered in recent years. Artsy Beaufort has become a somewhat laid-back, bohemian counterpart to Charleston, while Hilton Head's golf course- and resort-building spree has attracted thousands of monied retirees and second-home owners. Beaufort is the more racially diverse community, influenced both by military retirees and local African American sea islanders called Gullahs. The unique Gullah culture is highly valued in Beaufort, and the Penn Center on nearby St. Helena Island serves as its artistic and historical hub. Homes in Beaufort's historic district start in the $125,000 range, though $75,000 homes in other parts of town are easy to find. Hilton Head's home costs are much higher, starting at $175,000. Nearby Bluffton serves as a more affordable option.

Arts Scene

Though Beaufort's and Hilton Head's arts scenes both have varied opportunities, each town tailors offerings to its respective audience. In the university town of Beaufort, dance aficionados enjoy a local troupe and the Byrne Miller Dance Theatre, which attracts such groups as the Charleston Ballet and Nucleodanza to the USCB Performing Arts Center. The university also hosts the Beaufort Chamber Orchestra, with a five-concert season directed by maestro Fred Devyatkin. In Hilton Head, a larger group of metropolitan area retirees appreciate the Hilton Head Orchestra, whose ten-concert season at the First Presbyterian Church includes as many as 80 musicians.

You'll find roughly twice as many commercial art galleries in Beaufort as in Hilton Head. Clustered in the historic downtown, these galleries host regular Gallery Walks. Beaufort Art Supply offers art classes. Both the USCB Art Gallery and the Greer Gallery in Hilton Head hang touring shows, and the Hilton Head Art League exhibits both at Greer and at Sea Pines Center Gallery.

Local theater companies such as Beaufort

Little Theatre and Beaufort Repertory take to the boards at the Shed in Port Royal and the Port Royal Playhouse. The professional resident company of the Hilton Head Playhouse performs at Self Family Arts Center's Wallace Theater.

Art Talk

"It took ten years to raise the entire $10 million to build the Self Family Arts Center, but now we've done it and the building is debt-free," says Barb Lothrop, president of the Hilton Head Art League. "Our visual art exhibitions are juried by a seven-member panel of art professionals, so the shows tend to be of very high quality. We also have an outreach program for the island's schools and a workshop series that brings artists into Hilton Head from across the country year-round to teach at the arts center. Our association's gallery sold more than $45,000 in members' art in '97 and that's quite an achievement."

Painter Roger Steele observes that Beaufort's galleries are in a growth stage: "It's tourists from Charleston and Savannah coming here and buying art, and a new group of second-home owners buying local art for their places that are making things really happen right now. That's made a new crop of galleries pop up on the scene, so a lot of artists have heard about Beaufort and moved in from D.C., Philadelphia, and North Carolina. We've become the kind of place where an artist can make a fairly good living, and that's really turned the community around."

Essentials

Population: Hilton Head, 27,000; Beaufort, 11,000

Art Events: Gullah Festival and the International Piano Competition in February, Beaufort Art Association Annual Spring Exhibit in March, Any Oyster Roast and HarbourFest in July, A Taste of the Arts from September to May, Penn Center Heritage Days in November

Art Spaces: Altermann & Morris Gallery, Art Gallery at USCB, Bay Street Gallery, Creation Station, Frogmore Frolics, Gallery One, Garden Studio Gallery, Gloria Dalvini Gallery, Greer Gallery at SFAC, Indigo Gallery, John Stobart Gallery, Longo Gallery, Moonshell Gallery, Red Piano Gallery, Red Piano Too Art Gallery, Roger L. Steele Gallery, Smith Galleries

Hangouts: Blackstone's Cafe, Cheryl's Piano Bar, Harbourside Cafe, Hilton Head Brewing Company, Plum's

Bookstores: Authors Bookstore, Bay Street Trading Company, Firehouse Books, Port Royal Bookstore

Public Radio: WJWJ FM 89.9

Chamber of Commerce: Hilton Head Chamber of Commerce, P.O. Box 5647, Hilton Head, SC 29938, (803) 354-6431; Beaufort Chamber of Commerce, P.O. Box 910, Beaufort, SC 29901, (803) 524-3163

Woodbury, Tennessee

This small community of actors, artisans, and visual artists in the rolling hills of middle Tennessee has become one of Nashville's premier "edge cities." Largely responsible is the Arts Center of Cannon County, an exemplary facility that strives to makes Woodbury life a year-round arts festival. The nearby college town of Murfreesboro, less than 30 minutes west, provides employment and entertainment (a Nissan factory and Middle Tennessee State University's visual and performing arts programs respectively), while Nashville's big-time live music scene is just an hour away.

Lifestyle

Tennessee is growing fast, meaning that in places like Woodbury, real estate is a sound investment. The average home price here has risen from $70,000 to $80,000 in the past two years as lifestyle refugees from Nashville, Chicago, and other urban centers steadily trickle in.

That's not to say that Woodbury's valued rural lifestyle has changed . . . yet. But one issue facing this small art town is business development. More than a few Tennessee communities have already been ruined by cheap commercial sprawl and ugly mobile-home parks, and Woodbury needs to convince itself that holding out for something better will, in the long run, help retain the town's ambiance and valued quality of life.

Arts Scene

The reason Woodbury works as a small art town—and has the potential to become a cultural tourism hot spot—involves the Arts Center of Cannon County. This 11,000-square-foot facility delivers community theater, touring performing arts, classical music, visual arts exhibitions, arts festivals, and year-round arts education—and is seen as the focal point for Woodbury's social life. Take the ACCC's year-round PlayHouse Series of eight plays, each one performed at eight evening shows and numerous matinees for county schoolkids in the center's 250-seat performing arts theater. The plays regularly sell out, with the vast majority of ticket-buyers being theater-crazy locals. The PlayHouse Series had an amazing stretch of 25 consecutive sold-out performances for three of its shows in 1997 (that's 6,250 tickets—shades of *A Chorus Line!*). ACCC's theater programs are so popular that the center also produces two summer youth theater conservatory programs.

ACCC arts festivals include the nationally renowned White Oak Crafts Fair, the Festival of Quilts, and the Billy Womack Bluegrass Celebration. White Oak is the premier opportunity for national art dealers and folk craft collectors to buy middle Tennessee's highly prized fine-craft objects: baskets and chairs crafted from split white and other types of local oak. In recent years, other traditional art forms have proven popular with White Oak buyers, including handwrought iron, concrete sculpture, and hand-turned wooden bowls.

First American Bank underwrites the four-production ACCC Concert Spotlight Series, bringing folk-music acts, classical soloists, and touring theater to Woodbury. For local and regional artists there are exhibitions at ACCC's

Marly Berger Gallery, a 900-square-foot space that hosts ten annual one-artist and group invitational exhibitions.

For mid-career and emerging artists, one of Woodbury's advantages is its proximity to the Appalachian Center for Crafts in nearby Smithville. One of the nation's premier residency institutions for artists working in clay, fiber, glass, metal, and wood, the center attracts a nationally distinguished faculty for year-round classes in its 35,000-square-foot, state-of-the-art studio complex. Summer classes last only one week; during the school year the center is on a semester calendar and awards BFA degrees through Tennessee Tech. The center's three sales galleries exhibiting faculty and student work are legendary for their amazingly low prices. They regularly attract art dealers from major metropolitan areas looking for top-quality crafts.

Art Talk

According to Craig Nutt, master woodworker and visiting artist at the Appalachian Center for Crafts, the center's workshops are in a state of perpetual motion. "It's an incredible facility located in a drop-dead beautiful area," he says. "The equipment here is great and it's well-maintained, which allows the artists to reach their working speed with minimal effort and little wasted time. Every time I walk around at night the lights are on in these studios, with students burning the midnight oil. Our undergrads represent everything from professionals with strong reputations who come here to improve their skills to young artists taking courses in several areas as they decide on their career choices. Right now there's a huge interest in our blown-glass program; a lot of ambition is directed that way. The center's exhibition spaces work well as an income source for those students willing to create marketable work."

Scarlett Turney, a banker and actress, says ACCC's impact has been substantial: "The numbers of tickets we sell for these shows blows my mind sometimes. But, then again, there's a huge amount of talent right here in Woodbury, and we live in a community where all the employers support what the center does—giving people time off from work to attend rehearsals, plan fund-raisers, whatever's needed. Our audiences have grown far beyond the county line because we present an option for people who otherwise would have to drive into Nashville to see a live show. This small-town art center goes a long way toward exposing people in Cannon County to the wider world of what's happening in all the arts."

Essentials

Population: 2,200
Art Events: Dottie West Music Festival in June, White Oak Crafts Fair in August, Festival of Quilts and Billy Womack Bluegrass Celebration in October
Art Spaces: Arts Center of Cannon County, Appalachian Center for Crafts, Center for the Arts Gallery in Murfreesboro
Hangouts: Joe's Place, Main Street Deli, D.J.'s, Red Rose Coffeehouse & Bakery, Demos'
Bookstores: Williams Booksellers, Hastings, The Bookrack, Bookland
Public Radio: WPLN FM 90.3
Chamber of Commerce: Arts Center of Cannon County, P.O. Box 111, Woodbury, TN

Big Bend, Texas

The vast stretches of West Texas meet one of nature's most spectacular places in the Big Bend, a sparsely populated region that's turned into a magnet for artists escaping Austin, Dallas, Los Angeles, and San Antonio. Alpine (pop. 6,200), the largest town and site of Sul Ross State University, has developed a bona-fide gallery district. Marathon (pop. 400), home of the splendid Gage Hotel, has two very strong galleries of its own. Marfa (pop. 2,400) boasts one of the world's most renowned contemporary art institutions. Lajitas (pop. 150) has a gallery that doubles as the mayor's office. In addition to Terlingua's (pop. 125) two galleries, it sustains a music hall that draws many of Texas's top musicians. Some of America's finest cowboy artists and traditional Western craftspeople call Fort Davis (pop. 1,200) home. The area also draws outdoors lovers to Big Bend National Park, 1,100 square miles of near-wilderness bordering Mexico, and 287,000-acre Big Bend Ranch State Park. Just across the border in Ojinaga (home to the Pancho Villa Museum), a train to the spectacular reaches of Copper Canyon and the Pacific Coast stops at the depot.

Lifestyle

Ranching has always been Big Bend's economic lifeblood, but with each passing year, tourism exerts a greater impact. Among the visitors are a startling number of cultural tourists, who buy local art at places like the Terlingua Trading Post and the Evans Gallery. They also groove on blues shows at Railroad Blues, go two-steppin' at the Starlight Theatre, wander through Donald Judd's amazing minimalist art displays at La Fundación Chinati, and slurp down Tecates at La Estancia, Ojinaga's drive-in bar. Home prices have steadily risen, though it's still easy to find Alpine fixer-uppers for under $50,000 . . . and a near-palace for $125,000. The easygoing Big Bend infuses the soul with the sort of inspiration that places your life in context—and if you relate to that statement, this place just may be right for you.

Arts Scene

Donald Judd, one of the world's greatest and most successful contemporary artists, bought Marfa's decommissioned army base in 1986 and transformed it into a unique environment displaying his startlingly beautiful minimalist art. He then added more buildings inside city limits and turned those into galleries for other contemporary artists, studios for himself, and living spaces. Although Judd has died, the Chinati Foundation/Fundación Chinati remains and prospers as a contemporary art world gem. Judd's work regularly commands prices topping $100,000 at auction, but here it's on year-round display for free.

While no other contemporary artists working here have attained Judd's international stature, many do show at galleries in New York, Dallas, Santa Fe, and L.A. Why they choose to live here is simple: the Big Bend is an awesome place. Alpine now has such a concentration of galleries and artist studios that its twice-yearly Gallery Nights consist of more than a dozen venues displaying and selling art.

Alpine's viability as a cultural-tourist destination is enhanced by such events as the outdoor summer-stock season at Kokernot Theatre, in addition to the Studio Theatre's regular season. The college's well-selected performing arts series imports touring theater, classical musicians, comedians, and dance companies. Museum of the Big Bend, also on campus, exhibits local work through invitationals and one-artist shows. Its wildly popular annual Trappings of Texas show displays such traditional Western crafts as tooled saddles, sterling scarf slides, spurs, and holsters. Alpine's Big Bend Players community theater group offers three yearly productions.

All of the Big Bend's commercial galleries contain varied masterpieces created by this region's deep pool of artistic talent. Appreciate their virtues by driving the long distances from one small town to the next . . . it's time very well spent.

Art Talk

James Evans, photographer and gallery owner, says his art space is dedicated to making an unusual creative statement: "I'm strictly a photography gallery, and I represent photographers from all over the country, most of whom have worked in this area. Traffic through the gallery has increased as the Gage Hotel has become more of a destination, but for artists and galleries, staying in business is still a survival situation. There's a good market selling to tourists, but not enough of a market yet where you don't need to sell your work outside the area."

Clay Henry Jr., mayor of Lajitas, says an international group of cultural tourists responds positively to work created by the region's artists. "This place used to only sell imports from Mexico, but now I've got art collectors from New York and France stopping by my place to ask for advice on who the best artists are," Henry says. "There's a lot of Austin musicians building homes around here, and I'm thinking about turning my office and gallery space into a music hall—sort of an opryhouse on the Rio Grande. As long as I can keep my liquor license, I think it would work."

Essentials

Population: 10,000
Art Spaces: Adobe Hacienda Gallery, Cafe Cenzio, The Chinati Foundation/La Fundación Chinati, Chisos Gallery, El Museo de Pancho Villa, Evans Gallery, Fisher Hill Gallery, Front Street Books, Hallie's Hall of Fame Museum, Kiowa Gallery, Lajitas Trading Post and Mayor's Office, Marfa Art Gallery, Museum of the Big Bend, Ocotillo Bookstore & Cafe, Reata, Rinconada, Starlight Theatre, Terlingua Trading Post
Art Events: Texas Cowboy Poetry Gathering in March, Alpine Gallery Night in April and November, Mayor Clay Henry Jr.'s Cinco de Mayo Cabrito Cookoff, Chinati Foundation Open House in October, Marfa Lights Festival in September

Hangouts: Cafe Cenizo, La Estancia, La Kiva, Outback Bar & Grill, Railroad Blues, Starlight Theatre
Bookstores: Fisher Hill Gallery, Front Street Books, Ocotillo Bookstore & Cafe, Terlingua Trading Post
Public Radio: KTEP FM 88.5
Chamber of Commerce: 106 N. Third St., Alpine, TX 79832, (915) 837-2326

Kerrville and Fredericksburg, Texas

Rolling hillsides, flowing streams, an eye-popping wildflower season, and small towns built around town squares make Texas's Hill Country one of the nation's most beautiful regions. Add a first-rate music scene, affordable homes, distinctive fine craftsmanship, and traditional encouragement of the fine arts, and you have an artists' nirvana. The small towns of Fredericksburg and Kerrville are separated by about 30 miles of two-lane blacktop, yet each manages to have a distinct art personality. Taken together, the towns span the full range of visual and performing arts, festivals, and live music.

Lifestyle

Settled by German homesteaders, Fredericksburg retains much of its Old World charm. With its brewpub crafting decidedly German beers and its sausage plants cranking out some of the best bratwurst on the continent, it's no wonder that tourists have taken to the town's gemütlichkeit. These attractions, however, have proven a mixed bag for local artists and gallery owners, since Fredericksburg's reputation for great shopping (especially at the fabulous Homestead stores) far surpasses its galleries' renown. Kerrville, though just a short drive away, has cultivated an entirely different orientation. Here, cowboy culture is king, and such nearby towns as Bandera and Uvalde turn out top professional rodeo stars.

The entire region boasts some of the country's best year-round weather, attracting retirees who value both arts access and affordable homes set on enough acreage to support livestock. Expect to pay about $125,000 for an average-size place in either community or a house with a few acres just outside of town.

Arts Scene

Kerrville's Hill Country Arts Foundation is an exemplary small-town art center whose influence extends far beyond the Hill Country's horizons. Home to the Duncan-McAshan Visual Arts Center, the 722-seat Smith-Ritch Point Theatre, the 100-seat Pavilion Theatre, and several state-of-the-art workshop facilities for printmaking and other visual arts, HCAF is a first-rate performance, exhibition, and education center. Adults can choose from among 80-plus year-round art classes, many taught by top names in southwestern art circles. The center also manages a first-rate art gallery, exhibiting themed shows and invitationals primarily for local and regional artists. HCAF's performing arts programs include a Sunday music series and a pops series. The center also offers an exceptional theater season, utilizing both the indoor Pavilion Theatre and outdoor Point Theatre to present year-round family entertainment.

September through April, the Kerrville Performing Arts Society presents monthly concerts, featuring such luminaries as the San Antonio Symphony and the St. Louis Brass. Look for additional theater and music during the academic year at Schreiner College's Hanszen Fine Arts Center. Kerrville also weaves into its yearly calendar the Kerrville Folklife Festival, the Kerrville Wine & Music Festival, the Texas State Arts & Crafts Fair, and the Texas Heritage Music Festival.

In addition to three commercial art galleries, Kerrville also sustains the massive

Cowboy Artists of America Museum, dedicated to Western realist painters and sculptors. The museum has year-round special exhibitions, as well as art lectures and workshops. Fredericksburg supports three commercial art galleries and two fine crafts galleries.

While Fredericksburg's musical mindset tends to overindulge oompah, just outside of town the cherished Luckenbach Dance Hall conducts events such as Jerry Jeff Walker's Laborfest, a Hill Country musicians Sunday jam session, and regular gigs by Texas stars like Billy Joe Shaver and Don Walser. The Fredericksburg Music Club stages monthly classical concerts at the United Methodist Church, while the Pedernales Creative Arts Alliance sponsors summer bluegrass, blues, mariachi, and oompah concerts in Courthouse Square. A local B&B, Someday House, invites listeners to its back porch to hear Austin-based folk music.

Art Talk

Kathleen Hudson, executive director of the Texas Heritage Music Festival, says Kerrville's arts scene has a distinct identity: "We're not market-oriented as much as we're celebrating the arts for what they mean in our lives and culture. Art really does play a role in people's lives in Kerrville, and people living here know that and appreciate it. Our event is 17 years old and has turned its energy toward education programs during the festival's run and during the school year by bringing Texas musicians into the local schools."

Kim Roberts, manager of Fredricksburg's Whistle Pik Galleries, says the local art market does support galleries over the long run. "We've been in business for three years and have developed a good base of collectors though our exposure to Fredricksburg's walk-in traffic," Roberts says. "The walk-in traffic comes here from all over Texas, and by advertising the gallery nationally, we've developed an outside market for many of the 28 artists we represent. Some of our artists are local, but they're artists who are already established in their careers."

Essentials

Population: Kerrville, 20,500; Fredericksburg, 7,700

Art Events: Texas State Arts & Crafts Fair in May, Kerrville Folk Festival in May/June, Kerrville Wine & Music Festival and Texas Heritage Music Festival in September, Oktoberfest, Fredericksburg Food & Wine Fest and Texas Mesquite Art Festival in October

Art Spaces: Charles Beckendorf Gallery, Cowboy Artists of America Museum, Duncan-McAshan Visual Arts Gallery, Early Texas, Gracie's Art Gallery, Jack Terry Gallery, Java Pump, Kowert Art Gallery, Max Greiner Gallery, Pampell's Fountain, Whistle Pik Galleries, Woodstone Gallery

Hangouts: Choo-Choo's BBQ, Francisco's, Fredericksburg Brewery, Java Pump, Mamacita's

Bookstores: Books to Share, Main Book Shop, Pampell's Fountain

Public Radio: KUT FM 90.5, KSTX FM 89.1

Chambers of Commerce: Kerrville Chamber of Commerce, 1700 Sidney Baker St., #100, Kerrville, TX 78028, (830) 896-1155; Fredericksburg Chamber of Commerce, 106 N. Adams, Fredericksburg, TX 78624, (830) 997-6523

Rockport, Texas

For decades, Texas's coastal paradise has attracted wildlife artists inspired by the region's amazing variety of waterfowl, migratory birds, butterflies, and deep-sea fish. More recently, a new breed of coastal landscape artists has blended in with Rockport's already large artists' community, creating the critical mass necessary to sustain a significant art colony with strong reputation for quality art and art festivals. As word spreads about Rockport's supportive climate for artists and its affordable, high-quality lifestyle, more artists and art-loving retirees—especially those who like beaches and great seafood restaurants—are finding Rockport an ideal home address.

Lifestyle

Rockport is diverse enough to offer something for everyone, and what's not here is readily accessible an hour west in Corpus Christi, home to a contemporary art museum and performing arts center. Still, Rockport is very much a working-class community, where fishing and boatbuilding underpin the regional economy . . . an environment many artists find refreshing. The town's small business district is slowly renovating its older structures. Each year seems to bring a new gallery or two into town—some owned by early retirees who've left the urban jungle for the Gulf Coast's laid-back lifestyle.

Fancy developments such as Key Allegro are loaded with waterfront homes selling in the $250,000 range, while Rockport's older neighborhoods are filled with family-size residences priced around $75,000. Schools aren't the greatest, but the Rockport Center for the Arts, located in a gorgeous Victorian home on the waterfront, does a good job of addressing art education needs with year-round after-school classes in several creative disciplines.

Arts Scene

The ace up this small art town's sleeve is the Rockport Center for the Arts, a wonderful, multi-dimensional arts center in the process of expanding and updating its exhibition and educational spaces and building a much-needed performance space. The center offers year-round art classes for adults and kids, as well as rotating exhibitions. These exhibits range from regional invitationals to one-person shows by the likes of granite sculptor Jesús Bautista Moroles, a towering figure on the Texas art scene who chooses to live and work in laid-back Rockport's bucolic seaside setting.

Rockport abounds with great painters, and when artist Simon Michael opened his gallery here in the early 1960s he paved the way for the dozen or so serious art spaces the town has today. The art market here is strongest in winter, when snowbirds, cultural tourists, and birders flock into town to enjoy the mild winter climate, respected arts festivals, and easy access to such wonders as the Aransas National Wildlife Refuge, winter home of whooping cranes and hundreds of other winged species.

Until the art center's performance space is completed, local performing arts companies must make do with various venues. Rockport Ballet Academy uses a space in the old train depot, musicians such as bluesman John Grimaudo gig at Rudder's and the Boiling Pot, and the Repertory Theatre of America, a touring company based in Rockport, rehearses and stages its occasional performances at the high school auditorium and Rockport Country Club.

Rockport's arts scene has developed its own identity by growing slowly and responding carefully to the needs of community, artists, and cultural tourists. If, in the coming years, a few key pieces fall into place, this small art town could become one of cultural tourism's most successful economic development stories.

Art Talk

Lisa Bair, artist and owner of the Estelle Stair Gallery, has just completed extensive remodeling of the 100-year-old building housing her art space. "Rockport's always been a place where artists and galleries have survived rather than prospered," Bair says. "But with all the second-home building here by folks who mainly live in Houston, San Antonio, and Dallas, the market is really starting to pick up. Of course, it's still the sort of market where paintings, sculpture, and anything else sells well provided it has some element of Rockport in the image—though we do sell a surprising number of Hill Country landscapes as well. Rockport will always be a re-laxing and unstuffy place, but we need to keep educating the local residents that fine art goes beyond the definitions of wildlife art—and to keep telling the rest of Texas that great, interesting art is happening here."

Drexel Riley, founder and artistic director of the Repertory Theatre of America, says the art center's expansion into a performing arts space would be perfect for his company's long-range plans: "It would be hard to do theater in Rockport, regardless of when or what you're presenting, but I could see a successful winter season that had plays performed on Thursday, Friday, and Saturday nights, and maybe a summer outdoor season, provided you could do something about the mosquitoes. Our company is always touring and always using whatever space is available to perform in, but its hard to get actors to stick around if all they're doing is living out of a suitcase. Having a performance space here in Rockport and making a local season successful would be a great thing for the town. It's a developing community and a beautiful place to live, a place where every day feels like one more day I'm on vacation, sort of."

Essentials

Population: 6,500
Art Events: Rockport Art Festival in July, Fiesta en la Playa in September, Hummer Bird Celebration in September, Seafair in October
Art Spaces: Rockport Center for the Arts, Estelle Stair Gallery, Steve Russell Studio Gallery, Texas Maritime Museum, Simon Michael Gallery, Moroles Studio Gallery, Windway Gallery, Tejas Gallery, Seaside Gallery, Rockport Artists' Gallery, Little Gallery, Po Po's Gallery, Frame of Mine Gallery

Hangouts: Rudder's, The Boiling Pot, Crab-N Restaurant
Bookstores: Pat's Place, The Bookworm, The Book Shelf
Public Radio: KEDT FM 90.3
Chamber of Commerce: 404 Broadway, Rockport, TX 78382, (512) 729-9952

Round Top, Texas

With fewer than 100 full-time residents, the Texas Hill Country enclave of Round Top is an unusual small art town. This is a place where local visual artists manage to build thriving careers, where Shakespeare draws standing-room only crowds to a converted barn theater, where a twice-a-year antiques fair has developed into a county-wide blowout, where a 1,200-seat hall hosts sold-out classical music concerts, and where the local café not only has its own Web site and nationally distributed line of food products but also schedules creativity seminars drawing top names in corporate motivation and communications.

Lifestyle

Round Top's arts prosperity can be boiled down to one element: Houston money. Located in one of the nation's prettiest regions, about midway between Houston and Austin, Round Top has for the last decade been Houston's best excuse to drive two hours away from the city's concrete and crowds. Houses have been bought and renovated, farms have been turned into mini-ranches, festivals have sprung up like April bluebonnets, and a whole lot of dough has been tossed around in the process of furnishing the city folks' country spreads with art, antiques, and catered meals. Home prices in Round Top start around $150,000, while in nearby Carmine and Fayetteville similar residences cost half as much.

Arts Scene

Institutions and charismatic visionaries played leading roles in turning Round Top into a small art town. Concert pianist and native Texan James Dick, for instance, was the driving genius behind the International Festival Institute at Round Top, one of America's premier facilities for classical music performance and education. Beginning in 1971 with a single concert in an old schoolhouse, Dick has guided the institute through an impressive development stage. Today it sits on a 200-acre farm within city limits and holds nearly a dozen new buildings, including a massive 1,200-seat performance hall built by local craftsmen. The institute presents year-round recitals and concerts, some of which are broadcast on NPR's "Performance Today" series. It comes fully to life during June and July, when its Summer Institute for Advanced Study and Performance assembles dozens of the nation's most talented music students and classical music recording professionals for an educational and concert residency program.

Antiques goddess Emma Lee Turney is also a native Texan and a Round Top visionary. Single-handedly, she turns Round Top into the nation's most financially successful antiques marketplace twice each year through her Houston-based Round Top Antiques Fair. Thousands of antiques dealers and buyers crowd into this tiny town for Emma Lee's October and April events, filling every hotel bed and restaurant seat in the county for three-day spending splurges.

Yet another local visionary is restaurateur Bud Royer, whose Round Top Cafe actually won a Best Café in Houston award, even though Round Top is a bit outside that metro area's boundary. Royer, who is usually found sitting on his café's front porch, is famous for everything from pecan pies to pork chops and peach preserves. His wife, Karen, is famous in her own right for organizing Creativity Seminars at Round Top for corporate executives from Houston.

The University of Texas is involved here as well—through its Winedale Historical Center's two annual art festivals (held in April and October) and its main-stage Shakespeare season of three plays performed at the Theatre Barn in July and August (and one play during April's Springfest). Finally, in response to the bottomless pit of buyers for anything and everything related to local arts and culture, the Round Top Arts Festival has finally become an annual November reality. . . to which I say "Live Long and Prosper!"

Art Talk

Innkeeper Mary Stanhope says the Round Top Arts Festival has turned out to be a surprising success. "First it was a watercolor show, then in the past two years it's opened up to artists of all types, and that's brought in nearly 70 artists and more than 2,000 collectors on what once was a quiet November weekend," Stanhope says. "It's more than a walk-through show, because it gives kids an area where they can play for a couple of hours while the parents are spending their money, and there's food from Cajun to BBQ and live music both days. Round Top is full of good artists and good craftspeople working in all media, and we've now got serious artists living here working in things like studio glass and photography."

Folk artist P. J. Hornberger's studio/gallery attracts serious collectors. "I'm just one block off the town square in a small barn, but that [distance] seems to be enough of a bother to keep tire-kickers away without discouraging people who seriously want to find something different," Hornberger says. "My largest pieces sell best, and it's mostly to Houston people. Fall is the best selling time, but spring seems to bring through a lot of travelers from outside the state who are just finding out about Round Top. It was the antiques collectors who helped me get my folk art career started, and they've always been huge buyers of my work."

Essentials

Population: 81
Art Events: Springfest at Winedale in April, Round Top Antiques Fair and Square Fair in April and October, Shakespeare at Winedale in July and August, Oktoberfest at Winedale, Round Top Arts Festival in November, Second Shepherd's Play at Henkel Square in December
Art Spaces: P. J. Hornberger Studio/Gallery, Briar Patch Gift Shop and Nursery, Round Top General Store, Tin Star Company, Mostly Mesquite, Miller's Cedar Furniture & Crafts, Fitzwater Wood Crafting, Alice Darnell Gallery, Purple House Gallery, Stella's Beauty Salon & Gallery, Fayetteville Art Colony

Hangouts: Royer's Round Top Cafe, Klump's Restaurant
Bookstores: The Book Nook
Public Radio: KUHF FM 88.7
Chamber of Commerce: none

Park City, Utah

Park City's proximity to Salt Lake City (less than a half hour by interstate) has been both a bane and boom to this community's arts scene. While Park City offers ski slopes, art galleries, performing arts, restaurants, and art festivals, it does not have the "captive audience" geography that keeps tourists stranded (and spending) in places like Vail, Sun Valley, and Jackson. Nonetheless, this small art town has managed over time to put in place all the elements of a vibrant arts scene: commercial galleries, an arts center with exhibition and educational space, a community theater company performing in an historic theater, classical music groups, and, most important, a new performing arts center.

Lifestyle

As Salt Lake City's "back door" for outdoor recreation, Park City has seen its real-estate values skyrocket. Residents of L.A., Phoenix, and Salt Lake are Park City's main second-home owners, and when you combine their enthusiasm with the limited land available for home building, the result is a tight and expensive market loaded with overpriced condos and small homes starting in the $250,000 range. But here, unlike other western ski towns, artists can move "down valley" and find thousands of affordable houses—and they won't be shacked up in a double-wide on a desolate flood plain either.

Arts Scene

Over the past decade, many American ski towns have also turned into art towns—as has Park City. Though there's been a large turnover in the gallery scene in the past few years, Park City is the sort of place where art-business owners are willing to invest.

But history tells us that in this small art town, only the strongest survive. When the world arrives at Park City's doorstep for the 2002 Winter Olympics in Salt Lake City, the Kimball Art Center is certain to be around. The Kimball is ground zero for the state's premier summer arts festival, as well as year-round art classes for adults and kids, master summer art classes, touring national shows, exhibitions by local and regional artists, and much of the art action in local schools.

By anyone's estimation, the annual Park City Arts Festival is one of the Rocky Mountain region's best-run and most talent-filled art fairs. Over three days in August, the festival features more than 200 artists and dozens of performances by bands, children's entertainers, dancers, and theater companies.

Park City Performances, a theater company whose six-play season is a balanced mix of new works and chestnuts, presents its year-round season at the freshly restored Historic Egyptian Theatre, a downtown venue in the middle of Park City's gallery district. Rounding out the performing arts scene are summer performances by the Utah Symphony at Deer Valley, Park City Chamber Music Society concerts, Park City International Music Festival's summer concert season at tent and church venues, and the Park City Arts Council's Season Series.

When the Eccles Community Art Center opened its doors early in 1998, Park City finally had the 1,100-seat, state-of-the-art concert facility that its performing arts organizations deserve. The Eccles has also allowed Park City to stage top-name entertainment that was previously confined to shows in Salt Lake City.

For touring national bands, the favorite local venues are Cisero's Nightclub and the Inn at Prospector Square. Other clubs with live music are O'Shuck's, Mulligan's Pub, and The Cozy.

Art Talk

Robin Valline, owner of Old Town Gallery, says his gallery has prospered by serving a niche in the local market. "We once were a Western and wildlife art gallery," Valline says, "but because Park City was so strongly represented in that type of work, we transitioned over the course of several years into a contemporary art gallery. . . . [We represent] a national group of artists, most of whom have some sort of connection to Utah. One of the interesting trends of the past few years has been the lack of momentum in the art market for contemporary southwestern art, which once was a large part of our business. The Sundance Film Festival brings a flood of people into town, but few of them are buyers. I'd say our best months for sales are February, March, August, and September."

"We all have the Olympics in mind," says Cyndy Holz, house manager for the Eccles Performing Arts Center. "But this is also the state's fastest growing county, and one of the Eccles's main missions is to serve as an educational facility for the school district. Our facilities include a 180-seat black box and a 1,300-seat main stage, where in our first season we'll be presenting jazz, ballet, modern dance, and classical music. The Sundance Film Festival fills up the center on several evenings in January, and we'll probably also serve as a stage for Sundance Theatre. We're just 20 minutes from downtown Salt Lake City, so we'll be able to program events year-round and have substantial audiences turn out, regardless of whether tourists are in Park City itself."

Essentials

Population: 6,000
Art Events: Saturday night Sundance Film Series, monthly Gallery Strolls, Sundance Film Festival in January, North West Rendezvous of Art Exhibition in summer, Rocky Mountain Invitational Exhibition in July, Park City Art Festival in August
Art Spaces: Kimball Art Center, Taminah Gallery, Wild Earth Images, Park City Gallery, Old Town Gallery, William Duncan Galleries, Judy Taylor Artworks, Meyer Gallery, White Wolf Gallery, Coda Gallery, Nature's Art

Hangouts: Espresso Brothers, Wasatch Brewpub, Town Lift Brewery, Mulligan's Pub, Morning Ray Cafe
Bookstores: Dolly's Bookstore, A Woman's Place Bookstore , Summit Books & Coffeebar
Public Radio: KPCW FM 91.9
Chamber of Commerce: P.O. Box 1630, Park City, UT 84060, (435) 649-6100

Burlington, Vermont

The western border of Vermont's largest city is graced by lovely Lake Champlain, the town's greatest warm weather asset. And when the snow starts flying in late October, folks here catch ski fever, knowing that challenging resorts such as Stowe, Bolton Valley, and Smuggler's Notch are less than an hour's drive from downtown. Between the University of Vermont, Champlain College, Trinity College, and St. Michael's College in nearby Colchester, the Burlington area also boasts more than 14,000 college students . . . enough to support this town's dynamic live music scene as well as its alternative performing arts venues, dozens of coffeehouses, hundreds of restaurants, and several brewpubs.

Summer is warm enough for outdoor Shakespeare at Shelburne Farm's Coach Yard, while Burlington City Arts stages its very popular Battery Park Summer Concerts series outdoors on Thursday evenings. Winters are long, with short days and frequent whiteouts, which is why a fair portion of Burlington crowds into the Magic Hat Brewery and hoists a few from October through April. And for those who can't get enough of a good thing, the Ben & Jerry's plant is just a half-hour away in Waterbury.

Lifestyle

This community works best for those who relish outdoor activities and can handle the worst Mother Nature can dish out. Lake Champlain, at 136 miles long the largest freshwater body in the eastern United States, spills across the international border into Quebec, running almost to the suburbs of Montreal. Thus Vermonters can drive their boats to the Montreal

Jazz Festival in summer, and French Canadian boat owners can journey down to Burlington on summer weekends, tie up along the community's waterfront, and spend their bucks downtown.

Downtown Burlington's charms include the Church Street Marketplace, though its recent influx of national-chain tenants has greatly dismayed Burlington's vociferous "Made in Vermont" crowd. An 8-mile paved bike path winds through some of the community's prettiest neighborhoods, neatly avoiding the commercialized urban sprawl zone along Shelburne Road. Burlington's suburbs are generally growing at a modest rate. Housing is still very affordable, with average-size homes in reasonable condition selling in the $90,000 range.

Arts Scene

When it comes to the performing arts, Burlington's year-round events are hard to beat. Maybe it's the long winters, or perhaps it's simply the quality of what's presented and the social interaction that follows—but this is a community that loves going out for music, theater, performing arts, and nightclubs.

The Flynn Theater presents one of the nation's most exemplary performing arts seasons in a renovated space that anchors downtown Burlington's arts scene. The Flynn's MainStage series runs from early September through May, delivering a powerful schedule of nearly three dozen national, international, and regional performers at ticket prices from $14 to $40. The Montana Repertory, Ray Davies, Dee Dee Bridgewater, Merce Cunningham Dance Company, Michael Doucet, and Mandy Patinkin are just a few of the quality talents presented in a typical season, which also includes theater, opera, and world music. The Flynn also sponsors a children's performing arts season, an On-Stage series in its 120-seat black box, a Discover Jazz Festival staged across Burlington, and a comprehensive school outreach program.

The University of Vermont adds to the performing arts mix with the September-through-April Lane Series at the Flynn, the UVM Recital Hall, and the on-campus Ira Allen Chapel. The series nicely complements the Flynn's own season with classical music, Shakespeare, opera, and new music.

Burlington hosts several local theater companies. These include the St. Michael's Playhouse, Lyric Theatre at Trinity College, Champlain Arts Theatre Company at Champlain College, Atlantic Theater Company, and UVM Drama productions at the Royall Tyler Theatre.

The Vermont Symphony Orchestra uses the Flynn for its October-through-May Masterworks season that includes well-known orchestral pieces on Saturday evenings and an innovative New Attitudes series on Fridays, with guest artists such as Tish Hinojosa, Edgar Meyer, and Mark O'Connor. VSO, directed by conductor Kate Tamarkin, is famous for its Made in Vermont music festival in fall, when the entire orchestra goes on the road for a statewide, 12-performance tour to smaller communities. Burlington also hosts a Mozart Festival in July, a folk music festival in August, a free summer music festival in Battery Park and City Hall Park, the music-oriented Marketfest in September, and the Jeh Kulu Dance and Drum Festival in November. The Vermont Youth Orchestra, dedicated to music education and performance, is one of the nation's premier organizations of its kind.

Burlington's visual arts scene is a bit less fortunate, lacking sufficient infrastructure to support the town's enormous base of talented painters, sculptors, textile artists, jewelers, and fine craftspeople. A center for contemporary arts incorporating first-rate gallery spaces and studio classrooms would serve local artists well, as well as urban gallery owners and museum curators seeking fresh new talent.

That said, Burlington nonetheless does maximize the visual arts resources it has at hand. Knowing that local artists needed shows and that cultural tourists were eager to buy art, Burlington City Arts recently expanded its Firehouse Gallery. The top-notch Doll-Anstadt Gallery has staked a 2,200-square-foot claim to downtown's arts scene by representing local, regional, and national voices in sculpture, painting, and fine crafts. The Fleming Museum's Wolcott Gallery, the University of Vermont's Colburn Gallery, Fletcher Free Library, and the Flynn Theatre's gallery all infuse Burlington with significant art offerings. Even the Green Mountain Power Company headquarters has a gallery. Working Design Gallery, Robert Paul Gallery, and Frog Hollow offer some shows, and direct sales events like the South End Art Hop, an annual open studio tour in the town's favored art ghetto, give artists another way to pay their bills.

Burlington's Fleming Museum maintains a decidedly historical focus in its exhibitions, though it does present changing shows of work by living artists at its Wolcott Gallery. The Fleming also presents art lectures and after-school art programs for kids.

Alternative exhibition sites exist all over town, with coffeehouses such as the Daily Planet, Samsara, Uncommon Grounds, and Muddy Waters joining restaurants such as Sweet Tomatoes Trattoria, Halverson's Cafe, Isabel's, Red Onion Cafe, Magic Hat Brewery, Red Square, and Leunig's in showing local work. Cutting-edge spaces such as Rhombus Gallery and Exquisite Corpse Artsite offer shows of emerging talent (plus poetry readings, video art shows, and performance art pieces).

Burlington boasts an energetic nightclub scene led by three venues: Club Toast, Club

Metronome, and Nectar's. All three feature touring national acts, as well as local and regional bands of every possible stripe.

The legendary band Phish had its start in Burlington's club scene, and it has since helped other local bands garner national attention and recording contracts—bolstering the town's music scene just as R.E.M. did in Athens, Michael Martin Murphey did in Taos, and 10,000 Maniacs did in Jamestown.

Art Talk

"We've taken Club Toast in four years to national recognition as one of America's best nightclubs by presenting acts that sell out concert halls in New York and Boston," states co-owner Dennis Wygmans. "Audiences in Burlington are open to what's happening in the national music scene, and in this town it's possible for me to book four national acts each week, sell as many as 2,400 tickets a week for up to $17, and still have nights available for local musicians playing for a $2 cover charge. Four years ago Burlington's music scene was in dire straits, but because this and the other clubs have been successful, other venues are opening up around town and people have built full-scale recording studios to serve the local bands. If they want to work hard, bands can develop a strong local following in Burlington and then take that success to other places in New England and start a real career—I've seen it done a number of times."

"A third of our 26 artists are from right here," says gallery owner Stephen Doll. "There's a strong cultural awareness in Burlington, and what we try to do is appeal to the base of contemporary art collectors living in this area, as well as the cultural tourists who come down from Montreal and drive up from New York and Boston.... The quality of our space, which includes four galleries and two sculpture gardens, is what sets us apart from the other art galleries in the area."

"The reason why performing arts do so well in Burlington is because the Flynn Theatre has worked hard at making itself into an innovative presenter organization, and that has created the spillover effect of invigorating Burlington's club scene, theater companies, and visual artists," notes artist Bill Botzow. "Vermont is a rural state and a state filled with artists, which means that visual artists here are on equal terms with each other. So nobody from outside Burlington looks to visual artists in Burlington for something they can't find close to home. Burlington needs a community focal point for the visual arts, some place properly funded by private sector or public sources. Artists in Burlington need to be very innovative in terms of developing exhibition opportunities outside of the traditional loop of where artists show their work."

"The market for visual arts is varied here," says gallery owner Bob O'Toole. "But we also have a gallery [Robert Paul Galleries] in Stowe that sells 90 percent of its work to out-of-state visitors—from contemporary to Americana to Vermont landscapes. Burlington has always been a place where galleries come and go, but it's a different art market than the market in a resort town like Stowe, and a different season. About one-third of my artists are local, and the Stowe gallery is where I can sell the higher-priced pieces."

According to arts administrator Doreen Kraft, "Burlington City Arts has doubled the Firehouse Gallery's size, and we've embarked on a program to convert the upper floors of the old firehouse into studio classrooms and workshop space—hopefully, a whole building devoted to the visual arts. There needs to be some educating of the art–buying public on the need to support Vermont artists, but we can still draw as many as 500 people to one of our openings. Clearly, Burlington's developed a strong performing arts scene, one that also enhances the educational curriculum for the city's schools. For now, attracting Canadian cultural tourists remains an area Burlington has yet to fully develop. They're here in summer, but we need to present more to them than simply a shopping experience—most likely by demonstrating to business that the magnet effect of arts and cultural attractions can have a positive impact on their bottom line."

Essentials

Population: 39,000

Art Events: Arts Alive Festival in summer, Growling Pup Theatre Festival in summer, Discover Jazz Festival in June, Vermont Mozart Festival in July, Battery Park Summer Concert Series, South End Art Hop in September

Art Spaces: Clarke Galleries, Colburn Gallery, Doll-Anstadt Gallery, Exquisite Corpse Artsite, Flynn Gallery, Metropolitan Gallery at City Hall, Rhombus Gallery, Robert Paul Gallery, Wolcott Gallery, Working Design Gallery, Red Square

Hangouts: Magic Hat Brewery, 135 Pearl, Orbit Lounge, Samsara Cafe Sweetwaters, Vermont Pub & Brewery, Red Square

Bookstores: Adventurous Traveler, Barnes & Noble, Borders, Chassman & Bem

Public Radio: WVPS FM 107.9

Chamber of Commerce: 60 Main St., Suite 100, Burlington, VT 05401, (802) 863-3489

Montpelier, Vermont

Montpelier, the nation's smallest state capital, may have only 8,200 full-time residents—but it has a vibrant, diverse, and solidly supported arts scene that would be the pride of a city twenty times larger. In a bucolic setting where the tallest structure is the state capitol's gold dome, residents enjoy trout fishing, skiing, well-paying jobs, white-water kayaking, and pristine swimming holes right at their doorsteps. The community supports four colleges, a first-rate library system, farmers markets, a free bus system, lovely parks, and a golf course. . . everything one expects to find in a bustling state capital, except that Montpelier lacks the traffic jams and crime common elsewhere.

Lifestyle

Montpelier has affordable housing to accompany its extraordinarily high quality of life. Fixer-upper homes can be had for around $60,000, and for $85,000 home buyers can find spacious residences with lots of amenities, large yards, and safe neighborhoods.

Local schools offer art education programs, and one of Vermont's premier performing arts organizations, the Lost Nation Theater, directs Montpelier High School's first-rate drama program. The town supports a historical museum, and Middlesex, just a few miles away, has a military museum. Central Vermont is a land of small farms, and local dairies produce fine cheddar cheeses.

Arts Scene

Montpelier's artists have a receptive audience in the community's highly educated state workers. In recent years local artists have also benefited from a steady influx of arts-conscious urbanites, who participate in everything from the Onion River Arts Council's Celebration Series at the beautifully restored Barre Opera House to monthly downtown Art Walks.

Downtown has a half-dozen commercial galleries, many displaying local fine crafts. There's a fine-art gallery inside the governor's office at the state capitol, the Vermont Art Council's Spotlight Gallery is on State Street, and there's even a gallery at City Hall. Many of Montpelier's nearly 40 restaurants and cafés also exhibit art—and offer important alternatives for the region's emerging, newcomer, and even established artists.

One of Vermont's most distinguished art-world figures is the legendary painter T. W. Woodward, whose masterworks depict the lives of nineteenth-century African American laborers. He is memorialized at the T. W. Wood Gallery & Arts Center on Norwich University's Vermont College campus. This exemplary facility organizes everything from exhibitions of work by the state's living art treasures to art classes, art lectures, and excursions to major museums.

Lost Nation Theater's summer series hosts everything from Bertolt Brecht to Shakespeare at the 140-seat black-box theater at the City Hall Arts Center, while the Barre Opera House offers musicals, and the Vermont Philharmonic offers contemporary dance and more from September through May. Other regional theater companies include the Barre Players and the Valley Players.

Live folk music is presented at Bellini's

Restaurant, poetry readings at Barre Books, literary readings at Bear Pond Books, occasional classical concerts at the Bethany Congregational Church, and contra and folk dancing at the Capital City Grange. Summer in the tiny burg of Adamant brings the first-rate Adamant Music School, now in its 58th season, which attracts conductors, orchestral musicians, and soloists from across New England for July and August performances.

Art Talk

According to artist Alicia Lorenzo, "Artisan's Hand Gallery was started 19 years ago by local artists, and it's still going strong. Only Vermont artists exhibit their work at the gallery, and most of those artists are from central Vermont. There's a ready-made collector base drawn here by the state government offices, and we don't see as many cultural tourists as do other places in the state. The gallery's best-selling artist these days is a weaver, but everything from stained glass to photography and functional ceramics are here. The Friday Art Walks are a new thing for Montpelier, and they've been growing in popularity, provided the weather isn't too horrible."

"We've been a resident company in Montpelier since 1985," says Kim Bent, codirector of Lost Nation Theater, "and are involved in everything from our summer theater season to statewide touring to art residencies to directing local drama programs for the high school. We've survived by growing carefully and by striving to be a catalyst that serves this region and attracts new spending to the region in the form of private investments and cultural tourism spending. We're an actor-driven organization that doesn't look to other theater companies for models of how to survive and grow. We maintain ties to other theater groups, but we're too busy inventing our own organizational model to be concerned with how closely we are, or aren't, following what anyone's playbook says."

Artist Peter Keating says, "I moved here from Bucks County, Pennsylvania, and find that the market for my sort of landscape and traditional work is best in Woodstock's galleries. Vermont seems to show more interest in performing arts than it does in visual arts, except for the visitors who come here and discover the place to be loaded with great artists selling their work at affordable prices. I find this to be a stunningly beautiful place to work, a place of inspiration and long winters."

Essentials

Population: 8,200
Art Events: Summer evening band concerts on the State House lawn, blues and jazz shows sponsored by Lost Nation Theater, Downtown Montpelier Art Walks, Adamant Music School's summer concert series
Art Spaces: Artisan's Hand, City Hall Showcases, T. W. Wood Art Gallery, Phoenix Rising, The Painting Place, About Thyme Cafe, La Brioche, Capitol Cafe, Spotlight Gallery

Hangouts: La Brioche, Bellini's Restaurant, Main Street News
Bookstores: Bear Pond Books, Barre Books
Public Radio: WVPS FM 107.9
Chamber of Commerce: Vermont State Chamber of Commerce, P.O. Box 37, Montpelier, VT 05601, (802) 223-3443

Abingdon, Virginia

This historic town of 7,000 residents in southwest Virginia is flooded with arts. No other community of its size can match Abingdon's combination of two outstanding art centers, year-round professional theater in an historic, 1835 performance hall, arts festivals, restaurants that exhibit art, fine crafts galleries, and a huge base of local art talent. Moreover, within a 15-mile radius of this walkable and charming community in the Blue Ridge Highlands are the Paramount Center for the Arts, housed in a beautifully restored 1931 theater, Emory & Henry College, which presents an ambitious program of visual and performing arts events, and the nation's foremost concentration of bluegrass musicians, playing every weekend at regional community centers and fairgrounds. Abingdon is on the verge of becoming Virginia's premier city of the arts.

Lifestyle

Abingdon is situated in an affordable, safe, and naturally gorgeous part of the inland mid-Atlantic region. Retirees love it here—they are drawn especially by Abingdon's state-of-the-art, $3 million public recreation complex on a 20-acre campus, low greens fees at golf courses, senior arts programs, and discounts galore. Families can live in large homes on spacious lots in safe neighborhoods—for ridiculously low prices. A new three-bedroom home commands barely $125,000 here. For creative artists who enjoy nature and want easy access to a major airport (40 miles away), as well as a reasonable drive to D.C., Atlanta, Charleston, Charlotte, and Louisville, Abingdon can't be beat.

Arts Scene

The foundation of Abingdon's strength as an arts town comes from the sophisticated and professional presentations staged by the Barter Theatre, one of the country's most respected playhouses. For good reason, the Barter is the State Theatre of Virginia, a facility the entire state points to with pride. This renovated 1831 theater seats 500 for its 12-play, year-round, main-stage season. Barter Stage II, located across the street in a converted 1829 church, seats 141 for its black-box series of new American plays, children's theater performances by the Barter First Light company, summer theater camp, and lectures.

The William King Regional Arts Center, one of the town's two art centers and an affiliate of the Virginia Museum of Fine Arts, serves the entire region through exhibitions and workshops. The center has a museum-quality, 1,250-square-foot visual arts gallery for big-name shows and smaller spaces for rotating displays of local art. It also serves as a performance center for theater, dance, and music.

The Arts Depot is Abingdon's other community art center. The gorgeous facility, located in an historic former train station, exhibits the work of artists from throughout the region, offers studio workshops in a range of arts disciplines, serves as a performance space for the Highlands Center for Ballet Arts, and serves as a literary center for local poets, authors, and publishers.

Abingdon's unofficial headquarters for the local arts scene is the Starving Artist Cafe, which not only serves the state's best espresso but also rotates monthly exhibitions of traditional and contemporary work by local artists. Each show sells at least a few pieces, with local collectors being the most receptive audiences. On occasion, the shows are sell-out affairs, with buyers lined up at the cafe's doors, waiting for the 5 p.m. opening receptions.

The Abingdon area is also home to a rich tradition of folk crafts, such as quilting, basketry, and woodworking. Such crafts are showcased at local galleries including the Cave House, Dixie Pottery, and Abingdon Mercantile.

Artists looking for a little fun often head toward the Virginia Creeper National Recreation Trail, a 34-mile rails-to-trails project that's a magnet for joggers, families, horseback riders, and birders. In the nearby town of Bristol, the Paramount presents local and touring theater, as well as top-name music ranging from bluegrass to blues and gospel.

Art Talk

Rick Rose, producing artistic director for the Barter Theatre, says that audiences are a mix of locals and visitors: "We have a growing community of retirees from eastern cities, people who have gone to theater all their lives and want to keep going to theater. We also have a huge base of support from the region, local folks who appreciate new works and innovation. . . . We draw 120,000 ticket buyers annually, and many of them come from cities two hours away. The Barter's season presents standards everyone loves and new works most everyone wants to love—our audience is right there with us, giving us the freedom to present theater that reflects what's going on in this country."

"We can hang up to 30 paintings for a show, and our openings are hugely popular events," says Starving Artist Cafe owner Shawn Crookshank. "I've taken tables out of the cafe to accommodate some artists' work, because they deserve to be treated with respect for what they do. Local buyers are very active here, and anything priced under $500 sells easily, but I've also seen $4,000 paintings walk out of here. We don't take any commission—just connect artists with buyers."

Essentials

Population: 7,000

Art Events: Opening nights at Barter Theatre, Theatre Bristol season at the Paramount, Virginia Highlands Festival in August, Plumb Alley Day in May

Art Spaces: Starving Artist Cafe, William King Regional Arts Center, Arts Depot, Cave House Gallery, Abingdon Mercantile, Martha Washington Inn, Bristol Art Gallery

Hangouts: Starving Artist Cafe, Generations Cafe

Bookstores: Bookends, Main Street Books & Crafts, Abingdon Mercantile

Public Radio: WETS FM 89.5

Chamber of Commerce: 179 E. Main St., Abingdon, VA 24210, (540) 628-8141

Charlottesville, Virginia

This central Virginia community of 40,000 residents and 18,000 students has developed a national reputation as a great place to live—and for good reason. First, Charlottesville is home to one of the nation's best colleges, the University of Virginia. Second, its location 115 miles southwest of Washington, D.C., places it within easy reach of museums, international airports, and weekending cultural tourists. Third, this community has developed a strong cultural identity by supporting visual and performing arts, as well as an independent film festival, a great nightclub scene, classical music, and alternative galleries for up-and-coming artists.

Lifestyle

As Austin does in Texas, so does liberal Charlottesville contrast with Virginia's predominant conservativism. The community boasts dozens of alternative medical practitioners, a thriving gay and lesbian community, New Age festivals, and a varied art world. From plays and art shows produced by the local senior citizens center to the regular puppet and kids' shows staged at the Old Michie Theatre on Charlottesville's pedestrian mall, this town fulfills its residents' creative needs. Real estate prices have been steadily rising in the past few years, but for those put off by Charlottesville's $150,000 price tags, nearby communities such as Crozet offer homes in the $90,000 range.

Arts Scene

Charlottesville's smooth integration of town and gown has made this a community former students find hard to leave and relocating urbanites find hard to resist. The Charlottesville and University Symphony Orchestra, which performs its five-concert season under maestro Carl Roskott at UVA's Cabell Hall, embodies that integration. The town also supports two art-house cinemas (Vinegar Hill and Jefferson Theaters), the Virginia Discovery Museum (a kids' science and arts center), a local branch of the Virginia Museum of Natural History, a youth orchestra, a community performing arts center, a nonprofit contemporary art gallery (Second Street), the McGuffey Art Center, several commercial galleries, and dozens of alternative visual arts spaces at coffeehouses, cafés, and even churches.

UVA's Bayly Art Museum presents mainstream historic exhibitions but also operates an innovative, community-oriented contemporary art program that juxtaposes national and regional talents. The school's drama department stages the Virginia Film Festival each fall, bringing to town emerging screenwriting, production, and acting talent. The department also produces a main-stage season at Culbreth Theatre.

Local galleries have coordinated their First Friday exhibit openings and have smartly teamed up with the free Fridays After Five music series to draw May through October crowds onto the downtown mall. You'll find contemporary work at the Second Street Gallery and Fayerweather Gallery, while bözArt Gallery and the McGuffey Art Center's three exhibition spaces tend toward wildly experimental imagery. Downtown Artspace, located underneath the Jefferson Theatre, is the young, cutting-edge alternative, showing art with strong political and social themes. Coffee bars such as Mudhouse and Higher Grounds stage monthly exhibits that are integral parts of the First Friday scene and give younger artists needed shows.

Live Arts, the town's leading stage company, has earned a strong reputation for its smooth handling of new American plays. During summer, Ash Lawn-Highland, the country estate of former president James Madison, presents an arts festival encompassing opera, children's theater, and a live music series. Unfortunately, the opera company chooses to feed audiences old standbys, ignoring exciting new American work. Like many other small art/college towns, Charlottesville supports a thriving music scene, with avant-garde acts performing in the sushi bar/nightclub setting of Tokyo Rose, touring stars performing at Trax and the Outback Lodge, and jazz groups gigging at Michael's Bistro.

Art Talk

"We rotate the local art on our walls each month and don't charge commissions to the artists showing here," says Peter Castiglione, manager of Michael's Bistro. "Local visual art and local music are what we're about—it enhances our atmosphere and draws people in. Charlottesville's a word-of-mouth place, and local artists know we can sell three, four, or even five paintings from each show we do. We're a small town with an incredible base of local talent."

Jen Fariello, founder of Downtown Artspace, says her gallery/studio/darkroom/ performance space is popular with young local artists: "We like being adventurous, and we don't rely on sales to tell us what kind of art is important enough to be shown. We've been well received, our openings are always packed, and many artists see us as the best thing to happen here in a long time. There's a waiting list of artists who want to be part of the gallery."

"Our place sells lots of art, pieces priced anywhere from $250 to $4,000," says Nathan Wilson, manager of Mudhouse. "The walls are already booked one year in advance, and we're open to showing anything that gives young artists a chance to make a living."

Essentials

Population: 40,000

Art Events: Virginia Festival of the Book in March, Ash Lawn-Highland Summer Festival of the Arts, Labor Day Jazz Festival in September, Virginia Film Festival in October, First Friday openings year-round

Art Spaces: Artspace Gallery, Blue Hawaii, Central Space Gallery, Downtown Artspace, Fayerweather Gallery, Higher Grounds, McGuffey Art Center, Mudhouse, New Dominion Bookshop, Piedmont-Virginia Community College, Thomas Jefferson Center for the Protection of Free Expression, Thomas Jefferson Memorial Church, Second Street Gallery, Spencer's 206, bözArt

Hangouts: Blue Ridge Brewing Company, Boar's Head Inn, Durty Nellie's Pub, Michael's Bistro, Monticello Brewing Company

Bookstores: Barnes & Noble, Blue Whale Books, New Dominion Bookshop, Quest Bookshop, Williams Corner Bookstore

Public Radio: WTVU FM 89.3

Chamber of Commerce: P.O. Box 1564, Charlottesville, VA 22902, (804) 295-3141

Bellingham, Washington

Location, location, location is the magic potion that allows Bellingham's dynamic arts scene to flourish. Oh, yes, then there are those students at Western Washington University—the magic "target audience" that shells out its hard-earned bucks at nightclubs importing the latest indie bands from around the United States and Canada or at those training local performers intent on busting into Seattle's better-paying club circuit. Bellingham's 53,000 permanent residents also like their nightlife, which is why this community in northwest Washington can muster up the audience to support a respectable jazz club scene. But the rabbit in Bellingham's hat is its proximity to several million Canadians living just 45 miles north in the metropolis of Vancouver. Canadians routinely patronize Bellingham's arts scene because the prices—from seats at the Mt. Baker Theatre to local art displayed at Allied Arts Gallery to microbrews crafted at Boundary Bay Brewery—are serious bargains compared to those north of the border.

Lifestyle

One of the primary reasons Bellingham's arts scene has taken off like a rocket ship is that the weather along this part of the coast is so miserably dreary that most sane individuals prefer to stay put in the great indoors. If it rained this much in the rest of the nation, most U.S. cities would probably spend whatever it took to build a roof over their downtowns. Seriously, there are a few glorious months when locals can venture outside without carrying a spare umbrella (in case their main umbrella breaks), and

with all that free water, people manage to grow fabulous gardens.

Bellingham's real estate prices have risen sharply in recent years. Canadians hedging their bets have parked substantial amounts of their wildly fluctuating dollars here, pushing Bellingham's average home cost into the $160,000 range.

Arts Scene

Performing arts, visual arts, and music are all flourishing in Bellingham. Two very active presenters, the Mt. Baker Theatre and the Western Washington University Performing Arts Center (PAC), have staked out different, yet complementary territories in scheduling their acts, and just about every "name" performer making his or her way into Seattle is also booked into either Mt. Baker or PAC for a show. The PAC tends to bring an international group of dance, jazz, and classical performers into town, while Mt. Baker rolls the dice on everything from touring rock and roll to contemporary folk, children's theater, Delta blues, and ethnic dance. The shows are astounding not only in terms of their diversity but also for their lower-than-average ticket prices.

The Whatcom Symphony Orchestra presents its five-concert season at Mt. Baker, which is also the preferred venue for independent presenters such as the Pacific Northwest Jazz Alliance. WWU's music department uses the PAC's Concert Hall for recitals and performances by guest classical artists. The Bellingham Festival of Music uses the hall and several other venues for its August series of orchestral, chamber, and jazz concerts. The Bellingham

Chamber Music Society stages its concerts at the Whatcom Museum of History and Art, the town's most prominent visual arts exhibition facility. In its first and second floor gallery spaces, the Whatcom presents exhibitions by local and regional artists. Its ARCO Gallery is used for touring national and international contemporary shows and installations.

Between Bellingham and neighboring Fairhaven there are more than a dozen commercial gallery spaces, including Allied Arts Gallery, a nonprofit space, while at least twice that many coffeebars, cafés, and businesses support local artists by hanging their work. The local theater scene includes the Bellingham Theater Guild, which stages dramas, musicals, and comedies in its own playhouse; Theatre Three Company, which stages new and local works at Allied Arts, and WWU Theatre, which presents a main-stage season, a New Playwrights season, and an experimental season in the PAC's Room 199 black-box space.

Art Talk

Miriam Barnett, director of Allied Arts, keeps her organization's calendar focused on the local arts scene. "We try to serve as a venue for the emerging artists of the area as well as being an organization whose exhibitions survey some of the larger region's creative voices," she says. "This community has an incredible amount of talent and remains the sort of cheap and beautiful place to live that attracts artists. We have a lot of artists who don't sell their work locally but who have gallery representation in Seattle, New York, or L.A. and just stay at home and work quietly in their studios."

Tonie Sibillia Marlow, coowner of Blue Horse Gallery, says the declining value of Canada's dollar has crimped local art sales: "We used to get substantial business from Vancouver collectors for our originals, but now they've pretty much retreated to the limited-edition print market. What we do get a lot of are Canadian artists who want to sell into the U.S. market. Bellingham is close enough to Seattle that art buyers tend to wonder whether art exhibted in Bellingham galleries is really good enough, so I spend lots of time telling people how our local artists also sell their work around the country, and, yes, it is good enough."

Essentials

Population: 53,000 full-time residents; 11,000 students

Art Events: Northwest International Art Competition in summer, Tour d'Art Gallery Walk and Bellingham Festival of Music in August, Allied Arts Festival of the Arts in November and December, Solstice Gallery Walk

Art Spaces: Whatcom Museum of History and Art, Allied Arts Gallery, Scott Milo Gallery, Colophon Cafe, Artworld, The Little Gallery, Stuart's Coffeehouse, Cookie Cafe, Art Connects Gallery, Blue House Gallery, Chuckanut Bay Gallery, Roeder Home Gallery, Mark Bergsma Gallery, Earth Spirit, Fish Boy Gallery, Lucia Douglas Gallery, Gallery West, Good Earth Pottery, Meloy & Co. Gallery, Hamann's Gallery, Western Gallery at WWU

Hangouts: Boundary Bay Brewery, Orchard Street Brewery, Archer Ale House, Colophon Cafe, Stuart's Coffeehouse, Tony's Coffeehouse, Village Inn Pub, The Doublewide, 3-B Tavern, Cosmos Nightclub

Bookstores: Village Books, Watermark Books, Eclipse Books, Michael's Books, Barnes & Noble, Scott's Books, Rainbow Bridge Books

Public Radio: KZAZ FM 91.7

Chamber of Commerce: P.O. Box 958, Bellingham, WA 98227, (360) 734-1330

Olympia, Washington

Puget Sound's southernmost reaches have turned into safety net of sorts for artists, actors, writers, and musicians escaping the urban blur of Seattle, Chicago, New York, and other cities. What they find upon arriving in Washington's capital city is an inexpensive, arts-crazed, and extremely supportive community that seems to live and breathe for strong artistic statements . . . the kind of art that snaps the mind to attention and compels serious reflection. Maybe it's the weather, maybe it's the influence of Evergreen State College, or maybe it's just that Olympia is an arts community whose time has come. Whatever the reasons, we'll certainly be hearing about this small art town for decades.

Lifestyle

There's no overstating the influence Evergreen State University has had on Olympia's arts scene. Equally influential is the community's magnetic appeal to a diverse group of fringe, avant-garde, and abstract thinkers. Against all odds, many of these artists succeed to a startling degree. The local music scene is home to six record labels and was Nirvana's launching pad. The local performing arts scene somehow talked local and state government into building a 987-seat performing arts hall . . . and the list goes on.

There's an arts incubator aspect to Olympia—fueled by the powerful combination of cheap and plentiful studio spaces, a jungle of coffee bars, and a half dozen nightclubs presenting everything from regional bands to local heroes who have cashed in nationally to accomplished jazz musicians to touring national acts. When it comes to music, Olympia has lots in common with Oxford, Northampton, Wilmington, and Santa Cruz. If you want to move here, an average home will set you back around $150,000.

Arts Scene

The keystone in Olympia's arts scene is the Washington Center for the Performing Arts (WCPA), a state-of-the-art facility whose mainstage theater seats 987 and whose Theatre II accommodates 120. The center presents an annual series of touring national theater, music, and dance. But it certainly can't be called adventurous in its booking policy, especially when it has the chutzpah to toss *Forever Plaid, Porgy & Bess,* and *Damn Yankees* at the local audience all in one season.

The center's pandering to the mainstream has opened the door for Evergreen State College's Evergreen Expressions series—staged at the school's Experimental Theatre. The series brings a stellar list of cutting-edge filmmakers, dancers, and musicians into Olympia. The only thing wrong with Evergreen Expressions is that there isn't more of it.

A number of local groups perform at the WCPA: Olympia Symphony for its six-concert series, maestro Timothy Brock and the Olympia Chamber Orchestra for their four-concert season, Thurston County Community Concerts for its exemplary—though abbreviated—season of music, theater, and dance, Washington Shakespeare Festival for its three-week season of four plays in August, Abbey Players for its three-play season of comedies and musicals, and Olympia Junior Programs for its four-performance season of touring national children's theater.

Another kids' arts group, Creative Theatre Experience, holds a theater summer camp with both an educational and a performance focus. Olympia Little Theatre uses its own playhouse for a five-play season of dramas and comedies. Within a year, the State Theatre will become a beautifully remodeled home for Harlequin Productions, an ambitious local company presently using WCPA for its four dramatic, Shakespearean, and comedic productions. Harlequin will substantially expand its season once the 330-seat playhouse is complete.

Nearly a dozen commercial and cooperative visual arts spaces are concentrated downtown, and there's local art on the walls of practically every coffee bar, café, and pub. But Olympia's arts scene deserves its own visual arts center. Such a facility would help attract cultural tourists—and their arts buying power.

Art Talk

Scott Whitney, artistic director of Harlequin Productions, says his company's success still surprises him: "Olympia is the sort of place that's attracting folks from New York and L.A. who want a better place to live and who are amazed that this local theater company owns its own building. We took over the State Theatre, a downtown eyesore, and turned it into a place Olympia could be proud of. This all happened in eight years after a group of actors put up $400 of their own money to stage a show. Within five years we were selling out everything we did and just needed more space because we were turning away too many potential ticket buyers. This community responded to quality theater in a way nobody had ever anticipated."

Richenda Richardson, owner of Childhood's End Gallery, says the town's arts scene is largely supported by residents. "People living here take a great deal of interest in the art that's being created locally," Richardson says, "and most of our clients are collectors who have bought over a number of years. The state government creates a solid base of secure employment, so combined with the strong art being created through our local colleges, the pieces for an arts scene are in place. Artists who have graduated from those schools tend to stay in Olympia even if their career successes are more nationally based because this is a arts-supportive and easy place to live."

Essentials

Population: 37,000
Art Events: Procession of the Species Celebration in April, Spring and Fall Art Walks, Super Saturday and Dixieland Jazz Festival in June, Bon Odori Dance Festival in July, Music in Sylvester Park in July and August, Renaissance Fair in August, Olympia Film Festival in October
Art Spaces: State of the Arts Gallery, Mansion Glass, Childhood's End Gallery, Terra Gallery, Cornerstone Pottery, Loft Studio & Gallery, The Artists Gallery, Thompson Gallery, Looms, Lessons & Handiworks, Gallery IV

Hangouts: Fish Brewing Company, Titanic Brewing Company, Blue Heron Bakery, Batdorf & Bronson, Traditions Cafe, Kundalini Espresso, Otto's Bagels, All That Jazz Cafe, 4th Avenue Tavern, Fishbowl Pub
Bookstores: Budd Bay Books, Browser's Book Shop, Orca Books, Barnes & Noble, Four Seasons Books, Fireside Books, Oz Bookstore
Public Radio: KPLU FM 88.5, KAOS FM 89.3
Chamber of Commerce: P.O. Box 1427, Olympia, WA 98507, (360) 357-3362

Port Townsend, Washington

Victorian charm exudes from all corners of Port Townsend, a waterfront community in the northeast corner of Washington's Olympic Peninsula. While charm alone does not an art town make, the powerful one-two combo of a strong performing arts scene and a strong visual arts scene does.

What makes Port Townsend such a great place to live or visit is the overwhelming strength of its performing arts scene, namely the international-level programs staged by the Centrum Foundation. The foundation, housed on a decommissioned military base, gives Port Townsend a level of performing arts activity more commonly found in a major metropolis or Rocky Mountain ski town like Aspen. While the visual arts have a strong presence here, its Centrum that drive the cultural tourism sector of Port Townsend's economy.

Lifestyle

More than 10 miles of sandy beaches wrap around Port Townsend, and nearly every street corner in town is graced with spectacular views of Puget Sound, the Strait of Juan de Fuca, and the San Juan Islands. Port Townsend gets less rain than is normal for the coastal Northwest, though a relentless overcast prevails from late October to April. The bleak weather makes a fair share of the town's annual flow of new-comers from California think of other places to spend their winters.

Victorian homes are one of Port Townsend's claims to fame. While the best examples of these painted ladies have been carefully reno-vated, there are also lots of places that could use the loving care of an owner who knows a thing or two about carpentry. Housing costs are not outrageous. About $150,000 will get you into a quiet neighborhood where your neighbors might be a dulcimer maker on one side and a stay-at-home graphic designer on the other.

Arts Scene

The majority of Centrum Foundation programs are staged in summer. The season begins with a week of educational programs for talented youth, followed by two to four days of perfor-mances, primarily staged at the 1,400-seat Mc-Curdy Pavilion and the 280-seat Joseph Wheeler Theater. Centrum covers all the major arts bases—presenting festivals in jazz, blues, fiddle music, country blues, and classical music. For its jazz and blues festivals, Centrum fills every local nightclub and juke joint with full-tilt, late-night performances—gigs that don't even start until the main concerts at McCurdy have completed their encores. During each fes-tival, there's also a free noontime concert se-ries staged in Franklin Court. Into the middle of all the music, Centrum even slots a writers con-ference—loaded with big-name talent from around North America. Finally, Centrum stages a mid-winter Chamber Music Festival and over-sees a year-round artist residency program in the old military buildings scattered around its gorgeous facility.

Summer arts and crafts fairs take place in the waterfront setting of Pope Marine Park, which also serves as ground zero for wildly popular events such as the Wooden Boat Fes-tival and the Victorian Festival. Local theater is staged by the Key City Players, whose five-play season takes place at the company's 65-seat playhouse downtown, and by Bare Boards & Passion, a company that focuses on serious drama performed at the Sightlines Theatre at the fairgrounds. A winter poetry series, Sundays at One, takes place at the Rosebud Theatre, while the new NorthWest School of Documentary Vision brings a half-dozen filmmakers into town to show their works at a studio in uptown Port Townsend.

Two chamber music series help Port Townsend music lovers make it through the dark and damp Northwest winter. Turtle Bluff II Coffee Concerts are held Monday and Tuesday mornings. The Port Ludlow Arts Council hosts the Occasional Sunday series at the Bay Club.

Port Townsend Open Studio, a 30-member cooperative gallery, is dedicated to exhibiting local work, as is another cooperative space at the Franklin House Gallery. But though Port Townsend is home to a large group of talented and serious visual artists, for some reason this community lacks a visual arts center.

Art Talk

Artist Linda Jarvis says the Olympic Peninsula's population growth is fueling a strong art market. She explains: "We're a very diverse place in terms of the art styles represented in the galleries, and locally there are a number of artists living here who sell not only in Seattle but in galleries in Los Angeles and San Francisco. Our main buyers come into Port Townsend from Seattle, but in the past few years the second homes being built in the area have brought a whole new type of buyer into the galleries—the sort of person looking for high-end art. There are so many artists living here and so much growth that I think what this town needs are even more galleries."

Tracy Thompson, marketing and development coordinator for the Centrum Foundation, says that some events draw an international audience. "We're just a ferry ride from British Columbia, and whenever we stage the jazz and fiddle festivals the response from across the border is huge. The other events we do draw heavily from Seattle and Everett audiences, as well as from around the Olympic Peninsula. We figure we serve about 32,000 people a year, between our performances and our educational programs. It's taken us 25 years to evolve these programs, and we're still growing in our reach and goals for educating the schoolchildren of Washington."

Essentials

Population: 8,000

Art Events: First Saturday Gallery Walks year-round, Victorian Festival in March, Centrum Summer Season from June to September, Wooden Boat Festival in September, Kinetic Sculpture Race in October

Art Spaces: Port Townsend Open Studio, Bruskin Gallery, Earthenworks, Franklin House Gallery, Silverwater Cafe, Coho Cafe, Harmony Art & Antiques, I Create, Salal Cafe, Bread & Roses, Jaqua Gallery, Lateral Line, Artisans on Taylor, Lazelle Gallery, Northwest Native Expressions, Roche Gallery & Studio

Hangouts: Hilltop Tavern, Palindrome, Ajax Cafe, Town Tavern, Back Alley Tavern

Bookstores: The Imprint, Port Townsend Card Company & Discount Books, Phoenix Rising

Public Radio: KZAZ FM 91.7

Chamber of Commerce: 2437 E. Sims Way, Port Townsend, WA 98368, (360) 385-2722

Walla Walla, Washington

Anytime you have three colleges crowded into a town of 29,000 residents, you'll also get the critical mass of body piercing shops, tattoo parlors, brewpubs, coffee-bars, and juke joints needed to keep the students entertained. That's what you'll find in the eastern Washington agricultural town of Walla Walla ("many waters" in a local Native America dialect). Located in one of the nation's premier vineyard regions (with nine local wineries so far), Walla Walla is close to a respectable ski area, yet its valley climate still keeps residents warm from March through October.

Lifestyle

Prosperity is no stranger to Walla Walla, a town whose economy is based on agriculture, natural resources, and education. Because the local job picture is good, home costs tend to be higher than the region's norm, with average residences starting in the $125,000 range—though there are lots of cottages and fixer-uppers that sell below the six-figure level.

Of Walla Walla's three colleges, two—Whitman College and Walla Walla College—are residential. Whitman has high academic standards and a top-ranked liberal arts program. Walla Walla is a Seventh Day Adventist School with strong programs in music and visual arts. The third school, Walla Walla Community College, is a sprawling facility whose campus serves over 12,000 students.

Arts Scene

Like other places in the Northwest, Walla Walla operates on substantial amounts of highly caffeinated drinks, which is why a substantial chunk of downtown has been taken over by an army of cappuccino dealers. The coffeehouses mesh well with the town's galleries, which sponsor Third Thursday Art After Hours gallery walks each month. Unfortunately, there has been a high rate of turnover in these galleries, though several have managed to survive for the long term.

The Carnegie Art Center is Walla Walla's art education and exhibition facility. Its three galleries exhibit local and regional work, with some shows juried. The town's most prominent exhibition facility, and the only one with a respectable budget, is Whitman College's Sheehan Gallery. This modern space with a decidedly contemporary focus brings touring works by national and international artists to town. Walla Walla College's Harris Gallery limps forward—despite the budgetary scraps tossed its way by the school's administration—and manages to pull off several student shows and several regional shows each year. There's an exhibition facility at the community college, as well as at the Little Theatre, both of which show local art. One of the more unusual aspects of Walla Walla's arts scene is the contemporary sculpture cast at the Walla Walla Foundry. The facility has developed a reputation for quality and is used by top-name artists who sell in prominent urban galleries.

Cordiner Hall on the Whitman College campus serves as a venue for the region's performing artists, as well as for the occasional touring artist. Walla Walla Symphony presents its six-concert season at the hall from October to May. Whitman's Harper Joy Theatre offers a four-play main-stage and five-play black-box season, while the school's music department uses Chism Auditorium for faculty, student, and guest artist recitals.

Walla Walla College uses its Fine Arts Center for recitals by faculty, students, and guest artists. Walla Walla Community College presents its summer musical in the amphitheater at Fort Walla Walla Park over several July weekends. The community college uses the China Pavilion for theater productions and concerts.

Art Talk

Mark Anderson, managing director and owner of the Walla Walla Foundry, specializes in cutting-edge contemporary art that's shipped worldwide. "Walla Walla's in an important stage of its development as an arts community, one where the various arts organizations around the area are starting to pool their resources and decide upon the direction this community's arts need to travel," Anderson says. "Two indications of our emerging strength are the arts festival we're building around this summer's arrival of the Art Train and a downtown event that's being coordinated with the downtown business community matching artists up with business sponsors. Another major influence has been the increasingly active role Whitman College has been playing in its support of the arts scene through purchases of local art. That commitment to Walla Walla artists has gone a long ways toward validating the artistic integrity of the creative statements being produced by local artists."

Jill Zagelow, owner of the Paula Ray Gallery, says local art collecting habits are changing: "We've always had a group of fairly well-off people who bought their art out of town when they were on vacation. But lately it's been more the middle-income person who is becoming interested in Walla Walla, and that in turn is bringing some big local money back into the galleries. The past few years have seen a huge change in Walla Walla in terms of how people enjoy themselves, and there is this cigars, fine wines, espresso, and art culture taking root here that's been welcomed with open arms. . . . I'll always have to sell lithos to keep my doors open, but each year things get better and that's what's great about this town."

Essentials

Population: 29,000

Art Events: Third Thursday Art After Hours art walks, Walla Walla Sweet Onion Fest in July, Summer Sounds on the Plaza in July and August, Muddy Frogwater Classic Festival in August, Celebration of Regional Art in September, Italian Heritage Day Fest in October

Art Spaces: Sheehan Gallery, Harris Gallery, Carnegie Art Center, Fenton/Stahl Gallery, Paula Ray Gallery, Fotografiks, Painter's Cottage, Mildred Stewart Room Gallery

Hangouts: Mill Creek Brewery, Blue Mountain Tavern, Shady Lawn Antiques & Coffee, Main Street Coffee Company, Barnaby's Pub, Merchant's Ltd., Coffee Perk, The Green Lantern, Ancient Onion, Cynda's, Backstage Cafe

Bookstores: The Bookery, Book & Game Company, Earthlight Books, Logo's Bookstore

Public Radio: KWWS FM 89.7

Chamber of Commerce: P.O. Box 644, Walla Walla, WA 99362, (509) 525-0850

Berkeley Springs, West Virginia

A stunning location combined with an irrepressible creative spirit and a steady flow of cultural tourists has made this West Virginia art town a three-time repeater as one of the 100 Best. With a population of 875, Berkeley Springs is one of the nation's smallest art towns, but its local art scene never stops improving. New artists and art-business owners arrive each year . . . who in turn attract more weekend tourists, second-home owners, and culturally aware retirees from nearby D.C. and Baltimore.

In addition to its steady growth and high expectations, Berkeley Springs' Morgan Arts Council has recently become the proud new owner of a 40,000-square-foot, four-story downtown arts center called the Ice House. Its previous owners had no luck selling the unsightly structure, a former apple storage facility . . . then the council asked them if they'd be interested in giving it away. When those owners said, "It's yours," Berkeley Springs' place in small-art-town history books was secured.

Lifestyle

Considering that this sparsely populated, thickly forested corner of the state is just over an hour's drive from D.C., it's no wonder that it has attracted many urbanites tired of the city grind. Homes here average around $80,000. Those with a few acres run slightly over $100,000.

The town has historically been a favored getaway spot because of Berkeley Springs State Park, one of the nation's oldest thermal spas. Adjacent to winding streets filled with galleries and cafés, the park—with its manicured lawns, Roman-style bathhouses, and geothermally heated rivers—is a place of amazing beauty. It is also the site of a public tap, a year-round source of free, 74.3-degree drinking water that attracts a steady flow of devotees. The park has created a niche for homeopaths and massage therapists serving urbanites who come here for R&R.

Arts Scene

Local artists have two things in common: each has a favorite masseuse, and most spend time out at Tari's Premier Cafe, a cool joint serving everything from nachos and microbrews to lobster and Chardonnay. Tari's also sells and displays local art and hosts Thursday evening jam sessions for area musicians.

Music also thrives at the state park, which hosts a free summer concert series of blues, jazz, folk, and bluegrass acts. One of the newest developments on the regional arts scene is the Tom Netherton Show, a Lawrence Welk–style revue staged weekly at the Country Inn. Theater buffs can enjoy performances at Coolfont Resort's Pavilion and at the Ice House, though the latter is still under renovation. Nearby Martinsburg also offers a live theater season in its Apollo Civic Theatre.

The Ice House has been a major boon to the arts community. Though it's currently in a slow but steady process of renovation, the center already contains a sales gallery filled with local art, an exhibition space dedicated to local and regional shows, an arts workshop space, and a performance space. The completed Ice House will contain a dance center and pottery, printing, and weaving studios. Local artists and craftspeople also sell their work though a half-dozen gallery spaces in the town's historic downtown, which attract lots of cultural tourists.

As Berkeley Springs' reputation as an arts center has expanded, the Morgan Arts Council has increased its range of offerings. The council sponsors an artist-in-residence program at local schools, an ambitious exhibitions calendar at the Ice House, and wacky galas—like one that transformed the town water tower into a 100-foot-tall Water Wizard.

Art Talk

"We had owned a home for four years in this very welcoming community before buying an art gallery and making Berkeley Springs our place to retire," says Jenny Wheeler, who owns Mountain Laurel with her husband, Chuck. "We had been active collectors of contemporary crafts, so we already knew several of the local artists through their work. This area is loaded with great talents, sophisticated artists who work hard . . . . Baltimore and D.C. provide 60 percent of the gallery's traffic, and people from there don't blink at paying thousands of dollars for something they like."

Painter Jonathan Heath, who owns the Heath Studio gallery with his artist wife, Jan, notes that the community's art business has been steadily building: "People come here on weekends and really buy, and we're thinking of opening a new, larger gallery space. Artists need to apply themselves constantly to their work if they're going to make their living here from their art, but it can be done. On any given weekend we'll sell $2,000 paintings and 75-cent postcards. Opening the Ice House as an art center has had an amazing impact on this community. As many as 200 people turn out for art openings, and that's encouraged even more locals to try their hand at creating art."

Essentials

Population: 875
Art Events: Five Rings Visual Arts Festival at the Ice House and Concerts in the Park in summer, Artists' Studio Tour in August, Apple Butter Festival in October
Art Spaces: Bath House Health Center, Berkeley Springs Antique Mall, Capacon Art & Crafts Center, Heath Studio Gallery, Homeopathy Works, Ice House, Jules' Gallery, Mountain Laurel, STAR Theatre, Tari's Premier Cafe, Treasures & Treats, Woodworks of Berkeley Springs

Hangouts: Coolfont Lounge, Country Inn Garden Room, La Fonte, Tari's Premier Cafe
Bookstores: The Book Keeper, Mountain Laurel
Public Radio: WVEP FM 88.9
Chamber of Commerce: 304 Fairfax St., Berkeley Springs, WV 25411, (304) 258-9147

Lewisburg, West Virginia

Most people associate West Virginia's arts scene with homespun crafts and mountain music, and to some extent they're right—until Lewisburg pops up. This West Virginia community of fewer than 4,000 residents has used two powerful draws of the 1990s—cultural tourism and outdoor recreation—to build its economy, while improving quality of life for its residents.

The forested mountains outside Lewisburg's 236-acre historic district have attracted more than a few monied retirees in recent years—people seeking a few acres on which to build comfortable homes. With the area's growing base of fine craftspeople and artists, as well as urban families seeking a better place to raise their kids, Lewisburg has been able to sustain a depth to its arts scene that communities many times its size would envy.

Lifestyle

Lewisburg really gears up for its white-water rafting seasons—spring and summer on the New River and fall on the Gauley River—all of which attract hordes of visitors from Washington, D.C., Charlotte, and Raleigh. Winter brings a ski crowd through town on its way to Snowshoe and Silver Creek, while summer's West Virginia State Fair is Lewisburg's most crowded and crazy time—two weeks in August when huge crowds come for top names in country and bluegrass music and "suspend life as we know it," as one art wag says.

But this is still the sort of town where someone with a little cash and lots of home-repair talent can find a very affordable home. Handyman's specials in the $50,000 range abound, even within the historic district, while for $75,000 it's possible to find large homes with garages, shaded yards, and several bedrooms.

Arts Scene

For a small town that has no college and no nearby population center, Lewisburg sustains a surprisingly diverse and finely tuned arts scene. There are two important presenting organizations, Carnegie Hall and the Greenbrier Valley Theatre.

Carnegie, which just completed a $3-million, top-to-bottom renovation of its 500-seat performance hall, Old Stone Room art exhibition space, and art education workshop spaces, was a 1902 gift from Andrew Carnegie to a now-closed women's college. Today the Carnegie hosts a September-to-May performance season featuring classical music, dance, bluegrass, and touring theater. It also offers year-round art classes for adults and kids as well as a summer art camp.

Greenbrier Valley Theatre is a true anomaly for such a small community. Believe it or not, the 30-year-old GVT presents a two-month main-stage summer season featuring works by playwrights ranging from Neil Simon to Jean Molière, as well as new plays and commissioned pieces, all in a 170-seat converted-barn. GVT plays regularly to sold-out audiences, and it's now converting a downtown Lewisburg department store into a year-round 120-seat playhouse. The company oversees the Drama Club children's theater company, which has a board of directors staffed by kids and presents two plays in autumn and spring.

There are several visual arts and fine craft galleries in Lewisburg's historic downtown. The town's most prominent venue is the Old Stone Room at Carnegie Hall, which also hangs local art in its auditorium lobby gallery. Just a few miles east is the community of White Sulphur Springs and the Greenbrier Hotel, a top national golf resort and spa. Nearly a dozen art businesses cluster inside the hotel's Art Colony Gallery Row—representing everything from regional contemporary work to locally created jewelry and studio glass. But Lewisburg's galleries are also favored destinations for the hotel's monied clientele. Finally, Lewisburg has two live-music venues—Hobnobbery for weekend bluegrass and Roscoe's Cafe in nearby Fairlea for rock and blues.

Art Talk

Artists need to establish gallery connections elsewhere before coming to Lewisburg, according to painter Bonnie Fuoco, who moved here from Philadelphia. She explains: "There's a lot of support here for all the arts and a lot of support from other artists, but the local market is small and somewhat seasonal, so you've got to have things set up before moving here. Either that or just get a law degree and paint in your spare time. For myself, a landscape painter, this area has all the inspiration I need. Drive five minutes in any direction and you're in the middle of pastoral beauty."

"Sure, there are a number of tourists who make up our audience, but the majority of ticket buyers are locals," says Cathey Sawyer, Greenbrier Valley Theatre artistic director. "What people support here is simple: it's anything we do well. We'll have as many people turn out for a new play as turn out for a musical, and it's because local people like to be entertained. Once our downtown theater is finished, we'll switch to a year-round season, Wednesday through Sunday, with our off nights devoted to experimental works by members of our apprentice company—things that might not work for our main-stage audience, but which we can do as a way of giving playwrights a chance to see their work performed onstage."

Essentials

Population: 3,800
Art Events: West Virginia State Fair in August, Summersville Grape Stomping in September, T.O.O.T. in October, Season of Colors in October
Art Spaces: Carnegie Hall, Art Colony Gallery, Gallery 1897, Old Hardware Gallery, Wolf Creek Gallery, Tuckwiller Gallery, J. Fenton Gallery, Cooper Gallery, Clay Works, Ravenwood Gallery

Hangouts: Roscoe's Cafe, Julian's Restaurant and Coffeebar, Hobnobbery, Del Sol Cafe, The Bakery, General Lewis Inn
Bookstores: The Bookstore, The Open Book
Public Radio: WVPB FM 91.7
Chamber of Commerce: 105 Church St., Lewisburg, WV 24910, (304) 645-1000

Bayfield and Madeline Island, Wisconsin

The spectacular beauty of Lake Superior and the Apostle Islands National Lakeshore serve as the front porch for Bayfield and neighboring Madeline Island. Both places are loaded with artists and fine craftspeople, plus art galleries and a steadily improving range of performing arts events.

This Northwoods region is favored by artists searching for isolation and a strong summer art market, with cultural tourists from Minneapolis, Duluth, Milwaukee, and Chicago making the Apostle Islands a favored second-home and vacation destination. The attraction is a typically midwestern blend of friendliness, affordability, and easy access to everything from world-class fishing to secluded lakeshore cottages bordered by apple orchards.

Lifestyle

The northern lights make regular appearances here, and while summers are laid back and warm, winters are predictably brutal. During summer, a ferry carries visitors on the 20-minute ride between Bayfield and Madeline Island, while winter so deeply freezes this stretch of Lake Superior that locals actually drive cars between Bayfield and the island on the "ice road" (County Road H), a plowed pathway. When the lake's surface is freezing or melting, visitors make the journey aboard a propeller-driven "wind sled."

Madeline Island's property values have risen sharply in recent years—it's much easier to find a $250,000 lakeshore mansion than a $75,000 cottage. However, affordable Bayfield, where the region's schools and stores are located, offers housing in the $60,000 range.

Arts Scene

Madeline Island's LaPointe Center does everything possible to inspire, serve, and encourage the island's 180 year-round residents and 2,500 summer residents. It not only provides a beautiful exhibition space but also coordinates the local film society's summer programs at Positivity Polebarn, schedules ongoing classes in traditional crafts and visual arts, cultivates a community flower and vegetable garden, coordinates literary society activities, grants money to local artists for education, performance, and exhibition activities, and oversees the Positivity Children's Theatre summer camp. The island's retail offerings include a coffee bar/wine shop that sells local crafts. The Madeline Island Historical Society Museum, open four months of the year, has recently expanded its facilities.

The island's most prominent performing arts group is the Madeline Island Music Camp, which is currently building a performance and education center. The camp pairs talented students with seasoned orchestral professionals for a June and July series of chamber and virtuoso concerts.

Bayfield sponsors one of the nation's best summer performing arts festivals, the Lake Superior Big Top Chautauqua, staged under a massive tent on the grounds of Mt. Ashwabay Ski Area. Events include adult and children's theater, national-caliber pop and world music, and variety shows. Garrison Keillor comes here for live radio broadcasts each summer, as do performers such as Bela Fleck, John Gorka, Richie Havens, Taj Mahal, and Iris DeMent.

Other Bayfield musical opportunities include the July and August Bayfield Schubert

Festival, occasional classical concerts at Christ Episcopal Church, and free summer concerts in the park. Just north of town, the Red Cliff Chippewa Reservation hosts the region's hottest nightclub and an always-packed casino. Nearby Ashland features live music at the Railyard Pub, performances at Northland College's Alvord Theater, and the Black Cat Coffeehouse.

Art Talk

Shane Upthegrove, owner of Port Wing Pottery, says the regional base of artistic talent is surprisingly strong: "All my artists, and I have 20 of them, come from within a 40-mile radius of Port Wing [40 miles from Bayfield]. Artists come here because it's an easy place to live, less expensive, and inspiring. Some artists have their work selling in other parts of the country, others hold down day jobs so they can do their art, but one thing they all have in common is a commitment to not doing commercial work. Their art comes from inside of them, not from the mind of an interior decorator. I represent potters, painters, a pen maker, wood turner, wood carver, blacksmith, glassblower—they're all living right around here."

Phillip Anich, operations manager for Big Top Chautauqua, feels that his organization is expanding in several ways: "Our radio show is becoming huge, and we're starting to tour winter shows throughout the state, so in some ways we're becoming a performance troupe as much as we're a presenting organization. . . . These days Big Top Chautauqua is the magnet that pulls lots of new tourism into Bayfield. Our summer season is 70 shows long and attracts over 25,000 people—big numbers no matter where you are. Warren Nelson, our artistic director, is taking this organization into a new stage of development, with bigger name acts and expanded facilities. Right now we're considering putting in an outdoor stage that would allow us to present shows for as many as 3,000 people at one time."

Essentials

Population: Bayfield, 700; Madeline Island, 180
Art Events: Herbster Smelt Fry in April, Island Sea Symposium and Ojibwa Heritage Days in June, Bayfield Festival of the Arts, Whitefish Livers Big Saturday, and Red Cliff PowWow in July, Wooden Boat Festival in August, Port Wing Fall Festival and Superior Fall Breeze Fine Art Show in September, Bayfield Apple Festival in October, Christmas Boutique at Madeline Island Historical Museum in December
Art Spaces: Austin Miller Studio, Black Cat Coffeehouse, Chequamegon Bay Gallery, Donnalee Designs, Eckles Pottery, First Street Gallery, Kerr Studio & Gallery, LaPointe Center, Northern Great Lakes Center, M & I Bank, Mission Hill Coffeehouse/LaPointe Provisions, National Lakeshore Visitors Center, Oulu Glass Gallery, Port Wing Pottery, Stone's Throw, Superior Frame & Gallery, Tom's Burned Down Cafe, Washburn Historical Museum and Cultural Center, Waterfront Gallery, Woods Hall Craft Shop
Hangouts: Bell Street Tavern, Black Cat Coffeehouse, Grampa Tony's, Isle Vista Casino, Maggie's, Mission Hill Coffeehouse/LaPointe Provisions, Morning Star Espresso, Railyard Pub, Tom's Burned Down Cafe
Bookstores: Apostle Island Outfitters & General Store, Chequamegon Book & Coffee Co., LaPointe Provisions, Northward Bookstore
Public Radio: KUWS FM 91.3, WSCN FM 100.5
Chambers of Commerce: Bayfield Chamber of Commerce, P.O. Box 138, Bayfield, WI 54814, (800) 447-4094; Madeline Island Chamber of Commerce, P.O. Box 274B, LaPointe, WI 54850, (715) 747-2801

Door County, Wisconsin

With its spectacular location on a wooded peninsula jutting into Lake Michigan, Door County is called "the Cape Cod of the Midwest"—sort of a P-Town without the drag queens. This arts-crazed slice of paradise certainly qualifies as one of the 100 Best because of its peninsula-wide concentration of art galleries, performing arts centers, and open artists' studios. Urban musicians, actors, directors, and artists have long retreated to Door County during summer, transforming the peninsula's performing arts scene into one of the nation's most varied.

Cultural tourists from Milwaukee, nearby Green Bay, and Chicago not only keep the region's 50-plus art galleries going but also have spiked the local real estate market through a building spree of shoreline palaces. The results may not always be pretty, but the strength of Door County's arts-based economy provides year-round artists with the jobs and sales opportunities they need.

Lifestyle

While none of the peninsula's main communities of Fish Creek, Egg Harbor, Ephraim, Sister Bay, and Bailey's Harbor have more than 1,000 year-round residents, those same communities balloon to several times that size during summer. The county seat of Sturgeon Bay is the most populous, maintaining about 10,000 full-timers.

During winter local attention turns to having enough beer, brats, and firewood to get through the next blizzard—a frequent occurrence in this neck of the northern woods. In summer it's watch-out time on the two-lane

roads crisscrossing the peninsula, as vacationing urbanites in sport-utility vehicles terrorize the local deer and pedestrian populations. Local artists, actors, musicians, and gallery owners take advantage of the down time between Halloween and Mother's Day to prepare for the summer onslaught.

Real estate prices have escalated: an average home in Sister Bay now runs in the $150,000 range, while a home with waterfront access costs about $200,000. In the haughtier climes of Egg Harbor, expect to find shorefront homes in the $500,000 range.

Arts Scene

Fish Creek's Door Community Auditorium stages its seven-month season from June to December, bringing in theater, blues musicians, dancers, and contemporary folk singers. In August, the 750-seat facility also hosts the Peninsula Music Festival, maestro Victor Yampolsky's ten-concert series featuring top musicians drawn from national symphonies. Meanwhile, in Egg Harbor, the Birch Creek Music Performance Center, a summer music school, presents big band, percussion, and symphony concerts. The Midsummer Music Festival, a June chamber music series, serenades Ephraim, Sturgeon Bay, and Ellison Bay.

Peninsula Players Theatre, a professional summer and fall stock company, presents its plays on a 14-acre compound just south of Fish Creek. Peninsula Dance, a University of Wisconsin instructional troupe, stages much of its summer season at Fish Creek Town Hall. Open Door Theatre presents locally written and acted plays at peninsula venues and produces a weekly radio show about Door County arts. Just north of Fish Creek, Peninsula State Park's outdoor amphitheater is the summer headquarters for the family-oriented American Folklore Theatre. (Fall shows are indoors at Ephraim Town Hall.)

Art galleries are practically everywhere you turn in Door County. The Door County Art League maintains its Showcase Gallery in Sister Bay, while in Ellison Bay, the Clearing is a nonprofit exhibition space that offers summer classes. Ephraim has the Hardy Gallery, operated by the Peninsula Art Association, while Sturgeon Bay's exhibition and art-education hub is the Miller Art Center. Peninsula Players operates the Woodwalk Gallery, while the Door Community Auditorium maintains yet another nonprofit space, the Link Gallery. The peninsula's most prominent visual arts organization is the Peninsula Art School, a multidisciplinary facility in Fish Creek that schedules summer classes and residencies for adults, mid-career artists, and children.

Art Talk

Anne Haberland, who owns Edgewood Orchard Galleries with her husband, Minnow Emerson, says the county's arts scene continues to grow. "The art market has been very good, maybe too good because I sense there's some danger of art here losing touch with its motivation," she says. "The year-round galleries are attracting more visitors, and they do well when there's lots of snow on the ground. Lots of local artists choose to sell their work through their own studios. . . . It's a strong arts community, one that continues to attract more artists, galleries, and collectors each year."

Todd Schmidt, general manager of the Peninsula Players, says Door County audiences support all sorts of theater: "We have our usual summer-stock pieces, but then there's a core group that wants us to give them more, which is why we can do an *Amadeus* and a *Woman in Black* in one season. Most of our staff and actors come in from Chicago, and they love coming to this forested paradise. We use our rehearsal hall as an art gallery at night, and our Stagehouse can seat 470 in summer. Autumn productions can be a bit cold, so if you're planning to be here in October, bring your mittens."

Essentials

Population: 26,100
Art Events: Festival of Blossoms in May, Peninsula Art School Open House in July, Concerts on the Lawn in July and August, Peninsula Art Association annual juried show in summer
Art Spaces: Clay Bay Pottery, DeGraff Woodworking, Door County Scrimshander, Dovetail Gallery, Eden North Gallery, Edgewood Orchard Galleries, Frogtown Gallery, Gallery in the Garden, Gathering Art Gallery, Handverks Music, Jack Anderson Gallery, Joan Champeau Pioneer Gallery, Kathy Glasnap Gallery, Maple Grove Gallery, Millroad Gallery, Newport House Studio, Richard Mueller Gallery, Valle de Bravo, Washington Island Nature and Art Center, Water Street Gallery, Whitecaps Gallery
Hangouts: Black Locust, Cherryland Brewery, Door County Coffee & Tea Co., Karly's Bar, Orthober's Coffeebar, The Roadhouse, Shipwrecked Brewpub, Village Cafe, Windjammer Lounge
Bookstores: Bookworld, Caxton Books, Ltd., Ingrid's, Page's, Pastimes Books
Public Radio: WPNE FM 89.3
Chamber of Commerce: P.O. Box 406, Sturgeon Bay, WI 54235, (920) 743-4456

Jackson, Wyoming

Wyoming's ranching and cowboy culture combine with the majesty of the Snake River Valley, the Grand Teton Mountains, and awesome skiing in the town of Jackson, one of the West's most desirable communities. As with similar western communities, real estate values here have shot through the roof, though Jackson remains affordable compared to such kindred spirits as Telluride, Taos, and Sun Valley. The local population of 6,000 has seen an influx of real estate developers and second "mini-ranch" home owners, and many hardworking Jackson locals have been forced across the 8,400-foot Teton Pass to find housing in more affordable Driggs and Swan Valley, Idaho. Jackson's economy is easily the best in the state, though holding down at least two jobs to pay for one's ski lift pass is the norm.

Lifestyle

This small art town bordering Yellowstone National Park sits on the southeastern edge of a valley known as Jackson Hole. It shares its name with the massive, multi-terrained ski area that launched this region toward international fame. For Jackson's artists, gallery owners, and theater directors, the ski and national-park tourist seasons present a wealth of sales opportunities . . . as well as two shoulder seasons of watching few, if any, cultural tourists walk across their thresholds.

Condos in Jackson start in the $150,000 range, while average family residences needing a little repair can be had for $225,000. Second-home owners have created a tremendous surge of multimillion-dollar mansion develop-

ment, providing hundreds of locals with jobs. But locals complain that the newcomers frequently have minimal involvement with the community's friendly and talented full-time residents.

Arts Scene

Cowboy culture dominated the local visual arts scene up until recently, and many local galleries still sell western realism and Native American works. But some semblance of a contemporary art market has begun via a few commercial galleries, shows at the nonprofit ArtWest Gallery, and the art hanging from the walls of local coffeehouses, cafés, and swanky restaurants.

One major force bringing both change and national attention to Jackson's art scene is the National Museum of Wildlife Art, whose 51,000 square feet of gallery and archival space includes more than 1,200 paintings by the world's foremost wildlife, landscape, and western realist artists. Three of the museum's 14 galleries rotate exhibits to give contemporary landscape painting, photography, ethnic art, and fine crafts a first-rate venue previously unavailable in Jackson. The museum also has a children's gallery and hosts the Grand Teton Music Festival's Music on Exhibit winter concert series.

The town celebrates during the annual Fall Arts Festival, one of the West's most comprehensive art bashes, when the galleries, restaurants, and coffeehouses overflow with artists, cultural tourists, and out-of-town dealers seeking new talent. The Community Visual Art Association operates ArtWest Gallery, specializing in local and regional shows plus year-round adult and kids art classes, lectures, and foreign film. Jackson artists hope one day to build a community arts center consolidating these functions with a performance space for the Mainstage Theatre—an effort deserving of the town government's immediate attention.

The area's summer highlight is the Grand Teton Music Festival, directed by maestro Eiji Oue, a splendid celebration of classical and chamber music at the 740-seat Walk Festival Hall in Teton Village. The popular festival has expanded to offer a winter chamber music series at the National Museum of Wildlife Art.

Art Talk

Beth Overcast, owner of Center Street Gallery, says Jackson is becoming more accepting of contemporary art. "Our tourists are overwhelmingly from the East Coast, and they can't connect to western art," she explains. "I'm in business because I offer something different: contemporary artists from here and around the West that mostly are new talent to these tourists. Our growth has been well guided, and even though we're always in danger of becoming too glitzy, this is still a great place to be in the art business. Winters can be soft if the snow isn't great, but our summers will carry you right through the rest of the year."

Karen Stewart, executive director of the Community Visual Art Association, is closing in on her goal of a community arts center: "We've finally got the city and the school board to agree that the old Jackson-Wilson High School should be used as an arts center, so I'd say we're about five years from having it become a reality. In the past three years we've doubled our number of exhibitions, members, and classes, and still people are practically breaking our doors down. There's been a huge surge of interest in our programs from people in their 20s and 30s, an age group whose artists sell their work mostly through coffeehouses."

Essentials

Population: 6,000
Art Events: Grand Teton Music Festival and Mountain Artists Rendezvous Art Fair in July and August, Fall Arts Festival, Jackson Gallery Walk, and Art for the Parks Exhibition in September
Art Spaces: ArtWest Gallery, Betty Rock Coffeehouse and Cafe, The Cadillac Grill, Caswell Gallery & Sculpture Garden, Center Street Gallery, Images of Nature, Legacy Gallery, Martin-Harris Gallery, Mountain Trails Gallery, National Museum of Wildlife Art, Pearl Street Bagels, Sacred Trails Gallery, Trailside Americana Fine Art Gallery, Wilcox Gallery

Hangouts: Charlie's Jackson Hole Coffee Co., Kickin' Coffee Bean & Tea Co., Mangy Moose, Million Dollar Cowboy Bar, Shady Lady Saloon, Snake River Brewing Co.
Bookstores: Teton Bookshop, Valley Bookstore
Public Radio: KUWJ FM 90.3
Chamber of Commerce: P.O. Box E, Jackson Hole, WY 83001, (307) 733-3316

Scott Christensen, Painter

From his home base in the small art town of Jackson, Wyoming, painter Scott Christensen has developed a reputation as one of the nation's top landscape painters. His elegant creations bring to mind the works of American masters of the late nineteenth and early twentieth centuries. Christensen is represented by galleries in Jackson, Carmel, Scottsdale, and Dallas, and those galleries sell his works practically as soon as they receive them.

For Christensen, his surroundings are critical. "Jackson's one of the few places I'd ever want to live in, and yes, there are advantages and disadvantages to anywhere you go, but for me the advantages of being here far outweigh any complications," he explains. "I like being forced to say inside my studio by three feet of fresh snow, and I like being able to look out the windows and see the different light patterns of changing seasons.

"For me, taking a 10-minute walk down a hiking trail or running outside my studio to paint that last hour of transitory daylight is important to my work. I do a couple of hundred paintings outdoors every year, and even though only one out of twenty will ever see the inside of a gallery, those paintings are an important way for me to build my own library. Within an hour's drive of Jackson I can be in red rock canyons, on top of alpine peaks, or in the middle of agricultural flatlands—and its that sort of variety that keeps me balanced.

"I'm a firm believer in the power of a place, which is why I make the effort to hike these mountains with my materials strapped to my back. I can walk this landscape and see the porcupines, the bear, the elk, and the geese who we share this place with, and I can also better appreciate the natural changes this place experiences as the seasons change and nature reveals the beauty of her cycles of life.

"Jackson is the sort of area that reinforces an artist's sense of isolation and contributes to that important feeling of settledness that allows me to do my best work. I love the fact that if I'm here in my studio and just look up from what I'm doing I'll see some sort of cloud shadow pass across the tops of the mountains, or watch an elk come up to the stream in back of the studio and start foraging around for grasses. There's just something about living in a place where nature is so powerful that it compels you to grab your materials and rush out the door to paint something you know will be gone in 15 minutes. Yes, it's work, but it's also a lot of fun and it's how I've always wanted to paint and where I've always wanted to live."

Profile

Christensen recognizes the importance of not only teaching but also learning. "I don't teach art very often, but when I do its quite a bit of fun," he remarks. "Painters need to continually think of themselves as students, and one way to do that is to let other people know what you think good art is, which helps solidify those things you stand for in your career. It's also partly a matter of continually defining your borders, which helps an artist avoid falling into ruts.

"An artists' knowledge has to precede their execution. I don't think there's a how-to book written by the older artists I admire that I haven't read. As artists, it's our temperaments that are going to lead the way for our finding our individuality, and what's important for artists is to know enough about what they're doing so that when it comes time to make their own decisions about how much a painting can bear, they can determine what goes in as well as comes out and still have that painting hold up."

Christensen advocates working through problems instead of "shortcutting your way to the top." He explains: "For anyone who can paint well there's always going to be the temptation to try and work more rapidly than you have in the past, but that leads you into a situation where your paintings start showing what I call 'speed marks.' You can continually build up your subject matter and not deal with the question of what to leave in or take out of a painting, or you can really work at subduing the more difficult areas of a painting and painting down a piece to achieve a different result. Artists have to make the commitment to practice and flat out just go to work. . . . If an artist is willing to put in that sort of time and is able to perform their own critical thinking, then they will be ready to be expressive in the actual practice of painting.

"Once your career is established, it's easy to just show the art market what sells," Christensen concludes. "But if you want to keep your heart into what you are doing with your art, then you've got to orchestrate the maneuvers that will move you beyond the point where everything you do is some sort of rendering. You know, art is sort of like music in the sense that a truly beautiful composition includes notes that aren't played, notes that take place only in the imagination of the listener. And that's why the art of painting is a continual process in which the painter has to engage in accepting and rejecting what's going to be included in a piece."

The 100 Best Small Art Towns

Towns are listed by rank.

1 Northampton, Massachusetts
2 Santa Fe, New Mexico
3 Eureka and Arcata, California
4 Portland, Maine
5 Nelson, British Columbia
6 Burlington, Vermont
7 Panama City and Seaside, Florida
8 Loveland, Colorado
9 Hot Springs, Arkansas
10 Ashland, Oregon
11 Carmel, California
12 Nantucket, Massachusetts
13 Woodstock, New York
14 Taos, New Mexico
15 Sedona, Arizona
16 Aspen, Colorado
17 Niagara-on-the-Lake, Ontario
18 Sun Valley, Idaho
19 Port Townsend, Washington
20 Oxford, Mississippi
21 Provincetown, Massachusetts
22 Beaufort and Hilton Head, South Carolina
23 Wilmington, North Carolina
24 Mendocino and Fort Bragg, California
25 Charlottesville, Virginia
26 Hanover and Lebanon, New Hampshire
27 Martha's Vineyard, Massachusetts
28 Belfast, Camden, and Rockport, Maine
29 Door County, Wisconsin
30 Salida, Colorado
31 Key West, Florida
32 Keene and Peterborough, New Hampshire
33 Bozeman and Livingston, Montana
34 Telluride, Colorado
35 Baie St. Paul, Quebec
36 Grand Marais, Minnesota
37 Missoula, Montana
38 Moscow, Idaho
39 Jackson, Wyoming
40 Berea, Kentucky
41 Deer Isle and Blue Hill, Maine
42 Chapel Hill, North Carolina
43 Bellingham, Washington
44 Bisbee, Arizona
45 Easton, Maryland
46 Stratford, Ontario
47 Ithaca, New York
48 New Smyrna Beach, Florida
49 Portsmouth, New Hampshire
50 Durango, Colorado
51 Joseph and Enterprise, Oregon
52 Flathead Valley, Montana
53 Olympia, Washington
54 Santa Cruz, California
55 Cannon Beach, Oregon
56 Ruidoso, New Mexico
57 Eureka Springs, Arkansas
58 Big Bend, Texas
59 Helena, Montana
60 Park City, Utah
61 Vail, Colorado
62 Natchitoches, Louisiana
63 Berkeley Springs, West Virginia
64 Yellow Springs, Ohio
65 Montpelier, Vermont
66 Bayfield and Madeline Island, Wisconsin
67 Quincy, Illinois

68 Lawrence, Kansas
69 Abingdon, Virginia
70 Sandpoint, Idaho
71 Beaufort and Morehead City, North Carolina
72 Salt Spring Island, British Columbia
73 Ocean Springs, Mississippi
74 Athens, Ohio
75 Iowa City, Iowa
76 Ojai, California
77 Woodbury, Tennessee
78 Lewisburg, West Virginia
79 Peekskill, New York
80 Saugatuck and Douglas, Michigan
81 Athens, Georgia
82 Creede, Colorado
83 Round Top, Texas
84 Red Bank, New Jersey
85 Grass Valley and Nevada City, California
86 Jamestown and Chautauqua Lake, New York
87 Lanesboro, Minnesota
88 Cedar Falls, Iowa
89 Lambertville, New Jersey
90 Magdalena, New Mexico
91 Rockport, Texas
92 Kerrville and Fredericksburg, Texas
93 Stillwater, Minnesota
94 Northport, Alabama
95 Walla Walla, Washington
96 Mill Valley, California
97 Truth or Consequences, New Mexico
98 Easton, Pennsylvania
99 Flagstaff, Arizona
100 Homer, Alaska

Index